Torching the Fink Books
and Other Essays on Vernacular Culture

ARCHIE GREEN

TORCHING THE FINK BOOKS

and Other Essays on Vernacular Culture

FOREWORD BY ROBERT CANTWELL

The University of North Carolina Press

Chapel Hill & London

The following essays have been previously published and are reprinted here by
permission of the original publishers.
"Dutchman: An On-the-Job Etymology," *American Speech* 35 (December 1960).
"Hillbilly Music: Source and Symbol," *Journal of American Folklore* 78 (July 1965).
"Laborlore," in *Festival of American Folklife*, edited by Ralph Rinzler (Washington, D.C.:
Smithsonian Institution, 1971). Program book.
"A Folklorist's Creed and a Folksinger's Gift," *Appalachian Journal* 7 (Autumn–Winter 1979–80).
"Austin's Cosmic Cowboys: Words in Collision," in *And Other Neighborly Names*, edited by
Richard Bauman and Roger Abrahams (Austin: University of Texas Press, 1981).
"Tom Benton's Folk Depictions," in *Thomas Hart Benton*, edited by Linda Weintraub
(Annandale-on-Hudson, N.Y.: Bard College, Blum Art Institute, 1984).
"The Archive's Shores," in *Folklife Annual 1985*, edited by Alan Jabbour and James Hardin
(Washington, D.C.: Library of Congress, American Folklife Center, 1986).
"Stitching Patchwork in Public," in *The Conservation of Culture*, edited by Burt Feintuch
(Lexington: University Press of Kentucky, 1988).
"Remembering Jack Fitch, Pile Butt and Artist, on Labor Day 1994," *San Francisco Examiner*,
September 5, 1994. Op-ed piece.
"Kelly Girl," in *Calf's Head and Union Tale* (Urbana: University of Illinois Press, 1996).
"Torching the Fink Books," *West Coast Sailors* 62 (March 19, 1999). Union newspaper.

Library of Congress Cataloging-in-Publication Data
Green, Archie.
Torching the fink books and other essays on vernacular
culture / Archie Green ; foreword by Robert Cantwell.
p. cm.
Includes bibliographical references and index.
ISBN 0-8078-2605-7 (cloth: alk. paper)—
ISBN 0-8078-4920-0 (pbk.: alk. paper)
1. Folklore—United States.   2. United States—
Social life and customs.   I. Title.
GR105 .G738   2001
398'.0973—dc21   00-048931

05   04   03   02   01   5   4   3   2   1

CONTENTS

Archie Green at home, ca. 1993. (Photograph by Hazen Robert Walker)

Foreword

IN GOOD SPIRITS

Which side are you on? If only it were clear—as clear, at least, as it was for the striking miners in Harlan County, Kentucky, in 1931, whose song, "Which Side Are You On?," brooked no ambivalence. If you weren't for the miners, you were for the operators; if not the unions, the bosses. There was too much at stake for fine distinctions, and no room for compromise; disinterestedness looked too much like cowardice. And yet things are complicated, as every reader of these essays will acknowledge; to every story there are two or three or five sides—even the story of what now seem to be the irresistible developments in a global capitalism, whose miracles of marketing and distribution, underwritten by the communications revolution in which we all mostly happily share, bring in their wake such old-fashioned evils as speeded-up and sweated labor, not to mention prodigious new catalog-operator panopticons of worker surveillance. What is the situation of "folklore" in this brave new world, and where is the folklorist—whose affiliations are mostly, it seems, with the past and with distinctively nonglobal communities—to stand?

Like so many labor actions after the beginning of the Great Depression, the Harlan County coal strike seemed to those involved in it no mere local dispute—a community of workers against a family oligarchy—but an eruption, at a critical place and time, of a greater historical struggle whose outcome, it seemed, would determine the very character of the society of the future. More even than a debate about an economic system, it was a peculiarly American contest, ever and always revolutionary, between rights and powers, justice and tyranny, singing with a memory of the earth-shattering revolutions of the past and shining with a vision of a more perfect future that would follow from them.

But the absolutes of that moment have become the ambiguities of our own. To think in a system of ideas is one thing, to declare allegiance to it is another; and while political affiliation may be tactical, not ideological, we cannot but look on with dismay as those without the least ideological scruple capture the field of action. "My attention to politics . . . had always been more philosophical than practical," Archie Green writes in his afterword to this volume, "for I conceived politics in utopian rather than in backroom terms." Yet one cannot come away from a conversation with Archie Green — and will not come away from a reading of his essays — without finding herself troubled, again, by the strange new immediacy and intimidating pertinence of the striking miners' question. Which side *are* you on? Archie has spent the better part of his life endeavoring to answer that question — to bridge the gap between the contemplative and the active life, to reconcile intellectual responsibility with the responsibility we bear toward our fellow-beings.

As Archie's conversation, his example, his writing, and his speaking continually attest, we cannot, so long as we are creatures of particular times and places and are involved with one another in real situations and circumstances, finally avoid either the moral commitment *or* the intellectual honesty the question demands, for it demands *both*. However dispassionate, methodical, or rigorous we may aspire to be, we are ultimately, and necessarily, on one side or the other — or, at the very least, we are embedded in an interest, an affiliation, a loyalty perhaps, usually an undiscovered one, a place or position from which all we say and do must ultimately flow. And nothing we say or do, therefore, will be anything but a kind of reflex, a mere unconscious redundancy that enunciates and enunciates again that interest or that loyalty until we can incorporate with our view a consciousness of the principle from which it springs. And if, on consideration, we should discover it is a principle to which we cannot adhere, then we have no choice but to change, not merely our principles, but our place.

And that's the hard part. One must shake off indifference, listlessness, complicity, outright fear. The easiest way of life, for a person of principle, is never the best, as Melville knew. And that is why we find Archie Green always somehow practically inconvenienced in some arrestingly, even amusingly interesting way, he whose perpetually inquiring mind, indefatigable conversation, and ever-restless searching after principles of thought and action have never permitted him a comfortable place in the world of middle-class academics and intellectuals, many of whom feel acutely the incompatibility of their social place and their political position but like most human beings haven't the consistency or the fortitude to sever the connection between them.

Though perfectly capable, for example, of operating machinery — he was after all a shipwright on the San Francisco waterfront in the years before and after World War II, and later a building carpenter uptown — Archie does not, or will not, drive an automobile. Though endowed, furthermore, with a culturally rich urban-ethnic upbringing, a wide experience in manual work, and a superior education that includes a liberal arts degree from Berkeley and a doctorate from the University of Pennsylvania, as well as an astonishingly capacious and mercurial imagination and immense intellectual resources, he has never allowed himself to enjoy the material rewards and the cultivation of the personal life to which these achievements and gifts might have entitled him.

His Berkeley degree, for instance, granted in 1939 — especially given the impetus of a Ukrainian-Jewish heritage, with its emphasis upon education, intellectual achievement, and social aspiration — might have opened the door for an academic, public service, or professional career; but, drawn irresistibly instead to industrial work, he joined the Civilian Conservation Corps on the Klamath River immediately after college — certainly the most fateful decision of his life — and cast his lot for good and all with the ranks of the working class, dyeing himself so deeply with its colors that his own sons (the sons, it should be remembered, of a man whom we know now mostly as a historian, scholar, writer, and teacher) are themselves master electricians and, of course, union men.

But they came up when Archie was enjoying a modest living as a union carpenter — a career he abandoned, at age forty, to pursue an advanced degree; swiftly rising in a few years to a tenured position in the English Department at the University of Illinois, he gave *that* up to lobby, successfully, for the passage of the American Folklife Act, subsisting on small grants and a trickling of soft money from Washington's tiny folklife establishment. Having returned, finally, to the cozy apricot-colored house on Caselli Street in San Francisco, originally a working-class enclave which skyrocketing real estate values have transformed into one of the most expensive neighborhoods in the world (the gay synagogue across the street, once a frontier Mormon church, has just been remodeled to the tune of a million dollars by a major retail executive), Archie and his wife Louanne have so far not found sufficient reason to complain of the fifties-era kitchen or front room to make the home improvements that, it seems, are every day farther down on Archie's ever-lengthening agenda.

Archie Green has conscientiously, one might almost say religiously, followed the spartan and self-denying way of life one associates less with credentialed academics than with prewar union organizers, autodidacts, Wobblies, and other working-class intellectuals. One such is San Francisco's folk-etymologist Peter Tamony, Archie's early mentor, to whom he pays tribute in this volume, whom we remember for his researches into the meanings of *jazz* and *hip,* and upon whose work Archie has modeled the word-studies of *dutchman* and *fink* ("creative scholarship outside the academy") that also appear in this collection. Archie's description of Tamony's Mission District flat, where "hundreds of cardboard cartons" overflowed with "file cards, newspaper clippings, notes from remembered conversations, quotations from formal literature," fairly captures the aforementioned Caselli Street front room, in which there is seating space available for only one guest, the collection of boxes on the dining room table having overflowed the waist-high divider between rooms and onto both sections of the L-shaped couch and the better part of the floor space.

It is here, sitting in his rickety captain's chair, with a view out his wide front window of the sunny sidewalk and all the neighbors passing by whom he has known for years, as well as the newcomers to whom he has introduced himself and about whom he has learned more probably than they know about themselves, elbows on knees, sleeves rolled up, leaning slightly forward, that Archie continues the conversation on the politics of culture that began probably a century ago when his father, a Jewish harnessmaker from the Ukraine with several languages at his command and definite political views, led a youthful local cadre in the failed 1905 revolution against the czar. It is to his father's flight from the Cossacks, which took him through London and Winnipeg, where Archie was born, and finally to Boyle Heights, Los Angeles, that we owe the unlikely but fertile mixing of cultural traditions of which Archie is himself a kind of living archive and an avatar.

Sleeves rolled up: do not miss the significance of that. It means there is a job to be done. In America, as we've known since Whitman, it is

incumbent upon us—more than if we had been born into the compara-
tively fixed ranks and stations of a more settled European society—to
invent, more than just to "find" ourselves, the latter being the special
prerogative of privileged youth. This is particularly true for that broad,
variegated class of immigrant-Americans who supplied the labor force
of our belated industrial revolution, for whom a Jewish, Irish, or Ukrainian origin was both the linchpin of personal authenticity and a spike
driven into the heart of full constitutional equality and social acceptance; one could live neither with nor without it, for it was a badge of
oppression as much as of opportunity, a token of membership that was
also a guarantee of exclusion.

To the paradox of identity posed in those days by the conditions
of a new-formed industrialism, there was a variety of responses. One
was simply to embrace one's origins without apology, prolonging the
old way of life in an urban *shtetl* that was also, in a sense, an intellectual dead end, investing all of one's hopes in the influences—popular
culture and education above all—that would transform the next generation. Another was to import the political debates of the old country,
adapting them, albeit imperfectly, to America's maddeningly deceptive
system of class, status, and power, where the dream of revolution could
sustain itself only in a fervid romantic atmosphere purified by a kind
of willful rewriting of the national story and a methodical insulation
from its historical realities.

Still another was the heady promise of individual enterprise—and
the many success stories in those generations could not have but
strengthened the entrepreneurial faith—that could and did turn the
sons of fish peddlers and seamstresses into moguls and tycoons, even
if it could not actually install them in the ruling plutocracy after which
they nonetheless strove to model themselves. But once the industrial
expansion had exhausted itself and the working class had been parti-
tioned, floating either upward into an ever-less-secure but respectable
white-collar proletariat or downward into political invisibility, and the
productive system had begun its long deindustrialization, the question of origins, ethnic or otherwise, had, for want of a distinguishing
answer, largely ceased to be asked. In the general whiteout that is the
tendency of historical identity in a commercial society, working-class,
ethnic, regional, and other archaic instruments of identity-making re-
emerged in the various postwar revivalist movements—popular and
academic—that were the milieu in which an academic and public folk-

lore movement, the latter largely under the influence and tutelage of Archie Green, found a new reason for being.

The idea that underlay all of the tactics by which the immigrant worker had learned to make an accommodation with American society was the possibility, or the necessity, of rebirth, a basic paradigm that we find in every naturalization ceremony that ever converted a Pole or a Latvian or a Ukrainian into an American citizen—or, for that matter, the sons of Jewish shopkeepers into cowboys and banjo players. Like all such formative rituals, these ceremonies are defining as well as transforming; one's personal history tends to rally around them, looking forward to them and back upon them. They can become a force that is ultimately as likely to mire us as stubbornly behind the times as originally it brought us enthusiastically ahead or at least abreast of them. The ghettoized immigrant could not have followed his sons and daughters to the suburbs even if he wanted to; nor could the successful second-generation businessman, blessed by American democracy with safety and security, not to mention education and affluence, be anything but mystified by the anger, the cynicism, even the despair evinced by his children in the face of a society that turned out to be less than perfect after all. Even the third generation, having become the deeply compromised but still conscientious citizens that its own social revolution made it, cannot comprehend its own children, who sometimes seem oddly to have come from and to be going nowhere, and to know nothing—and moreover, to relish it with a kind of bitter but always amusing irony.

Archie Green's most singular strength, among many other strengths both intellectual and personal, is that he has somehow tapped into the sources of such transformations, and through each of the epochs of his life he has drawn upon them with renewed energy and confidence, girding himself once more to confront the challenges of a rapidly changing cultural landscape, always newly unintelligible in such unintelligible ways, yet without ever having relinquished the core of a personality that remains—and I have seen it through more than thirty-five years—unmistakably himself. While passionately allied to a position, a practice, a viewpoint, a strategy, Archie can, with equal passion but without discontinuity, discover ways to adapt the spirit of the old to the letter of the new; while perhaps figuring in terms of long-abdicated conflicts and the political language that attached to them, he nevertheless discerns the shape of the new crisis, the new debate, and stoutly, even cheerfully, enters the fray with undiminished conviction. And, in a way that can be startling to many of his younger students and protégés, he has consistently shown a capacity to entertain, to consider, and, when arguments on their behalf prove irresistible, ultimately to embrace and to accommodate new ideas. In this way he seems almost literally to be perpetually youthful—and even now, in his eighties, he returns again and again with a new interest, a new project, even with new acolytes just discovering him, and always, as he puts it, "in good spirits."

What may be the secret of Archie's prodigious energy is anybody's guess. His father—disputatious, opinionated, unstintingly political— lived well into his nineties. But intellectually speaking, at least some clue to it may be found, I think, in his discovery early in life of what we are wont to call, always a bit uneasily, folklore—or, more accurately, in folklore's discovery of him some forty years ago, when his own youthful fascination with "hillbilly" music and worker's language and lore on the one hand and with New Deal politics and the labor movement on the other, as well as his self-motivated scholarly work in these areas, proved negotiable both in the academy and, as Archie was soon to demonstrate, in the public sector. Still more to the point is his understanding of "folklore," which, as his friends and compatriots know, goes deeper than anything that can be readily formulated from his conversation or his writings, but which is somehow present, as a kind of intimation, at the juncture of his ideas and his practices.

Folklore, like poetry, is one of those things that we know when we see it, but which it is risky to identify too strictly with the *what,* rather than the *wherefore,* of what we've seen. Like poetry, it has its manifestations—in words like *fink* or *salmonbellies* or *dutchman,* in coal miners' songs, in artifacts like duck decoys or Thomas Hart Benton's paintings, in the skills of the pile butt or wood butcher—but always there will be new incarnations that, if we identify the thing itself too closely with the forms of the past, will escape our notice. It is somehow the spirit of the thing, springing like Archie's own good spirits from a burdened but unbowed imaginativeness, to which we must become sensitive. And it is Archie's consistent example, as well as the arguments he has brought to bear upon the whole range of his activities from labor activism to congressional lobbying to teaching, writing, and organizing on behalf of folklore, that more than anything else points to the nature of a uniquely human communicative power whose products— identify, preserve, classify, compare, and theorize about them as we will—remain precious precisely because the thing itself can only be traced or tracked, but never captured.

A word for that understanding might be, both in a chemical and a psychological sense, *sublime:* chemically sublime, on the one hand, because the substance of folklore, passing through an elusive vaporous state whose generative moment only the most stealthy and alert investigation can hope to detect, will transform itself into another, different substance, still equally itself. ("Dutchman," in Archie's case study, moves like a stolen gem from the giant bolster on a ship's hull, to a printery where some thirsty pressmen have been surreptitiously tapping the pipes running along their wall from a saloon next door, to the carved lions guarding the entrance of the New York Public Library. Each transition of the linguistic kernel, from expression to expression, exposes in the play of continuity and difference, tradition and innovation, the irresolvable paradox of meaning, which like a struck match must consume itself in order to shed light.) And psychologically sublime, on the other, because Archie's career, and even in a sense the pattern of his thought, can be understood in its successive stages as sublimations of one set of opportunities, structures, and codes into another set that derives from it—an achievement that is morally of the highest order, as it calls upon us to detach our life force from its vital sources in order to attach it again to the valid purpose and living possibility with which history has confronted us. This is always a crisis of darkness, and no one can weather it who is too jealously tied to things, whether material or intellectual.

In this sense folklore, for Archie Green, has become the field in which the ideals to which he attached himself in youth, the men and women he admired and upon whom he modeled himself, the struggles that shaped his historical sense and the ideas surrounding them, are all alive and well in new forms and configurations: the liberal confidence in the role of government inherited from Roosevelt; the admiration for working people of every stamp and the fascination with the traditional skills they use to materially shape our world, as well as the expressions and stories from which they derive dignity and strength; the dedication to the shipwright's trade and the trade union; the great investment in ideas and words and the ability to deliver them, especially in a workingmen's institute or union hall; and above all an undying curiosity about what amounts to the epidemiology of culture as it moves, viruslike, from mind to mind, use to use, with its infinite capacity for self-replication and adaptation.

These influences and interests are evident now in sublimated form, as when with great wit, animation, and invention Archie addresses a meeting of public folklorists—for example, in the memorable lecture that formed the basis of the essay "Raven, Mallard, and Spotted Owl," cited in the bibliography appended to this volume. His aim is "to make common cause among cultural conservation professionals"; he carries us, with brilliant metaphorical leaps, emblematically, through the history of folklore as it moves from myth and narrative to material culture to performance and social staging, gradually literalizing the avian totems he has summoned up—the mythological raven, the utilitarian duck decoy, even a mine canary and an oil-soaked cormorant—and arriving at last, with the spotted owl, at the ecological trope through which he suggests both the extensive web of social relations in which folklore is enmeshed and the inescapably political implications of cultural work in the public domain.

Readers of this collection will become familiar with the ideological underpinnings of Archie Green's work as vernacular etymologist, labor historian, folklorist, and cultural ecologist—studies that, as he reports in "A Folklorist's Creed and Folksinger's Gift," have made him a consistent champion of self-determination in every sphere and at the same time aligned him with historical, natural, and cultural preservationists, positions that by virtue of their traditional class and party alignments, the one flowing mainly from the left, the other mainly from the right, have not always necessarily been amiable bedfellows. What unifies these commitments is perhaps the cultural idea, essentially a *theory* of folklore, suggested by Archie's self-described political orientation, which he inherits from the Industrial Workers of the World. Archie is a self-described "anarcho-syndicalist with strong libertarian leanings," a "left-libertarian." The vocabulary takes us back to the precinct office, union hall, and settlement house debates of industrial America before the war on fascism, wherein liberal, socialist, anarchist, communist, and other reformist or revolutionary ideas vied for dominance in a clamorous conversation agitated by the appalling injustices and the concomitantly inflamed idealism of the industrial age, a debate in which to participate at all one needed to discover one's place and speak both from and to it.

As a political synthesis, the anarcho-syndicalist position posited a society constituted by voluntary cooperative associations as a hedge against the encroachments upon personal, social, and political liberty that inevitably flows from institutional power. Anarcho-syndicalism hence implies, necessarily, some form of resistance to the tendency of power to concentrate and to centralize itself, as well as to strictly formulated political regimens or programs and their inherently coercive influences: resistance, perhaps, to ideology itself. The trade union, understood as the industrial form of the voluntary association, would, by virtue of its ownership of the means of production—that is, as a "syndicate"—enjoy preeminence in such a system, first among equals in a participatory democracy administered, but not governed, by federations or leagues of industrial workers.

But from the "anarcho-syndicalist" formulation, absent a specifically political context, one might also derive an outline of a process of social communications and the sociopolitical formations that follow from them: a sketch, if not exactly a completed picture, of a society constituted by face-to-face communities or communicative networks, "voluntary" in the sense that they have been formed out of consanguinity, circumstance, proximity, or affinity, or in any case not ideologically or institutionally, and "cooperative" in the sense that these same commonalities have conferred a set of shared or overlapping purposes and values. In such a society, moreover, these communities, however established and governed, form the social medium of a complex and extensive web of human communications in which informal, colloquial, and unofficial "folk" cultures, epitomized perhaps by the traditional communities normally thought of as "folk" but far from exclusive to them, vie coequally with constituted authority, institutional influences, and official culture—themselves understood more as formations than as powers—for audibility, influence, and allegiance.

What Archie calls his "libertarian tendencies," then, would follow inevitably from this picture of society, since the libertarian position places a premium on the freedom of association that practically and philosophically precedes the idea of voluntary community and generally sets the principles of self-governance and self-determination, individual and collective, above the organized structures of social coercion that even representative democracy, with its tyranny of the majority, in effect must adopt. But Archie's libertarianism has a collectivist rather than the more familiar individualist focus, because it is in such affiliations as the trade union or the enclaved folk community, particularly in their oblique or actively oppositional orientations to hegemonic or "official" culture, that individuality finds both its political meaning and the social location in which individual identity is grounded. Which is to say: you and the side you're on are one; to know one is to know the other.

Because property is precisely what the traditional libertarian position takes for granted, the mercantile and agrarian overtones of traditional libertarianism are missing in Archie's analysis. His is, rather, a kind of cultural libertarianism, fitted to a system in which the necessity of retailing one's labor in the marketplace, the historical source of worker disenfranchisement and alienation, instead guarantees — through the freedom granted to declare and assert through work one's primary allegiances — social membership, cultural legitimacy, and political participation. What others have called "cultural democracy," a Leninist shadow-program for equal rights of cultural expression, is in Archie's scheme driven not from above by cultural lieutenants but from below in and through the social formations, neither classes nor social strata but cultural communities, flowing from myriad culturally embedded choices, independent because they *are* so embedded. The language, then, is socialist; but the spirit is Jeffersonian.

Whatever the character of Archie's libertarianism, we can best know it perhaps by its *bête noir,* Stalinism. His conversation, his speeches, and his writing are consistently haunted by the Stalinist specter that would fashion out of pure tyranny a society dedicated to the glorification of the State — a specter that, precisely because the work of cultural conservation so easily lends itself to high-minded but ultimately coercive plans and schemes, he will not allow us to forget. "The same leaders who ordered tanks into Tiananmen Square," he writes, "destroyed Buddhist temples and language schools in Tibet. . . . Those who scrapped an energy-conservation policy for the United States energized death squads in Central America. The term *cultural genocide* links the death of individuals and communities to the extermination of their expressive forms." This formulation in effect turns the Marxist universe upside down, founding it not upon a mode of production or "material base" but in the deep generative power of a liberated cultural expression that, like *dutchman* or *fink* or even the "material base" itself, erupts like the exotic microorganisms in a deep ocean vent at the juncture of earth and world.

In the understanding of culture we are, it seems, approximately in the age of Mendel before the discovery of the gene, knowing something of its operations and its issues but largely in the dark as to its actual agents. We have too readily assigned culture to personality, or vice versa, or too willingly confined it to the manifest "works" that contest or enforce it. Or we have, in the other direction, too ambitiously thrown its mantle over the whole of the human creative enterprise, sacrificing whatever distinctiveness the idea had to begin with. But Archie's politically derived cultural outlook begins to suggest, I think, how "folklore" is far more than a kind of special case or epiphenomenon of culture, its "archaic" or "marginal" or "residual" form; it is an instance, and a particularly trenchant and revealing one, of our cultural behavior generally. We may, therefore, discover ways of translating "folkloric codes into public action."

To the folklorist of Archie's stamp, "culture" is that body of tacit and habitual ideas, understandings, and practices, enlisted by us in the appreciation of being and the performance of life, in which we recognize, communicate, and reaffirm our membership in a particular human community, our "cultural" community. These communities, of course, are many, and our affiliations multiple, but they are neither indefinitely diffuse nor hermetically concentrated. From this viewpoint, postmodern society begins to look like an extensive skein of "folk" cultures flourishing at *every* social level, whose very evolution out of the totalizing industrial, bureaucratic, and technical infrastructures of modernity has enabled us to distinguish more clearly between what is cultural and what is social, what is cultural and what is psychological, what is cultural and what is economic or technological.

A "folk" culture traditionally so called, while often set in conscientious opposition to concentrated power or energized by unsystematic but persistent subpolitical resistance, typically springs up in those sequestered, if not altogether isolated, social enclaves or moves along the momentary synapses of social contact, to dance like electrical discharges among the ever-shifting configurations of human mobility and extension that form the imaginative milieu, the cultural ground, of social life. If we habitually identify folk culture with its incarnations—the quilt, the fiddle tune, the duck decoy, to use Archie's own examples—it is only because the vanishingly ephemeral movements of information at the folk level cannot be observed in and of themselves any more than the movement of a gene (to which cultural information has recently been compared), can be observed except by its traces. We can only seize upon it in those manifestations that, like the colloquial expression, the remembered ballad, or the crafted artifact, register and embody the movement of that information and the adaptation of that information to new settings and purposes, or at best track the already vanished pathways and the moments of imaginative arcing by which a cultural idea has found its way from one set of circumstances to another.

Hence the science of folklore is always, in a sense, one step behind the game, always arriving just as the other has left, with only a foot or a fingerprint to mark its presence. These deposits, as human productions, are intrinsically interesting, intriguing, or beautiful, and it is inevitable that we shall collect, study, celebrate, and seek to preserve and perpetuate them. At bottom, though, the fascination of folklore — what has drawn so many of us obsessively into its vortex — is in the movement itself, because however momentary and partial our picture of it may be, that movement intimates a global information network of vast historical extent, one as surely embedded in the technics and the organics of human communications as our World Wide Web is embedded in a historical infrastructure of fiber optics and copper cable. It is this movement, and the matrix in which it occurs, that we designate when we use the word *culture*.

This is the realm in which Archie Green has always worked. His heart will quail to a lonesome mountain song, his eye rove through the patterns of a patchwork quilt, as much as anyone's; but, as his studies of *fink* and *dutchman* and especially *hillbilly* indicate, his real interest is in tracing the genesis of an idea or an expression from its origin to its exfoliation, through hundreds of instants of imaginative and practical origination and invention, into the multitudes of discrete situations in which we find it. This is the way Archie learns the cultural landscape and how to maneuver in it — a neverending process, its horizon ever receding, but one that bestows a kind of immunity, like Brer Rabbit's from the briarpatch, from the fixed perspectives, the entrenched positions, and the quarrelsome ideologies that — although we must adopt them in order to discuss, debate, or articulate at all — we only ultimately embrace at our peril. Herein actually lies, I suspect, some of the truth of Archie's inexhaustible energy, his capacity for intellectual and moral growth, his adaptability to changing times and interests.

It is in this realm, too, that Archie's extraordinary investigative skills show forth most brilliantly. For there are few, if any, bibliographies, card catalogs, search engines, or websites to guide us into the strong-holds or along the thoroughfares of folk culture, which are but the ephemeral traces of oral and mimetic transmissions that no sooner have completed themselves than they disappear. Such an investigation, sleuthlike, intuitive, built on hunches, memories, notions, associations, and half-conscious perceptions, can only have been shaped in the very medium within which it works, by a kind of habituation to the embodied character of folk-cultural knowledge. One has to have a nose for it—there is no other way.

Consider, for example, Archie's seminal essay, "Hillbilly Music: Source and Symbol," which permanently installed the study of commercially recorded Appalachian music in the canon of academic folk-lore and surveyed the ground upon which all subsequent histories of country music have been written. Like any academic essay, this one represents long hours in a library; and, indeed, Archie's ability to maneuver in a library owes much to his graduate training in library science. But the story he has constructed from his research emerges as a palpable body out of a phantasmal rush of ephemeral and esoteric material including newspapers, magazines, record catalogs and albums, discographies, radio logs, photographs, disc labels, company records, and personal letters, as well as the more customary dictionaries, encyclopedias, journals, and books—and all these are in addition to a surrounding chatter of conversations and interviews, hundreds of hours of them over a ten-year period, which are the real milieu of the study.

Any historical study involves such an investigation of primary material, no matter how transient; what strikes the reader of this essay, and of the others in this collection, however, is not so much *what* the writer has used as the almost uncanny prescience with which he has used it. How, one asks, can he have known to look, for an essay on hillbilly music, into the *American Mercury* for 1928 or the "Index to the Films of John Ford"? And where on earth could he have found *The Columbia 13/14000-D Series: A Numerical Listing*? Once one has grasped the extent of the accumulation of information necessary to create the article's basic narrative, it emerges as a wonder that Archie's research can have consumed only ten years; twenty-five would be more like it.

On casual perusal, then, Archie Green's brand of scholarship, with its unlikely turns and unexpected disclosures, strikes us as almost paranormally inspired, and in much the same way, I would suggest, as Whitman's poetry, in which many years' accumulation of ideas, impressions, images, sensations, and words resolve themselves into a rhap-sodic utterance indicative, it would seem—for this way poetic illusion inclines us—of a mind as fleet as faerie dust, an experience as wide as continents, a sympathy as unbounded as a god's. From this perspective one begins to understand what those cardboard boxes, spreading over Archie's couch and floor, are all about. Neither poetry nor scholarship comes out of cardboard boxes, of course, but from memory, under-standing, and imagination, and still more from patient application and dedicated, coherent labor. Whether in the Southern Folklife Collec-tion at Chapel Hill or cluttering the front room of his house on Caselli Street, Archie's accumulated archives represent his years of collecting; but collections do not make scholars. Archie's collections map the pro-longed reflections of his mind as well as its more wayward peregri-nations—a terrain of times, places, and people whose topography he knows as surely as he knows the San Francisco bus routes and whose major and minor thoroughfares he has charted for us in his work.

Which brings us to the matter of Archie's unique and in many ways eccentric writing style. Though learned, cosmopolitan, and profes-sional, Archie writes with neither the facile allusiveness of the *belle lettrist,* the glib self-assurance of the highbrow journalist, nor the convo-luted abstraction of a university academic. Rather, his writing is work-manlike in more than the usual metaphorical sense, his voice poised between the articulation of subject matter on the one hand and the *constructive* activity of writing on the other. He demonstrates as much as he assays, audibly organizing, assembling, and building as much as narrating, expounding, or explaining. The debt of his style is owed as much to the evening meeting at the workers' institute as it is to the morning lecture hall, as much to the trade weekly as to the academic journal, while still other traces—of brochure and sleeve notes, chap-books, even op-ed pieces and, I would suggest, blueprints and work orders—linger amongst its lines.

Several features, both rhetorical and grammatical, characterize the style. Among the most noticeable of these is the ceremonial pause, in which his assembled audience, like a tour group clustered around a mechanical or scientific demonstration, becomes nearly visible, and in which he points to or explains what, rhetorically or intellectually, he has done or is doing: "To mark Alan's enthusiasm, I . . ." or "Here I explore. . . ." Equally characteristic is his tendency to develop an idea around a particular symbol, emblem, or event, often one of marked currency or immediacy, by which he ties his subject on the one hand to the political present and on the other to the historical past: the spotted owl, then everywhere in the newspapers, is a prime example. Today it might be Littleton or Kosovo; but always the connection is made in a way that finds in the immediacy of such events more deeply recurrent meanings. Finally, and most pervasively, Archie's writing shows a general hankering after verbal efficiency or economy, indicated by a systematic and sometimes mannered erasure of connectives, plurals, and particles, as well as by a conspicuous favoring of possessives: "The Archive's Shores," the "conversation pole's base."

Taken together, these stylistic habits help us to locate Archie as a writer. As he writes he demonstrates, in effect practically apprenticing his readers to the craft. Critically concerned to anchor his ideas in the memory of his readers, and at the same time to set them afloat upon the stream of the times in which they live, he links them to familiar images or objects in a provocative context of immediate relevance that both locates the audience to which he is writing and suggests the deeper significance of topics that, superficially at least, would seem to have little to do with what official culture has for its own purposes magnified or glamorized. Finally, this writing style represents above all a sense of providence or frugality in the use of his medium.

In *all* of these respects, Archie's writing betrays the hand of the tradesman in the literary salon, caulking the joints in the discursive hull (to use the figures of Archie's own trade), bolting the rhetorical decking to the argumentative framework, plugging the bolt-holes and applying a protective varnish. We are under his tutelage as well as his instruction; though we may not take away with us the precise equations in which he has embodied his ideas, we will surely take away the images or symbols around which, ultimately, we may advance our own designs as well as originate our own tricks of the trade. But most important, we will absorb what is finally the most consistent of messages in Archie's use of language, which is that the resources of the world, natural or cultural, are precious and finite, and that it is incumbent upon us not only not to waste them but to put them to good use—which is to say, for a *collective* good. One senses that Archie approaches a scholarly essay much as he might a job of work: an end to be attained—say, a hatch to be squared or a bulkhead plumbed—and a fixed supply of materials— say, a certain weight in bolts or rivets and a certain number of board-feet of teak rail or deck pine; the craftsman's problem is first to assess, then to estimate, and then to plan, and thence to bring into the best possible alignment the materials and the aims of the work.

These syntactic and rhetorical habits prove meaningful in ways that help link the writing to the imaginative traditions in which Archie came up, especially in such essays as "Stitching Patchwork in Public" or "A Folklorist's Creed," designed originally as public addresses. In these, the elision of the common particle and the substitution of singulars for plurals becomes a kind of naming of parts, imparting to common nouns something of the singularity of their "proper" cousins; this often lends an emblematic texture and heroic resonance to his topic reminiscent of socialist realism, the "waterway and museum case" or the "natural habitat and editorial column" becoming by implication scenes of political or social contestation and almost epic struggle, "from boardroom to courthouse, fireside to streetcorner" or "Pacific shore to Virginia Tidewater." Here he shows his strong rhetorical affinities to Thomas Hart Benton's visual images (analyzed in "Tom Benton's Folk Depictions")—panoramic, narrative, and symbolic, their original particularity emancipated by a kind of liquefaction of outline, frank coloration, and a reconfiguration of the conceptual space in which they occur, suggestive of a kind of gale of popular energy sweeping through the multitudinous scenes of the national experience and drawing them up into transitory figures of social meaning.

The effect of the style is to efface the introspective or even narcissistic bourgeois "author" in favor of an inclusive, impersonal voice couched in a symbolic, or as he would have it, totemic, common language: "We seek to preserve fiddle tune and guitar run, barn sign and scrimshaw token. But day by day news pours into parlor, den, or office about social inferno, new horrors confronting people and environments." The hortatory tone and the structural as well as rhetorical reliance on symbolic forms lends itself to symbolic manipulations that often transcend specific arguments or particular claims, permitting the coexistence of otherwise incompatible outlooks and inspiring, typically, concluding bursts of new ideas, questions, and themes.

All this brings home what anyone familiar with Archie and his work understands at once, which is the sheer impossibility of capturing in the written word the gorgeous rhetorical arabesques, the ever-mounting terraces, stratum upon stratum, of reference, the stunning associative leaps of his intellectual monologues. To listen to him talk is often to be, at first, confused or bewildered, as the apparently disconnected ideas and images, most of them held in the ghostly half-life of a never-completed sentence, accumulate like a crowd of restless spirits until with an almost audible orchestral swell a sense of the intricate interconnectedness of each idea to the other begins to brighten one's intellectual sky, and Archie's point—and it will be a point, sometimes, that one may hold onto for years to come—appears triumphantly on the horizon.

Archie Green is a brilliant talker. His manner is digressive: sentences interrupted in mid-phrase, parenthetical asides that soon advance like a tidal wave over what moments earlier had been the topical ground, passionate interjections from today's paper or the weekend book review (especially if it involves Washington's latest political imbecility), clever—often unbelievably clever—interpolations, high-level reconnaissance flights over history or literature, sometimes withering excoriations of tyrants, knaves, and fools, who are never, in Archie's discourse, in short supply or very far away—all delivered with intense urgency and conviction, or, as the case may be, with easy good humor, or in whatever way the occasion, whether a public meeting or a private consultation, calls for. At times he is a man talking to men, the bared forearm pumping, one side of his mouth bearing the greater part of the burden, the gaze turned to survey whatever is at the other end of the room or outside the window—one can almost feel the afternoon shadow of a ship's hull crawling over the scene where we, his confederates, have convened on the docks to mull, to strategize, to rendezvous. At other times he is the congenial and gentle father-figure, his shining face and good-natured smile presiding over the transformation of a casual aggregate of idle interests and half-hearted intentions into ardent convictions and a crusading spirit. Private or public, Archie's words can be galvanizing.

To repeat, then, it is as much through Archie Green's example as through his writing that we come to know him. I have already alluded to his inexhaustible energy, his uncompromising commitment and his tacit insistence upon it in others, leavened by strict intellectual rectitude and its openness to argument, change, and growth, his seemingly unlimited capacity to transform the imperatives of one place and time to the opportunities and requirements of another.

What I haven't yet mentioned is that the writer so frugal with written words and so prodigiously liberal with spoken ones is a man of huge intellectual generosity. In a time when ideas have assumed virtually the status of trade secrets in an academic marketplace tense with the ordeals of promotion and tenure, when the presses are flooded with academic titles that spring from little more than cocktail-party conceits and dining-table paradoxes, and when open intellectual exchange has almost fallen silent, Archie Green, who I suppose has ideas to spare, is prolix, almost profligate with them. He has none of the usual sense of proprietorship; to him ideas are, in a sense, an abundant natural resource, whose planting, cultivation, and harvest are a general benefit requiring labors best distributed among those best equipped to perform the work. He gives them away freely, especially to young scholars most in need of them. There is scarcely a program, an exhibit, a festival, a book, or any other project in the field of public folklore in the last thirty years in which Archie has not had some hand, and much academic, scholarly, or theoretical work for which Archie has provided, not only the original impetus, but devoted guidance and persevering moral support.

"Have you heard of the Archie Green doll?" went the joke, not so long ago, in folklore circles. "Wind it up, and it'll introduce you to someone you ought to know." It is consistent with Archie's idea of culture that he should always seek to place his work and ours in the midst of the busy human scene, where the chatter, the rush, and the buzz of life continually replenishes the deep social reservoirs from which we fill the wells of our own natures. *Here,* in discourse, discussion, disputation, and all the forms of human intercourse such activity implies, we walk the bridge Archie has built between action and contemplation, intellectual integrity and political commitment. Of all the urgently instructive examples Archie's life provides, this is perhaps most urgent of all: that we are social beings, and that from pride and selfishness nothing, of any kind, is ultimately to be gained. Some of us, perhaps, are more shy and reclusive, less socially confident, than others; not all of us came up in the teeming urban environment that shaped Archie's gregarious nature. But even the most retiring soul can recognize in Archie Green an object lesson in the extent of our relations, our complete dependency for all that we are upon them, and the powerful engine of moral, intellectual, and spiritual energy they are. Like it or not, it is the side, the side of our common humanity, that we are on.

Let us return, then, for a moment, to the automobile, in which Archie will be perhaps a willing, and certainly a voluble, passenger, but never a driver. One only has to spend a day with him in his beloved San

Francisco to grasp the reasons behind this otherwise eccentric and, it seems, highly uncooperative and sometimes inconvenient policy. Consider, first, how profoundly *political* is this posture in an automotive age. Its reverberations extend from the petty designs of quotidian errands and daily interactions through the layered economies and interests of municipalities and states, through politics-as-usual to the federal government and finally to the transcontinental megacorporation, the oil cartels, and international relations. But all that is not, finally, at least not immediately, the point. He is not really, as he sometimes likes to claim, a cultural Luddite. The point is that the automobile is isolating; it sets us apart. It is a social and environmental predator, and like the water carrier in the Chinese folktale who would not build a waterwheel, the slave has enslaved the slaver. As surely as we are becoming the servomechanisms of our computers, we long ago succumbed to our cars, our highways, our repair bills, and our insurance policies, all at the expense of the sociality that from infancy onward is the heart and soul of our humanity—what symbolically or actually we will have, one way or another.

Archie travels in his shoes—and on the buses, trains, and trolleys that circulate like so many savory old stories around San Francisco Bay, plunging him into the welter of contacts, conversations, recognitions, and encounters that is life in the great peninsular city for those who have acquired the cultural skills to live it. From the bookstore owner on Potrero Hill, to the retired pile butt in the lower Mission, to the archivist at the public library, to the filmmaker in the Haight, to the record producer up in El Cerrito, Archie's connections, these and dozens more, those of fifty years' standing, of only yesterday, or of days to come, are the nodes of a high-voltage grid of human energy that extends from Archie's captain's chair on Caselli Street down to the bus stop on Eighteenth Street and to every corner of the Bay and beyond to union and hiring halls, libraries and classrooms west and east, to the Smithsonian Institution and the Library of Congress, but most of all throughout the widespread generation of students who have been his protégés, now themselves striving, as they enter their own majority, to return to a still younger generation something of what he gave them by following so far as possible his ever-enlightening example.

Think of him, then, footloose, in his dungarees and knit cap, on the city sidewalks or on the bus, with a reference to track down, a typescript to copy, a letter to put in the mail, a friend to meet, acquainted, it seems, with everyone from the postman on the corner and the building contractor at work across the street to the editorial page editor and the union boss, moving eagerly from conversation to conversation, turning perfect strangers into cultural informants at a moment's notice — the natural, the architectural, and the social landscapes that he knows by heart touched for him in every feature with the lives of noble but uncelebrated people whose fables and chronicles, but more important, whose *work,* full of unexpected heroism, dignity, beauty, and genius, he has been teaching us all his life to read and to appreciate. It is a paradigm — a *para-dim,* as Archie might say — of the world, real and imagined, in which he lives, one in which the capacity for living, or what we call culture, is no unsolicited gift, but the outcome of selfless labor in the trade of being human. It is a traditional skill — and like all such skills, we must honor, practice, preserve, and share it, lest it be lost forever.

Robert Cantwell

Torching the Fink Books
and Other Essays on Vernacular Culture

Dutchman

AN ON-THE-JOB ETYMOLOGY

A t mid-century, the chief arena for ethnic conflict in America is often a city schoolyard. In bygone years such conflict occurred in the mine, mill, workshop, and construction camp—the industrial front. Immigrants who came to build a new nation had first to face bigotry and hostility on the job. Ironically, as each group achieved status, it vented its spleen on newcomers surging up from below.

Today, job conflict between national groups is submerged. Unions, employers, churches, schools, and government educate toward mature democratic behavior. However, a residue of ethnic hostility lives on in the language of the trades. An apprentice or new worker learns the argot and slang of his special calling. Along with a host of esoteric technical and trade terms, he picks up hidden reminders of the past in the form of pejorative language—the language that downgrades, demeans, destroys.

No one who has rubbed shoulders where men work together has escaped the half-playful banter between national and even native regional groups. This vocabulary of slurs and slanders is applied directly to persons. However, a special type of depreciatory nomenclature has been applied to tools, mechanical devices, and work processes. Long after a minority group is integrated, or has completely vanished from the trade, the tool name lingers on as a faint reminder of early aggression or conflict.

Phrases in this category that I have heard in actual usage in San Francisco building construction and waterfront employment are: *German planer, Irish buggy, Irish confetti, Irish rosette, Jew nails, Mexican drag line, niggerhead, Norwegian steam, Polack screwdriver, Portugee lift, Portugee pump, Swede hand axe,* and *Swede rule.* Any construction stiff or factory hand could

"On the Ways," by unnamed artist. From Richard Finnie,
Marinship *(San Francisco: Marinship Corp., 1947).*

extend this brief list from his personal vocabulary. A study of the origins of these terms would portray the grim story of the adjustment of immigrant to industry.[1]

Very early in my own apprenticeship as a shipwright in San Francisco I was exposed to a single ethnic work-process term that, unlike the unpleasantries cited, was ameliorative and complimentary. The word was *dutchman;* perhaps it caught my ear because it was used in a pleasant, friendly manner.

The setting was dramatic. We were high on the hull of a huge vessel under construction on the ways. I was helping two skilled Scottish shipwrights, Ben Carrwardine and James Allan, who were fitting the twin hawse pipes into the bow. The circular bolster—five feet in diameter, heavy, and as irregular as a mushroom with a hole in its head—would not fit snug to the sheer of the shell. We twisted and turned, pushed and pulled, cajoled and cursed the huge casting, but to no avail. Finally, Carrwardine said, in exasperation, "Let it go! We'll put in a dutchman." I was mystified, but soon observed the two journeymen cutting and shaping heavy bands of steel to insert in the gap left between the bolster and the ship's shell. Then a welder skillfully joined casting, dutchman, and shell together, in itself a difficult and trying job.

Later, I quizzed Carrwardine on this peculiar usage. Why did he

---

call the steel insert that hid the multiple errors of the patternmaker, foundryman, loftsman, and shipwright a *dutchman*? He replied that *dutchman* was a term applied by carpenters to a patch or an insert in woodwork. Often it was placed to hide a miscut, a bad joint, or poor workmanship. Sometimes it served to replace a natural defect in the wood, such as a pitch pocket or knot. When the dutchman was inserted by a skilled mechanic, it would be so smooth and clean as to avoid detection. Because shipwrights constructed both wooden and steel vessels, the term was applied to both wood and metal.

Carrwardine's theory of the origin of the term was that it started in San Francisco after the Gold Rush. Great numbers of European craftsmen came to California to seek fortunes at the diggings or with their tools. German cabinetmakers, furniture hands, wood carvers, piano builders, coopers, and carpenters flocked to El Dorado. When fellow workers observed their skill in inserting patches, they extended the slang name of the group to the work process itself, and *dutchman* is the term employed to this day.

Some sixteen years passed before I was prompted to look into the etymology of *dutchman*. I had heard it so often and on such a variety of jobs that the explanation of the origin had receded into a cranny of my memory. In the spring of 1957 I learned that George Korson was engaged in a study of the folklore of Pennsylvania Dutch coal miners.[2] When informed of Carrwardine's usage, he requested details and confirmation. Was the term applied directly to old-country German mechanics, or did it possibly come from Pennsylvania Dutchmen seeking their fortunes in California? Unfortunately, Carrwardine had died during the war, and I had to turn elsewhere for the answer to this question. Peter Tamony, San Francisco etymology, kindly gave me access to his library, and I began to explore.

The first lexicographer to recognize *dutchman* as applied to a work process was John Russell Bartlett in the *Dictionary of Americanisms:* "A flaw in a stone or marble slab, filled up by an insertion."[3] Some years later, Edward H. Knight issued the first portion of his definitive three-volume *American Mechanical Dictionary,* later published in London under the title, *The Practical Dictionary of Mechanics.* Knight defined a *dutchman* in carpentry as "a playful name for a block or wedge of wood driven into a gap to hide the fault in a badly made joint."[4]

The *OED,* the *DAE,* and the *DA* added numerous examples of the term as used by craftsmen, but did not offer clues to its origin. However, Mitford M. Mathews cited in the *DA* a choice usage by a group of Butte, Montana, printers during frontier days. The *Evening Intermountain* pressroom was underneath a large saloon. Beer lines ran from a next-door storage cellar into the printery and across the ceiling of a corner of the composing room. One day an inquisitive printer discovered that the pipes contained beer. A hand drill was obtained, a hole was bored and then corked tight with a small steel plug known as a *dutchman*. The bartenders knew that things were amiss, but the tapped pipe was well camouflaged. One year later, after their annual mulligan, the printers began to drink quite heavily. Before long, a drunken printer either forgot to replace the *dutchman* or was too drunk to secure it tightly. When the kegs ran dry, of course, the source of conviviality on the *Intermountain* was discovered and the practice brought to an end.[5]

Long after the Butte story had passed into folklore, V. E. Leighty, of the University of Michigan while writing on printer's argot offered a partial explanation of the meaning of the term. He stated that *dutchman* was used when a compositor, finding some loose type in a locked form, drove in a toothpick or matchstick wedge to tighten the type. Leighty observed that

> the term does not appear in Moxon's *Mechanick Exercises,* 1683, nor in Smith's *Printer's Grammar.* Hence it seems to appear too late to have any connection with the humorous and opprobrious compounds with Dutch which arose from the animosity engendered by the Dutch wars of the seventeenth century.[6]

Both Leighty and Carrwardine agreed that the term is not pejorative. Was the shipwright correct in placing its origin in California? Armed with my new knowledge, I interviewed in July, 1957, two old-time San Francisco carpenters.

Henry Kendall had begun as a millwright apprentice in the Spreckles Sugar House on the San Francisco waterfront in 1906. He laughingly referred to himself as an earthquake carpenter, thereby revealing a bit of folk etymology. In the rush to rebuild the city after the holocaust, many new, untrained men entered the trade to throw up jerry-built housing. Although Kendall is conceded by his peers to be a superb journeyman, he dates his time of origin in the craft with the mock-critical epithet. Kendall told me that *dutchman* was known to all the old mechanics in the Sugar House, both natives and those from other parts. He had not considered it an ethnic word, good or bad, since it was such a common and basic trade term. He was quite surprised when I conveyed Carrwardine's theory to him, for he had never heard it in all his years of growing up and working in San Francisco.

William Kelly had come to the West Coast from Boston a few years after the 1906 earthquake and fire, and started his apprenticeship in an Alameda planning mill. When he first joined the union, there were two mill-cabinet locals in San Francisco, the German Local and the American Local. In those days woodworking firms were often combination shops with the German mechanics doing fine cabinet work upstairs, and the Americans doing production work downstairs. He added by way of good-natured explanation that the Americans were really "Duke's Mixture"—simply any millmen who were not German. Kelly also was surprised to hear Carrwardine's theory, and offered as his hunch that the term might have been used in the East prior to the Gold Rush.

Bartlett recorded *dutchman* in his *Dictionary* in 1859. It is a good rule of thumb in language study that a word circulates orally many years before it gets into print, and often for some time in print before it is rewarded by being placed in a dictionary. If *dutchman* was first applied by American mechanics to compliment the skill of their German fellows, when and where did the act of extension occur?

The first woodworkers in the New World were colonists and pioneers who felled trees, cut logs into lumber, and built their own crude implements. While the nation was still young, the invention of specialized woodworking machinery set the stage for factory production of wood products. It was only after the application of the steam engine to saw mills, and the introduction of the circular saw and related tools, that cheap, rapid, mass production of finished lumber, furniture, sashes and doors, and stock trim was possible. Hence it was in the decades of the 1830s and 1840s that mill-cabinet and building entrepreneurs reached out to Germany and other European areas for skilled help.

Writing in the New York *Harbinger* on January 10, 1846, a journalist observed:

> There are persons who are constantly watching for German emigrants who can work at cabinet making, even going on board of ships before the emigrants have landed, and engage them for a year at $20 and $30 and their board, or the best terms they can make.[7]

The early machine woodworking trade was centered in the growing cities of the East Coast, Boston, New York, and Philadelphia; then it gradually spread to Cincinnati, Chicago, and Grand Rapids as the forests of Wisconsin and Michigan were opened to lumbering operations.

Some place, some time, perhaps in an East Coast cabinet shop in the Age of Jackson, a native tradesman complimented the craftsmanship of a German mechanic and a new word was born. Neither lexicographer Bartlett nor shipwright Carrwardine is here to give his sources. Perhaps a curious reader would like to present his own etymology for *dutchman*.[8] Of particular value would be trade journal or workingmen press usages of the term in the days of early German immigration into the United States.

NOTES

1. Several of these terms are glossed by me in "John Neuhaus: Wobbly Folklorist," *Journal of American Folklore* 73 (1960): 189–217.

2. George Korson, *Black Rock: Mining Folklore of the Pennsylvania Dutch* (Baltimore, Md., 1960).

3. Boston, 1859, p. 134.

4. New York, 1874, p. 765.

5. Anecdote by Bill Burke in WPA Writer's Program, *Copper Camp* (New York, 1943), p. 94. The word *mulligan* occurs in the following sentence on that page: "Just after the Butte-Anaconda printer's annual mulligan, a moist affair that lasted several days, many of the boys suffered from parched throats." According to such sources as the *OED, DAE,* and *DA, mulligan* refers to stew, soup, or an alcoholic drink. Burke's extension of the term to a celebration seems unreported prior to this instance.

6. "Some Composing Room Terms," *American Speech* 13 (1938): 268–74.

7. Quoted by Frederick S. Deibler, *The Amalgamated Wood Workers' International Union of America* (Madison, Wis., 1912), p. 35.

8. In "Recovered" (in "The Talk of the Town," *New Yorker,* September 3, 1960, pp. 20–21), Walter Beretta, marble carver who restored the New York Public Library's terrace lion, offered a reporter an explanation of *dutchman*. Surgeon-sculptor Beretta "mended the lion by cutting recesses several inches deep wherever the stone was damaged, and fitting new pieces of stone therein. These pieces are known in the trade as dutchmen, and Mr. Beretta thinks the name comes from the fact that the pieces are nearly always square, whence 'squarehead,' whence 'dutchman.' In our experience, it is Scandinavians and Germans who are called squareheads, but perhaps the 'dutch' here is the common corruption of '*Deutsch*.'" The item goes on to mention a special adhesive, made

in Germany from a secret formula, which serves to fix the dutchmen in place. After the adhesive has hardened, "the stone is carved to look exactly like the original. Over the years, the Library lions' Tennessee pinkness has faded to New York gray, so the dutchmen in the uptown lion were bleached to make them as nearly invisible as possible."

Hillbilly Music

SOURCE AND SYMBOL

illbilly, the word, has been used both pejoratively and humorously in American print since April 23, 1900. On that day the *New York Journal* reported that "a Hill-Billie is a free and untrammelled white citizen of Alabama, who lives in the hills, has no means to speak of, dresses as he can, talks as he pleases, drinks whiskey when he gets it, and fires off his revolver as the fancy takes him." We do not know how early the term began to circulate in speech. William Nathaniel Harben, 1858–1919, a north Georgia writer, must certainly have heard it during his Whitfield County youth. In his novel, *Abner Daniel* (1902), he used "passle o' hill-billies" in a vernacular context. When the spate of publications appeared after 1870 based on slow "Arkansaw" trains, one such pamphlet by Charles S. Hibler, *Down in Arkansas* (1902), featured a full description of The Hill Billy tendered by a guide to a trio of out-of-state land speculators in the Ouachita Mountains. The stereotype moved quickly from novel and pamphlet to academic attention, for J. W. Carr, University of Arkansas professor, in his first word list from the state's Ozark section reported the expression in 1903 speech, "You one-gallused hill billies, behave yourselves." [1]

There is no point in documenting the obvious by noting all the contemporary nuances — negative or comic — that describe the Southern mountaineer or backwoodsman today. Two snatches of folksong, however, add biting twists to the term as well as relate it to specific areas of agrarian conflict. In the Kentucky tobacco wars of 1907 organized farmers sang derisively of their dissident neighbors. "Oh poor old hillbilly, oh, where do you stand, / While the Dark Tobacco Planters Association is forming its clan?" In Texas, some years later, sharecroppers

"Hill Billies," by Okeh Records artist,
in Talking Machine World, *April 15, 1925.*

and muleskinners chanted, "I'd rather be a nigger an' plow ol' Beck, /
Dan a white hill-billy wid a long red neck." [2]

What brought this figure to the surface of print and speech from
Georgia to the Ozarks at the turn of the century? We do not know; nor
do we have any acceptable etymology for the word. One possible clue
on origin might be found in a pair of Scottish colloquialisms, *hill-folk*
and *billie*. The former was deprecatory, for it designated a refractory
Presbyterian—a Cameronian—a rebel against Charles II. Scots hill-
folk and hill-men in 1693 were noted for zeal, devotion, and prudence
in seeking isolation away from their rejected monarch's rule. *Billie* was
used in Scots dialect as early as 1505 as a synonym for *fellow, companion,
comrade,* or *mate*. The words *hill* and *billie* might well have been combined
in the Highlands before the first austere Cameronian took refuge in
the piney uplands of the New World. Historical speculation aside, we
know the word in print only from 1900 and only as an Americanism.

Hillbilly, a combined word, has lent itself to further combination, for in many of its recent appearances it is found linked with the nouns—*music, song, ballad, singer, folio, act, show, record.* The *OED* places such a new combination for *song* in 1932, and the *DA* for *ballad* in 1949. One student of American speech commented that radio itself brought the mountain nickname to acute and general public consciousness in the 1930s.[3]

By 1951 the association of the hackneyed image and music was so fixed by mass media that a scholar felt impelled to undercut the linkage. He wrote: "We may safely discount the picturesque hallucination of screen and radio, that ballads are a monopoly of 'hillbillies,' a race of gaunt, bearded primitives, drinking whiskey out of tin dippers and singing ballads when they ain't feudin'."[4] Seemingly his discounting efforts were ineffective, for in a 1962 dispatch from Germany a London official stated, "It is no longer considered in good taste among American diplomats to display an awareness of hillbilly music or to discuss the poetry of Walt Whitman."[5]

Perhaps the Foreign Service will shuck off folksy informality and its poetic accouterments, but it is not likely that American speech, letters, or scholarship in the near future is going to break the bond stated in the combination, *hillbilly music.* My task, then, is to ask why a pejorative-humorous term was first extended to a viable form of traditional folk music and to seek answers to the queries of when, where, and how the act of extension took place.

Two scholars who have listened to the music under consideration offer these preliminary guides. "Hill-billy music seems to be a super-hybrid form of some genuine folk elements which have intruded into the mechanism of popular culture." A dual formulation states: "Of or pertaining to commercialized folk or folkish songs (or the performers thereof) largely derived from or aimed at white folk culture of the southern United States, beginning in 1923. Of or pertaining to that style—a blend of Anglo-Irish-Negro folksong and American popular song—on which the commercial tradition was based and developed."[6] Whether an ultimate definition stresses time, locale, ethnic group, vocal and instrumental style, or the dialectic antithesis and synthesis between Folk and Mass Culture, it is necessary at this juncture to note that the term *hillbilly music,* however defined, has been employed for three decades as a rubric covering a kaleidoscopic variety of sub-forms: old time, familiar tunes, Dixie, mountain, sacred, gospel, country, cowboy, western, country-western, hill and range, western swing, Nashville, rockabilly, bluegrass. *Hillbilly* can cover all available (recorded and published) white commercial country music or it can be equated simply with one limited type or recent period; for example, *Time*'s folksong expert reports that *bluegrass* is a polite synonym for *hillbilly*.[7]

It is obvious that mountain folk sang and played music long before the word *hillbilly* was printed and before it was coupled with *music*. Language extension is not a chaotic process isolated from other culture forms. It is my thesis that the term *hillbilly music* was born out of the marriage of a commercial industry—phonograph records and some units of show business—with traditional Appalachian folksong. My paper is restricted largely to early matrimonial days: pre-1927, pre-Jimmie Rodgers, pre-Carter Family, and frequently pre-electrical recording processes.

The search for an adequate etymology, if one turns to talking machine history, can lead into a discographic jungle where the danger is that a meaningful area in American studies will be lost under a growth of esoteric labels and master numbers. It is basic to our purpose to know who recorded the first hillbilly disc, and when, but it is also more important that we ask who sang such music at home, Snopeses or McCaslins. On first hearing a hillbilly ballad or breakdown, do we visualize the mountain over which the Trail of the Lonesome Pine coiled, or the coves of Frenchman's Bend in Yoknapatawpha County? When we listen to these tunes do we hear the voices of shiftless, landless outcasts or of free and upright herdsmen and yeomen? Are we listening to the music itself or rather to pre-cast aural images? Do we deprecate the music because it is sentimental, banal, saccharine, or do we judge it as the product of an eroded or decadent culture? James Agee linked his talents with photographer Walker Evans to evoke the life of Alabama cotton tenant families in the depressed 1930s. If the authors of *Let Us Now Praise Famous Men* (1941) could have supplied to each reader a kit of Okeh 45000s, Brunswick 100s, or Columbia 15000s, how much more powerful would their book's impact have been!

Why have hillbilly records been on hand for four decades with the minimum attention from the Academy?[8] Why is it so difficult to break the aural blockade even today? David Reisman suggests a clue. "Things that strike the sophisticated person as trash may open up new vistas for the unsophisticated; moreover, the very judgment of what is trash may be biased by one's own unsuspecting limitations, for instance, by one's class position or academic vested interest."[9]

Not only does High Culture frequently downgrade the artifacts that document hillbilly music—record, folio, radio transcription, barn dance show, rural drama—as trash, but for two centuries it has labeled the very people who produced the music as poor white trash. Fanny Kemble, after a visit to antebellum Georgia, wrote of the pinelanders as "the most degraded race of human beings claiming an Anglo-Saxon origin that can be found on the face of the earth—filthy, lazy, ignorant, brutal, proud, penniless savages."[10] Frederick L. Olmsted, George M. Weston, Hinton Rowen Helper, and J. E. Cairnes—travelers, historians, sociologists—elaborated and pyramided the dismal scene. Nor was it confined to the writings of outsiders. Shields McIlwaine surveyed fictional treatment of the poor white and found that pejorative nomenclature ran from Byrd's *History of the Dividing Line* (1728) through Caldwell's *Tobacco Road* (1934).[11] At one time or another Southern local colorists used these analogs for *poor white: lubber, peckerwood, cracker, conch, sandhiller, redneck, cajun, woolhat, squatter, clayeater, sharecropper, linthead, swamprat, tarheel, hillbilly.* My personal vocabulary of such catchnames was enriched by an Oklahoma sailor buddy (and Bob Wills enthusiast) to include *ridgerunner, appleknocker, cherrypicker,* and *turdkicker.*[12] Yet no country boy who carefully transported his guitar across the Pacific favored us with music labeled under any other tag than *hillbilly.* The very fact that only one of the names for a poor white was attached to the music and persisted, leads back to the time and circumstances of the christening.

There exists a semi-official baptismal narrative, reported in *Collier's* (1938) and subsequently picked up and used by others.[13] Like many a folk tale it bears some resemblance to historical fact, but it is so telescoped that it is both unfair to the actors it names and to those it leaves unmentioned. In a nutshell, reporter Kyle Crichton tells us that Ralph S. Peer of Okeh records[14] found Mamie Smith in 1921 to start the boom in race records (blues, jazz, and sacred material recorded by Negro artists intended for sale to Negro audiences), and later recorded Fiddlin' John Carson to start a similar hillbilly boom.

Peer himself richly deserved Crichton's praise and even more. He was at one time a successful businessman, a recording company pioneer, a music publisher, a completely unsung folksong collector, and a camellia grower. In 1954 he won a London Royal Horticultural Society gold medal for his gardening skills. There is no mention in his obituaries of any award from the American Folklore society; nor did any folklorist or historian publish an interview with Peer while he lived.[15] We can only speculate now as to whether he perceived his role to any degree as a cultural documentarian of the first rank.

Peer was regarded by his colleagues as modest and not given to exaggerating his position. He stated his role so briefly as to underplay it. In a letter to *Variety* he identified himself "as the person responsible for the discovery and development of the hillbilly business." In a letter to me he wrote, "It is quite true . . . that I originated the terms 'Hillbilly' and 'Race' as applied to the record business."[16]

The story begins, then, in Okeh's New York office, but this is like tagging a link in a continuous chain. More properly it has at least five separate places of beginning: an Atlanta fiddlers' convention; a Fries, Virginia, textile mill; a Gap Creek, North Carolina, mountain farm; a Galax, Virginia, barber shop; and curiously, a Times Square motion picture theater. In the period June, 1923–January, 1925, Ralph Peer was the director who brought a company of actors together from their various locales and who integrated their skills in a new drama. He welded isolates into a movement in the sense that the hillbilly record industry achieved an esthetic unity like other movements in art and letters. Alternative captions for Peer's achievements — genre, idiom, tradition — have been used to separate hillbilly music from other forms. He and his colleagues thought of themselves only as businessmen selling a new product — native white folksong freshly recorded and packaged — to a buying audience from whom the music had originally come. It took eighteen months to season Peer's creation and another two years, January 1925–December 1926, to give it a broadly accepted public name. There was no single day in this forty-two-month continuum when a given person broke a champagne bottle and launched the vessel Hillbilly Music.

Actually, students of Americana know that comic derivatives and "concert improvements" of folksong, as well as some traditional folk music, were available on cylinder or disc in the 1890s. An exhaustive survey of the pre-race and hillbilly recorded corpus is badly needed.[17] In essence, much of the material was presented by rustic monologists or black-faced comedians to brighten up the gloom in late Victorian parlors. The potpourri of rural dances, minstrel routines, laughing songs, country fiddling, and concert offerings was neither integrated nor specially categorized by the industry or public. However, it was well received. Alma Gluck's "Carry Me Back to Old Virginny" was the first Victor Red Seal disc to sell over a million copies and, needless to say, many of the purchasers felt they were getting a real view of plantation mores. Victor also did well with Charles Ross Taggart, a pre–World War I raconteur in the same vein as Uncle Josh from Pumpkin Center (Cal Stewart). Taggart added snatches of folk music to his routines on discs with such titles as "The Old Country Fiddler in a New York Restaurant." Then, as now, the media offered restyled vulgarized, folk-like songs as well as authentic pristine selections under a bewildering set of labels. The 1901 Columbia cylinder catalog identified the already traditional "Arkansas Traveler" as the "description of a native sitting in front of his hut scraping his fiddle, and answering the interruptions of the stranger with witty sallies." But two decades later this same piece performed by Joseph Samuels was cataloged by Okeh as an Irish instrumental. Between 1901 and 1923 there existed no established category for recorded native folk music.

This is not the place to ask whether the camouflaged comedians and country fiddlers who first introduced folksong to record buyers were traditional or not (although it is a vital question). In this period no recording executive, or folklorist either, had any reason to ask. Such questions were formulated only after Ralph Peer and his associates opened a field, bounded it, and provided a name.

What was Peer's milieu when he recorded his first white folksinger? In 1920–21 the record industry had scored heavily with the rapid climb to popularity of race record star Mamie Smith and her followers. The general postwar economy was already sluggish, when a new competitive menace arose to challenge the medium. Radio was still a utilitarian message service during the war, but on November 2, 1920, Pittsburgh station KDKA broadcast the Harding-Cox election returns, and soon Westinghouse researcher Frank Conrad was reading newspapers and playing records over and over again from this primitive studio. New York station WEAF began selling time, and radio was its way to big business. The record industry was directly challenged. "Almost overnight, radio sneaked into the picture and the novelty of tuning in music and static from a distance, combined with the convenience of no cranks to wind and no records to buy and change, began sending the sale of platters downward."[18] Edison's progeny was in trouble in 1923.

There were many responses to depression. One was receivership; another was intense plugging of tested items; a third was involvement in the process of changing the phonograph's role from a utilitarian talking machine to a piece of home furniture; a fourth was the quest for new material and a new market. At this juncture Polk C. Brockman,[19] a young and imaginative Atlanta record dealer, conceived an idea of great consequence. He had grown up in a mercantile family and had entered his grandfather's furniture store, James K. Polk, Inc., quickly taking over the phonograph department. By 1921 the firm was Okeh's largest regional outlet with particularly heavy sales of the new race records. The young Atlantan convinced Okeh executives Otto Heineman and W. S. Fuhri to give him a wholesale distributorship, and Brockman soon met Peer in New York City. Brockman's business trips to headquarters were frequent; on one such trip early in June 1923, he found himself in the old Palace Theater on Times Square viewing a newsreel of a Virginia fiddlers' competition. Struck by a novel idea, he took out his memorandum pad and jotted down "Fiddlin' John Carson—local talent—let's record." His next step was to arrange for an Atlanta recording expedition. Brockman recalls that Peer had no particular type of talent in mind but wanted anything that might stimulate lagging sales. Both men went South via an extended Chicago detour for an Okeh dealers meeting held in conjunction with the National Music Industries annual convention. Meanwhile, Okeh engineers Charles Hibbard and Peter Decker proceeded to Atlanta with the acoustical recording equipment. Brockman rented an empty loft on Nassau Street, off Spring Street, from a suspicious landlord. With an associate, Charles Rey, he rounded up his artists—Warner's Seven Aces, a local collegiate dance band; Eddy Heywood, a Negro theater pianist; Fannie Goosby, a young blues singer; and Fiddlin' John Carson. A number of other performers—the Morehouse College Quartet; Kemper Harreld, violinist; Lucille Bogan, blues singer from Birmingham; Charles Fulcher's novelty jazz band; and Bob White's syncopating band —also recorded but, apparently, not all their material was subsequently released.

Atlanta marked Okeh's initial out-of-town expedition and the first day of any major company to record traditional artists of either race in the South. There was no way for the local press, at that time, to assess the session's eventual significance. On June 12 the *Atlanta Constitution* radio columnist noted that the General Phonograph Company of New

York was in town to record the Seven Aces—stars on the newspaper's own station WGM.[20] Three days later the *Atlanta Journal* carried a more detailed story on the event:

"Canned music" recorded by local musicians will be made for the first time in Atlanta by the Okeh company, of New York, it was announced Friday by R. S. Peer, production manager of the company, who is completing arrangements here for the recording of selections by a number of local musical organizations. About thirty recordings will be made at the laboratory of the company on Nassau street, including selections by the Morehouse college quartet of negro singers, "Fiddlin' John" Carson, the Seven Aces, and other organizations. Manufacture of the records here is made possible by a recording machine recently invented by an engineer of the Okeh company, which lowers the high cost of producing the records away from the home laboratories.[21]

Fiddlin' John Carson recorded on Thursday, June 14, 1923.[22] Initially Peer did not respond to Carson's vocals and felt his singing to be "plu perfect awful."[23] But Brockman knew the fiddler's potential audience—the great numbers of rednecks and woolhats who had flocked into Atlanta's mills and factories since the days of the city's reconstruction. Carson was very well known to these people. He was born in 1868 on a Fannin County Blue Ridge Mountain farm and, at the age of ten, began to play his grandfather's instrument—a Stradivarius copy dated 1714, reputedly brought to the north Georgia hills from Ireland in 1780. Carson fiddled during his years as a young race horse jockey in Cobb County, and, when too large to ride, he competed at the annual Atlanta Interstate Fiddlers' Conventions. Here in the city he was able to scrape out a living with his bow between intermittent jobs as a textile hand and building trades painter. He fiddled constantly at political rallies for friends Tom Watson and Eugene Talmadge, on trolley cars and at street corners presenting topical ballads to casual audiences, at the many Civic Auditorium fiddlers' conventions, and, finally, on the then-infant radio.[24]

On March 16, 1922, the *Atlanta Journal* had established station WSB with a 100-watt transmitter as the first commercial broadcasting unit in the South, and on June 13 it increased its power to 500 watts. Three months later, on September 9, Fiddlin' John Carson made his radio debut as part of a novelty program. It was several years before another old fiddler, Jimmie Thompson, inaugurated Nashville's *Grand Ole Opry*. Carson had been preceded on WSB by a few folk performers: a Negro quartet from the federal prison in Atlanta; a north Georgia mountain quartet from Miss Berry's settlement school; the Atlanta Primitive Baptist Sacred Harp Singers; the Reverend Andrew Jenkins, a blind evangelist-newsboy and gospel singer. Other folk artists followed Fiddlin' John: Clayton McMichen, Charles and Miles Whitten, Ted and Boss Hawkins, Riley Puckett, and Lowe Stokes, who formed an old time stringband (The Hometown Boys); Dave and Andrew Hendrix, Jesse Jones, and Horace Thomas, a Negro jubilee four; Bob White, a blues-ragtime cornetist and jazz group leader. WSB's manager, Lambdin Kay, put Carson on the air in 1922 for the same reason that Brockman put him on wax in 1923, his appeal to a hitherto untapped market; yet there was no direct tie-in between WSB's pioneer country music broadcasts and Okeh's recordings of the same music. Carson's first recorded selections were "The Little Old Log Cabin in the Lane / The Old Hen Cackled and the Rooster's Going to Crow." When Peer expressed misgivings at the initial session in the improvised studio, Brockman offered to buy 500 "right now"—in reality, as soon as they could be pressed in New York. Peer acceded and issued the item as an uncataloged special without a label number for local Atlanta consumption. He could not imagine a regional or national market for the disc. In fact, the first Okeh press releases on the southern session to a national trade journal featured the Morehouse College Quartet and Warner's Seven Aces. Meanwhile, in Atlanta Brockman prepared for Carson's new debut. A scant four weeks after the Nassau Street session the 500 records arrived via Railway Express. The Elks were in town for the 59th reunion and were invited to a small but festive old time fiddlers' competition in Cable Hall, 82 Broad Street. On Friday night, July 13, Carson played both recorded numbers on the Cable stage in front of a large German phonograph with a morning glory horn and did a brisk sale of his own unnumbered discs across the footlights. He was pleased. Brockman recalls the mountaineer's quip, "I'll have to quit making moonshine and start making records."

Peer's early reservations vanished when Brockman reordered Caron's record. On July 19 the *Atlanta Journal* commented that the fiddler's two most famous tunes were on sale at local distributors and soon they were played for WSB's appreciative audience. The uncataloged special was now, late in July, given label number 4890, and, hence, was automatically placed in Okeh's popular series: dance bands, sacred, Hawaiian, Broadway tunes, novelties, instrumentals, standards. There was no thought of special nomenclature, nor was there any problem in classification, for Carson's disc at this time. On August 3—a day of national mourning for President Harding—Okeh placed special release ads in both Atlanta papers for the current records of such popular best sellers as Vincent Lopez, Billy Jones, and W. C. Handy, as well as the new local favorites, Warner's Seven Aces, The Morehouse Quartet, and Fiddlin' John Carson.

Carson's entry in Okeh's catalog meant that his pieces were available in August and September beyond the Atlanta market. Early in November Brockman sent the fiddler to New York to record a dozen more selections and to place him under an exclusive Okeh contract. Peer released a second Carson disc, coupling a bathetic and a vulgar piece, "You Will Never Miss Your Mother Until She Is Gone/Papa's Billy Goat" (4994), and began to sense the outline of the coming boom. Now Peer recalled that his New York office held a test pressing of some material similar to that of the Atlanta fiddler. In the spring of 1923, Henry Whitter, a Fries, Virginia, millhand—a self-educated guitar and harmonica player—had journeyed to the city to seek fame and fortune. Somehow, he had persuaded the Okeh concert and studio band director, Fred Hager, that he could do better as an entertainer than as a cotton spooler. The tests, instrumental combinations and ballads, were made, perhaps to get rid of the brash youngster, and put away on a shelf. But late in 1923 Peer sent them down to Brockman, the new country music expert, for advice. His reaction was positive and the songs, "Lonesome Road Blues/The Wreck on the Southern Old 97" (40015), were issued very early in 1924. The latter went on to make ballad as well as juridical history.

We now know that Carson sparked Okeh's hillbilly movement although Whitter preceded him by some four months as a recording artist.[25] Peer had two country hit sellers on hand; Brockman began scouting for similar talent. A cornucopia opened. Okeh engineers in Atlanta found themselves listening to an array of local talent: The Jenkins Family—Blind Andy, Irene Spain, Mary Eskew—offered standard gospel numbers; Land Norris accompanied himself on the five-string banjo; J. Douglas Swagerty, the Druid Hills, Presbyterian Church Choirmaster, sang hymns. Bascom Lamar Lunsford, an attorney and also an early Blue Ridge folksong collector-performer, responded to a recording session's announcement and journeyed, at his own expense, from Marion, North Carolina, to Atlanta to contribute two traditional songs. While a Georgia Sacred Harp unit sang "Wondrous Love," Fiddlin' John Carson's string-band, The Virginia Reelers, became the first group to record the social music of the area. Not to be outdone, in July, guitarist Henry Whitter took a fiddler and a five-string banjoist to Okeh's New York studio to record as The Virginia Breakdowners. Finally, during Okeh's first expedition to Dallas, Texas, in November, Chenoweth's Cornfield Symphony Orchestra appeared and the long parade of wildly exaggerated or grotesque band names—poking fun at the idiom from within—was on.

These were 1924 recordings. Peer was presenting neither gimmicks nor innovations but was seeking material to sell to conservative rural or rural-derived audiences. In these halcyon days Peer's performers could not have broken away from traditional folk style even if they had desired to do so. Within the first year following Carson's debut, Okeh presented a full sampling of folk material in straightforward style: sacred, secular, ballads, lyrics, vocal solos, instrumental combinations. These items were released initially in Okeh's 4000 pop series which gave way early in 1924 to a 40000 series. By the end of 1924, there were some forty folksongs scattered in this series and an Okeh executive felt the need for a distinctive sales category—an inclusive name that would identify this music to its audience. The June 1924 monthly supplement distributed by dealers to announce new releases had identified A. A. Gray, Tallapoosa, Georgia, fiddler, as a Southern hill-country musician.[26] The comparable December supplement identified two current discs by Carson and by Whitter as "old time tunes" played "in the real 'old-time' way," and parallel to other headings—Dance, Vocal, Irish—it listed "Old Time Tune" Records. (Brochures for July through November are not presently available to me; hence the precise selection date for the new title is unknown.) Okeh had previously pioneered by selecting the name *race records* for its Negro 8000 series; now it had an old time group within its 40000 series. By January 1925, a little six-page, accordion-fold brochure was printed with the title *"Old Time Tune" Records* (equivalent to *Foreign Language* and *Race Records* special catalogs). By May 1925, the ninety-two-page Okeh *Complete Catalog* carried an Old Time Tunes section and this name was used in subsequent publicity material for many years. The qualifying combination, *old time,* probably had been connected to *music* in the context of a southern fiddlers' convention or religious revival meeting, since both functions made extensive use of traditional folksong.[27]

It is interesting to speculate on what chance the new modifier had as the overall name for the genre. In retrospect, it had very little chance, for the February 1925 Okeh supplement announced a new release, "Silly Bill/Old Time Cinda" (40294), by The Hill Billies. The second *"Old Time" Tunes* special catalog followed in April and added another disc by the group, "Cripple Creek/Sally Ann" (40336). The provocative copy read:

> Hear, folks, the music of the Hill Billies! These rollicking melodies will quicken the memory of the tunes of yesterday. The heart beats time to them while the feet move with the desire to cut a lively shine. These here mountaineers sure have a way of fetching music out of the banjo, fiddle, and guitar that surprises listeners, old and young, into feeling skittish. Theirs is a spirited entertainment and one you will warm to.

The *Talking Machine World* (April 15, 1925) printed a life-like pen and ink drawing of The Hill Billies. The sketch was soon reproduced in Okeh's May supplement alongside photos of dance band leader Vincent Lopez and Negro monologist Shelton Brooks. How then did the noun *hillbilly* find its way onto the labels of two Okeh discs released early in 1925 and into consequent printed media? The answer involves a southern string-band whose members came from Watauga County, North Carolina, and Grayson-Carroll Counties, Virginia. These two areas are well known to folklorists for the richness of their tradition. They come close to being the scholar's ideal and idealized "singing community."[28] These three counties, significantly, nurtured the skills of the band members who were destined to name their region's music.

John Benjamin Hopkins, farmer, house-builder, and North Carolina state legislator, like many of his Watauga County neighbors knew the songs and fiddle tunes prevalent in the Blue Ridge Mountains. His wife, Celia Isabel Green Hopkins, knew the old ballads and church music as well as her husband's repertoire. After their marriage in 1878, they reared a large family of boys and girls, all with musical talent. In 1904 the elder Hopkins moved the brood to Washington, D.C., where he found employment in the Census Bureau. His hobby was organ building, and he taught several of his boys piano and organ tuning. Seemingly, they taught themselves to play any available instruments.

In 1910 Al, Joe, Elmer, and John—ages twenty-one through eleven—formed an Old Mohawk Quartet and began entertaining in Washington's Majestic Theater. Music was to remain Al's main concern for the rest of his life.

About 1912 Mr. Hopkins built a large family house at 63 Kennedy Street in Washington's then open-field Northwest section. In the hot summers Mrs. Hopkins took the younger children back to their Gap Creek home farm. Daughter Lucy, until her recent retirement a Washington public school music teacher, recalls a variety of fiddle tunes, hymns, old ballads, and pop songs from both homes. In the early 1920s the eldest son, Jacob, had established a country hospital-clinic in Galax, Virginia. Many anecdotes cluster about his early use of musical therapy—bringing local banjo players into the hospital to cheer his patients. Doctor Hopkins was renowned and active as a surgeon and musician. As his practice grew, he brought his brother Al down from Washington to act as hospital office manager and secretary. Meanwhile, brother Joe, a Railway Express agent at White Top Gap, Virginia, had become an itinerant guitarist between regular jobs. He, too, gravitated towards his brother's office on his "bustin" trips.

On a Monday morning in the late spring of 1924, Joe found himself in a Galax barber shop where one of the young journeymen, Alonzo Elvis "Tony" Alderman, kept a fiddle on the wall. The guitarist and fiddler became friends at once, formed a duet on the spot, and began to make music. Tony cut no hair that week. On Saturday Al came for a shave—and for his brother—and joined in the harmony. Word of the new trio reached John Rector, a Fries general store keeper and five-string banjo player of local renown. In fact John had just recently returned from New York City where he, Henry Whitter, and James Sutphin had made three string-band records for Okeh as The Virginia Breakdowners. There seemed to be a great deal of competition among the Grayson-Carroll musicians. Rector felt that the Alderman-Hopkins' talent and his banjo could outshine the Breakdowners. Since he was looking for an opportunity to make the exciting New York trip to stock up on fall merchandise, he asked Al, Tony, and Joe if they wanted to record.

The boys were agreeable, for they preferred music to their respective trades. Tony's musical skill was considerable. As a lad he had played the trumpet in his father's Dixie Concert (brass) Band. From his many uncles and a particular family friend, Ernest V. "Pop" Stoneman, he had learned to fiddle at mountain dances. Tony's memory of the summer New York trip is both clear and amusing. It took three days in Al's 1921 model T Ford to reach the city where Rector had arranged a session with Clifford Cairns, Victor A & R (Artistic and Repertoire) man.[29] In the studio Joe, John, and Tony used guitar, banjo, and fiddle while Al took vocal leads as well as acting as the group's leader. Also he turned the piano into a country music instrument—a precedent infrequently followed by subsequent string-bands. Good techniques for recording mountain string-bands were not yet perfected in 1924. The music was still relatively unknown in the industry; there were problems in balance and placement. Tony recalls the scene:

> We played in front of a big horn, banjo ten feet back in the corner. I was fiddling like mad on a fiddle with a horn on it which I couldn't hear. John Rector couldn't hear me either, and no one could hear the guitar. Nobody could hear anybody else, to tell the truth. Victor played the record back to us and my father could have done better on his Edison! (No reflection on Victor; it was us.) So we went home a little sad and ashamed that we had not done better.[30]

Fortunately, the quartet was not daunted by its failure. In January 1925, they planned a trip to the Okeh studio—this time in Rector's new Dodge. The weather was cold; hence they improvised a hot brick heater for the journey. To break the long trip from Galax north, they descended on the Hopkins family residence in Washington for shelter. Mr. Hopkins asked his two sons and their mountain companions, "What d'you hillbillies think you'll do up there?" His paternal jibe was to prove effective. In the city, having learned from their previous failure with Victor, the band members were in good form. Ralph Peer supervised the session and recorded six pieces. At the end of the last number Peer asked for the group's name. Al was unprepared. They had no name and he searched for words. "We're nothing but a bunch of hillbillies from North Carolina and Virginia. Call us anything." Peer, responding at once to the humorous image, turned to his secretary and told her to list The Hill Billies on her ledger slips for the six selections.[31] The recording-christening date was January 15, 1925; labels, as well as dealer release sheets, were soon printed and by February the first disc with the new band name was on the market.[32]

Meanwhile, en route home the boys had qualms about their choice. Tony seemed particularly sensitive: "Hillbilly was not only a funny word; it was a fighting word." Although he had grown up in an isolated log cabin at River Hill, ten miles southwest of Galax, he was in no sense backwoodsy or backwards. His father, Walter, was a self-educated surveyor and civil engineer, a justice of the peace, and a man of literary and musical skill. Tony felt that his family might be critical of the undignified name selected up North and half wished that he could reach Peer to alter the band's name.

But back in Galax the boys encountered an old friend who was to tip the scale in favor of the new name. "Pop" Stoneman had already journeyed north on September 1, 1924, to record for Okeh "The Ship That Never Returned/The Titanic" (40288). He, too, like Rector, had felt that he could improve on Whitter. Stoneman's first record was not yet released at the time of The Hill Billies' Okeh session. Naturally he was most curious about their luck with Peer. In response to his query, they reported success and the christening. "Pop" laughed until tears came to his eyes. "Well, boys, you have come up with a good one. Nobody could beat it." [33]

Following the New York success the band put on its first live show in a Carroll County high school under its Peer-selected name. Dr. Hopkins had died earlier on July 26, 1924, and there was no incentive for Al to stay in Galax. He now turned his father's Washington home into band headquarters, and following the release of their initial record the boys began a heavy schedule of personal appearances in nearby states, as well as radio work in the capitol city. About March 1929, as The Hill Billies, they made their broadcast debut on WRC with the theme song, "Going Down The Road Feeling Bad." Al's mother frequently accompanied her boys to the station and joined in singing the old ballads that were interspersed between the breakdown instrumentals and humorous skits. Fan mail began to come in addressed to The Hill Billies. Simultaneously, record buyers and radio listeners responded to the new association, *hillbilly music.*

The full story of the band that named the music is reserved for a separate paper. A few events, however, are salient to this account. On May 8, 1925, the Mountain City, Tennessee, Ku Klux Klan sponsored a tremendous fiddlers' convention,[34] and, among others, invited The Hill Billies, having heard them on WRC broadcasts. At the gathering Charlie Bowman, a young country fiddler from Gray Station, near Johnson City, Tennessee, joined the band. He was the first of many newcomers to augment the original group's rank. Not only did he contribute his fine talent and humor at the time, but in later years he was to convey much of the band's story to discographers and folklorists.[35] Following Mountain City a heavy schedule of personal appearances from South Carolina to New York commenced—at schools, vaudeville shows, fiddlers' competitions, political rallies, and even a White House Press Correspondents' gathering before President Coolidge. Much of the road work was correlated with trips to New York for recording sessions. On the final trip early in 1929 the band made a film sound short for Vitaphone that was released as a trailer with Al Jolson's *The Singing Fool*. It was certainly the first movie to couple the sound and sights of hillbilly music. A few years later Al Hopkins died following a car accident at Winchester, Virginia.[36] The band did not survive his death.

Ralph Peer's contact with The Hill Billies occurred during one memorable session. Later in 1925 he left Okeh for Victor but the band he helped launch did not go along with them. Instead, it went over to the recently combined Vocalion-Brunswick companies to work with A & R man Jimmie O'Keefe. All their post-Okeh discs were released for dual sales purposes as The Hill Billies on Vocalion and as Al Hopkins and His Buckle Busters on Brunswick. For personal dates they used both names interchangeably. During one New York recording session they were surprised to see on the Hippodrome Theater marquee lights, The Ozark Hillbillies. They responded to the competitive threat by having a Washington lawyer incorporate (January 21, 1929) their group—complete with an embossing seal and stock shares—as Al Hopkins's Original Hill Billies. But the gesture was of no avail. Other bands, singers, and units in show business appropriated their name. In time, they accepted the rivalry philosophically—especially when *hillbilly* became the generic term for southern country music.

Until this point I have developed a unilinear narrative from Carson's June 1923 Okeh session through the incorporation of The Original Hill Billies. In reality this development did not flow on an even or straight plane. It is not likely that one group alone could have had such an important neologistic influence unless other conditions were propitious in the record industry. My personal research had focused on the crucial Okeh label. Other students have explored the many companies that climbed onto the hillbilly music bandwagon. Here only a sketchy outline of a few key persons and events is listed to provide the backdrop against which The Hill Billies' name got away from its band.[37]

It was early in 1924 when Ralph Peer and Polk Brockman first sensed the dimension of the old time tunes boom, and many of their rival company colleagues were as quick as they were in their response to the new idiom. (The recording industry is notorious for the speed with which it covers hits—quick pressings by different artists of best sellers.) The talent was there in Atlanta waiting to be discovered. Columbia executives found Riley Puckett, a blind street-singer and guitarist with a sweet tenor voice. He had brought his songbag to the city from Alpharetta, Georgia. Also from rural Georgia was Gid Tanner, a Dacula cotton farmer and fiddler.[38] Late in February they made Atlanta test pressings and on March 7–8, 1924, they were in Columbia's New York studio repeating the earlier Okeh pattern. Puckett sang and picked his way through "Little Old Log Cabin in the Lane" with fiddle accompaniment by Tanner. For the coupling, "Rock All Our Babies to Sleep," he yodeled a bit, thus introducing a technique that was destined to longevity in country music. Their disc (107-D) was released on May 20 in Columbia's popular series, and the Georgians were soon followed north by two ladies from Sylva, North Carolina, Samantha Bumgarner, banjo, and Eva Davis, fiddle. "Big-Eyed Rabbit/ Wild Bill Jones" (129-D) was their vocal-instrumental debut.[39] Next came a blind minstrel, Ernest Thompson, from Winston-Salem, North Carolina, who could play twenty-five instruments. Just as Puckett had used Carson's "Log Cabin" for a first record, Thompson covered Whitter's "The Wreck of the Southern Old 97," linking it with "Are You from Dixie" (Columbia 130-D).

The specific identity of the sales and recording executives who so quickly established Columbia's eminence in the hillbilly field is not yet determined. Probably, the credit was shared by W. S. Fuhri, a phonograph industry pioneer and Okeh's general sales manager in 1923 prior to becoming a Columbia vice president in 1924, and Frank Walker, a talent scout with particular skill in recording race artists. By November 1924, Columbia printed a booklet, *Familiar Tunes on Fiddle, Guitar, Banjo, Harmonica, and Accordion,* designed to list the records of Tanner, Puckett, Thompson, and others "whose names are best known where the square dance has not been supplanted by the fox-trot."[40] This publication became the first exclusive compilation of traditional folk material gathered by the then very young hillbilly record industry. By January 1925, the firm had enough folk material to begin a Columbia 15000-D series, Familiar Tunes—Old and New, paralleling its own 14000-D race offerings. At this time Okeh was still releasing country material on pop labels. Hence, Columbia was the first company to see the possibilities in an exclusive white folk series. By October 1925, Okeh followed suit with a similar 45000 Old Time Tunes category, and, eventually, nearly every American record company established some type of hillbilly series.

The second firm to emulate Okeh in 1924 was Vocalion, finding three traditional and colorful Tennessee performers for starters. Blind George Reneau, still in his twenties, had come down from the hills to play his guitar-harmonica combination on the streets of Knoxville. Discovered by a local Sterchi Brothers record distributor in May, he was sent to Cliff Hess, Vocalion's New York A & R man, to cover Whitter's initial disc. Reneau's version of "The Wreck on the Southern 97/Lonesome Road Blues" (14809) was the firm's opening bid for the new market. During July it was released in the Red Records pop series and soon led to a Special Records for Southern States listing in public announcements. Next came "Uncle Am" Stuart, a 73-year-old safe and vault salesman, champion fiddler, and raconteur from Morristown, Tennessee.[41] In the first week of June he was in Manhattan recording "Cumberland Gap/Grey Eagle" (14839). While in the Aeolian Hall studio, he favored New York's WJZ radio audience with a program—perhaps the first Tennessee mountain music to be broadcast in the metropolis.

The third and most influential Vocalion pioneer was "Uncle" Dave Macon (The Dixie Dew Drop): banjoist, entertainer extraordinaire, shaper of the developing commercial country music tradition.[42] His first offering was "I'm Going Away to Leave You, Love/Chewing Gum" (14847). Macon's seventh released disc, "All I've Got's Gone/Hill Billie Blues" (14904), was recorded in July, 1924, and issued at the year's end, a few months before The Hill Billies record was on the market. To my knowledge, Macon's blues, which opens "I am a billy and I live in the hills," is the first in a long series of songs using the catchy word *hillbilly* in a title. Also, it is the first record label to bear the term. The song is actually Macon's reconstruction of a W. C. Handy recomposed folksong usually called "Hesitation Blues"—the name Macon used when he sang it in personal appearances and on the air.[43] Today we lack knowledge as to why or when he altered or renamed the old song. Was "Hill Billie Blues" part of his early theatrical repertoire or was it put together for recording purposes? Nor is there evidence of any special role for this particular disc in extending the term. Seemingly, Macon never asserted any semantic priority as did both Peer and Hopkins for their January 1925 meeting.

During 1924 three competitors—Okeh, Columbia, Vocalion—had entrenched themselves in the hillbilly arena, and, finally, the largest and richest unit of the American record industry, Victor, decided to enter the field. Its own personnel could not have escaped notice of competitive sales by the new country artists in the area roughly bounded by Roanoke, Atlanta, and Knoxville. Because the three firms who had discovered Carson, Whitter, Tanner, Puckett, Reneau, and Macon were New York–based and geared to national distribution, it was inevitable that the new discs would sell themselves simply by being in the catalogs. Nevertheless, in May 1924, Columbia began to advertise such records with full pages in the monthly *Talking Machine World,* a handsomely designed and well edited dealers trade journal. Of the initial Tanner-Puckett disc Columbia stated: "No Southerner can hear them and go away without them. And it will take a pretty hard-shelled Yankee to leave them." In June the firm's copy writer exclaimed that "The fiddle and guitar craze is sweeping northward," and Okeh, not to be outdone, announced that "the craze for this 'Hill Country Music' has spread to thousands of communities north, east, west, as well as in the south and the fame of these artists is ever increasing." By September Okeh had to remind the trade again via a full page, two-color ad that Fiddlin' John Carson's records "were the very first of their kind ever offered."[44]

During November 1924, Victor made its own discreet announcement to the trade:

> The old-time fiddler has come into his own again with the music loving public and this fact is reflected in the demand for records of the music of the old fiddlers. The Victor Talking Machine Company has taken cognizance of public interest to issue an attractive four-page folder for dealer distribution with a cover design showing the fiddler presiding over the old-time barn dance, and a caption of "Olde Time Fiddlin' Tunes." In the folder are listed four records by Fiddlin' Powers and family, three records by A. C. (Eck) Robertson, and two Southern mountaineer songs on a record by Vernon Dalhart with fiddle accompaniment. The back of the folder is used to call attention to a negro spiritual record by ex-Governor Taylor of Tennessee and his Old Limber Quartet, and two novelty records.[45]

Victor's press release writer could not have known that Dalhart's record was destined to nationalize hillbilly music; nor could the writer have sensed any irony in his item's juxtaposition of Robertson's and

Dalhart's names. On June 30, 1922—a year before Peer's Atlanta expedition—Victor had recorded in its New York studio a pair of traditional fiddlers, Henry C. Gilliland from Oklahoma and A. C. Robertson from Texas, playing a solo, "Sally Gooden" (Robertson), and a duet, "Arkansaw Traveler." [46] The southerners had journeyed to New York to break into records following a trip to the 1922 United Confederate Veterans' Reunion at Richmond, Virginia. Victor did not release the pair's beautiful, archaic tunes (18956) until April 1923—well before Okeh's similar disks were on the market. Robertson was fully as traditional as Carson, Tanner, or Stuart; however, the Texan's piece led to no trend, let alone movement, within this major company. Whether Victor was unable or unwilling to exploit folk music in 1922 we do not know. However, by the fall of 1924, apparently induced by one of its own very popular artists, Victor made a cautious entry into the hillbilly area.

Vernon Dalhart, born Marion Try Slaughter in the bayou region of east Texas, had come to New York in 1912 as a light opera tenor and had succeeded on the stage.[47] By 1916 he turned to a new recording career, favoring the sentimental and popular pieces of the day including much pseudo-Negro "plantation" material. An apocryphal story tells us that Thomas Edison himself launched Dalhart's recording career because of a favorable response to "Can't Yo' Heah Me Callin' Caroline?" But the Texas tenor had heard enough traditional folksong—Anglo and Negro—in his boyhood to be able to leave both Victor Herbert and Stephen Foster behind in favor of his down-home folk style.

We do not know now whether Dalhart was prompted by someone in the record industry to turn to the new field of country music or whether he followed his own instincts, but for the Edison firm during the summer of 1924 he covered Whitter's railroad ballad accompanied by his own mouth-harp and Frank Ferara's Hawaiian guitar. "The Wreck on the Southern Old 97" (Edison Diamond Disc 51316) was backed with an Ernest Hare black-face song. It was issued in August, and in a month the ballad was dubbed for release on Edison Blue Amberol Cylinder 4898. Neither disc nor cylinder made a special stir, but their good sales did help Dalhart persuade his Victor executives, one of whom was Nat Shilkret, to let him record the ballad for them. Dalhart now coupled "The Wreck of the Old 97" with his cousin Guy Massey's piece, "The Prisoner's Song" (19427). It was released on October 3, 1924, entered in Victor's *Olde Time* folder, and went on to make history by selling more than seven million copies and precipitating complex legal battles.

The fascinating story of these two songs and this particular record has been commented on in writing that ranges from erudite Supreme Court decision to popular fiction by Harry K. McClintock (Haywire Mac). Here we need pause only to note that Dalhart's nasal "Wreck" and banal "Prisoner's Song" nationalized old time music. Victor 19427 quickly reached a coast-to-coast market where records by Carson, Tanner, Macon, and the Hopkinses had had chiefly local or regional appeal.

A previous Victor disc, "It Ain't Gonna Rain No Mo'" (19171), by a Chicago radio artist, Wendell Hall, had been the company's best seller late in 1923 and early in 1924.[48] Although Hall's song, self-accompanied on ukulele, was based on a country dance tune and was widely covered by other artists and labels it had no direct influence on the new genre. The public accepted "Rain No Mo'" as a pop item and "Prisoner's Song" as a hillbilly piece. Why the difference? Dalhart's songs followed a trail blazed by traditional folksingers; Hall's piece was a novelty. Also, Victor was willing to exploit Dalhart as a country singer. In their 1920–23 catalogs they had described him as a Century Theater light opera tenor. After the release of 19427 this publicity was deleted, as were his operatic and standard discs. In fact the company made a conscious search for southern mountain material for him.

When in February 1925 Floyd Collins died in a Kentucky sand cave, the public was galvanized. His dramatic rescue attempt was covered by nationwide press and radio; his death struggle was excruciatingly slow; many symbolic elements were sensed in his story. Polk Brockman, still searching for good sales material, asked (by telegram from Florida) his own Okeh recording artist in Atlanta, the Reverend Andrew Jenkins—blind newsboy, evangelist, poet, and musician—to write a Collins song. Until this time each pioneer hillbilly performer had come into the studios with his own stock of traditional ballads. But now "Blind Andy" composed a new one on demand for a music industry executive. Jenkins's daughter, Irene Spain, recalls the scene on her front porch after the receipt of the assignment. The news story was known to both of them from press and radio. As her father composed, accompanying himself on the guitar, Irene took down the words. Within four hours she scored the music and sent text and tune on to Brockman.[49] She now recalls, wistfully, that if she had known it was destined to be a million seller, and an American folksong as well, she would have added a few grace notes to color its melodic simplicity.

Brockman gave "The Death of Floyd Collins" to Fiddlin' John Carson for recording on April 14—26 days after Collins was found dead in his cave—but Carson's Okeh version did not take hold. In time, it caught the ear of Dalhart, who recorded it for Victor on September 9, 1925, in New York. It was coupled with another fresh topical item, "The Wreck of the Shenandoah" (19779), composed by Carson J. Robison under the pseudonym Maggie Andrews (his mother's maiden name), and announced in the November supplement. However, in December the dirigible piece was dropped (at the request of Commander Lansdowne's widow) in favor of another Jenkins song, "The Dream of a Miner's Child"—itself a recomposition of an earlier English parlor ballad—and the new pair (19821) was Dalhart's second national hit. "The Wreck" he had gained from tradition; "Floyd Collins" he gave to tradition. The public made no such distinction. Instead, it began to link his dolorous contemporary pieces with the older ballads, as well as the string-band social music and southern rural humor available on discs. The industry was most acute in helping its consumers relate the new topical pieces to old ballad themes and styles. Victor's supplement writer for November described the "Shenandoah/Collins" disc in these terms:

> Popular songs of recent American tragedies. They belong with the old fashioned penny-ballad, hobo-song, or "come-all ye." The curious will note that they are even in the traditional "ballad" metre, the "common metre" of hymnodists. They are not productions of, or for, the cabaret or the vaudeville stage, but for the roundhouse, the watertank, the caboose, or the village fire-station. Both have splendid simple tunes, in which the guitar accompanies the voice, the violin occasionally adding pathos. These songs are more than things for passing amusement; they are chronicles of the time, by unlettered and never self-conscious chronicles.[50]

The year 1925 to the phonograph industry is marked by Western Electric's introduction of the electrical recording process—a revolutionary technological change. The year can also be seen in retrospect as including the national acceptance of Dalhart's "Prisoner's Song," the release of The Hill Billies' first record, the launching of Columbia's exclusive Familiar Tunes series, followed by Okeh's Old Time series, and the beginning of Nashville's role in country music. Chicago's WLS *National Barn Dance* had begun on April 19, 1924, and Nashville's WSM *Grand Ole Opry* (first called *WSM Barn Dance*) on November 28, 1925.

One additional event important to hillbilly music was Victor's discovery in mid-1925 of Carl T. Sprague—ranch boy, World War I cavalryman, Texas A&M athletics coach—with a songbag of traditional cowboy ballads. His "Bad Companions/When the Work's All Done This Fall" (19747) was released before Dalhart's "Floyd Collins." Victor, slow in discovering the lode in mountain music, compensated by opening wide the field of recorded western music. Very conveniently, the buying public identified and related the two in spite of important stylistic and regional differences. A significant step in the blurring of the genres was the addition of sound to western movies in 1928. Westerns, from their origin, had already developed to include historical epics, occupational tales (metal mining, railroading, logging), and melodramas set anywhere and anytime on the frontier beginning with the French and Indian War in the Alleghenies. The line between mountain and cowboy movies was no stronger or higher than a barb wire fence. One of the very early horse operas directed by John Ford in 1918 was actually titled *Hill Billy*.[51]

Western films had always required some music, whether Rossini or American folksongs in concert arrangements by such native composers as Lamar Stringfield (North Carolina) and David Guion (Texas). By 1930 the piano and organ gave way to the voice—initially homespun and flavored by campfire smoke and rodeo dust. The first silent star to introduce authentic cowboy pieces to "talkies" was Texas-born Ken Maynard. He had made his way to acting via an apprenticeship as a young Army Engineer and a Ringling Brothers Circus rider. He could sing the old songs and he could fiddle. Maynard's 1933 film, *The Strawberry Roan,* was written around the popular ballad; it was one of the few full length feature movies based on a folksong. In 1935 Gene Autry, soon followed by Tex Ritter and Roy Rogers, inaugurated a cycle of elaborate and colorful musical westerns.[52] They, and other Singing Cowboys, now turned from traditional sources to newly composed screen songs that quickly fed back into hillbilly repertories. Autry and his progeny were of equal importance to the phonograph and the movie industries. The film's perforated sound track itself became an artifact tending to fuse mountain and western music—old and new—into a single artistic form and marketable commodity.

The stage complemented the cinema in creating synthetic outdoor songs. When *The Ziegfeld Follies of 1934* presented the national hit "The Last Round-Up," its Boston-born composer, Billy Hill, providentially was named with the inverted noun. His song was instantaneously accepted in New York, Nashville, and Cheyenne. In the decade from Carl Sprague to Billy Hill–Gene Autry, the American cowboy's legendary glow, as well as a Hollywood tailor's version of his dress, moved onto the WLS and WSM barn dance stages. Mountain boys born in Piedmont textile villages, Cumberland coal camps, and Great Smoky lumber towns were costumed in cowboy togs by Nashville. Hillbilly musicians had now acquired a ready-made uniform,[53] and, more importantly, a heroic and dramatic mythology. It was to help record-radio-screen fans, as well as persons within show business, compensate for the bleak color in the Poor White portrait.

In the formative years of folksong recordings the industry received an unsolicited gift in the campaign for its new product. We have no consumer polls to tell us how Broadway and book and magazine publishers were simultaneously selling their own views of southern mountain tradition. Frederick Koch's University of North Carolina student actors and writers—The Carolina Playmakers—had stimulated interest in regional folk drama in the early 1920s. A number of New York plays in 1923–25 took up such themes: *Sun Up, The Shame Woman, Hell-Bent fer Heaven, Ruint, This Fine-Pretty World.*[54] In March 1926, Rose Wilder Lane published a popular novel, *Hill Billy,* with an Ozark setting, in which she used play-party songs that she had heard in the region.[55] Her title was common in the Ozarks; did she select it because of the prevalent interest in mountain music or was her choice coincidental? We do not know; we know only that the new combination *hillbilly music* caught on against a backdrop of urban as well as rural drama, circuit vaudeville as well as medicine tent show, middle-brow fiction as well as cracker barrel tale sessions.[56]

The parallel between the music industry's reaching out to Carson and his peers and concomitant discoveries by writers is striking. In March 1925, *Century Magazine* first printed Stephen Vincent Benét's delightful literary ballad, "The Mountain Whippoorwill: How Hill-Billy Jim Won the Great Fiddler's Prize." The poem's narrator is an orphan child who pictures his parents as fiddle and bird; he wins the Essex County Fiddlers' Show. Benét had heard old time music at Highlands, Macon County, North Carolina, where he summered between 1911 and 1915 while his father was stationed at the Augusta Arsenal. The ballad was written in New York early in 1925 almost simultaneously with the release of the first disc by The Hill Billies. It is highly unlikely that the poet ever met fiddler Tony Alderman, but he epitomized Tony in his work. Although Benét got the tune of the boxwood fiddle as well as the tone of hill dialect into "The Mountain Whippoorwill," nowhere did he label the fiddlers' music as *hillbilly;* the term was reserved to name the hero.[57]

Today no chronicle is available that reports whether a country dweller in a remote general store, or someone in a big city music shop, perhaps influenced by drama, poetry, or fiction, first asked for a record of hillbilly music; nor do we know what radio fan first sent a letter to a station requesting a hillbilly song, but we do know that by 1926 Vernon Dalhart was as much in the public domain as Babe Ruth, Rudolph Valentino, and Will Rogers. There existed a need for a nationally known tag for "The Prisoner's Song" that was as catchy as *jazz* or *pop.*[58] *Hillbilly* filled the need. Words rush in to fill vacuums. Something of the exact process can now be reconstructed.

It is possible that *hillbilly* and *music* were linked in speech before 1923; we have no such evidence today. We can use the *Talking Machine World* to trace the word's extension to music in print after December 1924, when the journal first listed Macon's "Hill Billie Blues" (Vocalion 14904) in its Advance Record Bulletin. By the following April the word moved from song title to name of a string-band in the first released story on The Hill Billies. In November it was applied within the trade to a general category of records when an Edison cylinder sales director commented to a *World* reporter on the relationship of farm prosperity and the firm's extensive mail order business. The Edison official found that rural demand "is largely for Blues, Coon songs, and Hilly-Billy numbers." Finally, in December 1925, a feature writer in a long article was impelled to comment on "the popularity of hill-billy songs."[59] He was correct in assuming that record dealers, song publishers, and public buyers of music could identify his category.

During 1926 the association could be found in print beyond trade journal pages. In January a Columbus, Ohio, newsman caught a Washington WRC broadcast of The Hill Billies. He responded to their skill and humor with a perceptive review that revealed his own knowledge of folk music and his awareness of the negative overtone of their name. He wrote: "These Hill Billies, as they wished to be called, came from the mountain regions of our southern states with a collection of old-time melodies, some of which have never been written down but have been passed on from fiddler to fiddler through the generations. . . .

It was far and away the best program of its kind we have ever listened to."[60] He had not heard them before but he liked their music and accepted the string-band's title. His response was personal. The next step was a generalized response that linked music and title.

At year's end *Variety* (December 29, 1926) presented its annual show business roundup. What was fresh; what did music editor Abel Green use for industry front page news? He wrote:

"HILL-BILLY" MUSIC

This particular branch of pop-song music is worthy of treatment on its own, being peculiar unto itself. The "hillbilly" is a North Carolina or Tennessee and adjacent mountaineer type of illiterate white whose creed and allegiance are to the Bible, the chautauqua, and the phonograph. The talking machine's relation to the show business interests most. The mountaineer is of "poor white trash" genera. The great majority, probably 95 percent, can neither read nor write English. Theirs is a community all unto themselves. Illiterate and ignorant, with the intelligence of morons, the sing-song, nasal-twanging vocalizing of a Vernon Dalhart or a Carson Robison on the disks, reciting the banal lyrics of a "Prisoner's Song" or "The Death of Floyd Collins" (biggest hillbilly song-hit to date), intrigues their interest.

Not only was Green the first writer, to my knowledge, to combine *hillbilly* and *music* in print, but he went to the heart of show business's exploitation of the new product. In later years he was to reconsider and modify his early view of the Southern mountaineer and his songlore,[61] opening *Variety*'s pages to sympathetic treatment of the idiom, but his 1926 front page feature brings into focus cultural and esthetic problems that are still current. Green in 1926 had heard the term *hillbilly records* from music business colleagues—publishers, bookers, talent scouts—Tommy Rockwell, Ben Selvin, Jack Mills, Louis Bernstein, Ralph Peer, "Korky" O'Keefe. Even though the executives used it freely in speech, they were cautious in applying it in advertising media. While their copy writers continued to coin euphemisms—Songs From Dixie, Old Southern Tunes, Old Time Singin'—the public continued to use the common label. It was not until 1929 that Sears, Roebuck actually entered *hillbilly* as a tag for records in its catalog, followed by Montgomery Ward in 1930. A 1933 Okeh brochure finally identified its own 45000 series as Hill Billy, and after 1935 the adventurous

Decca company issued several *Hill Billy Records* catalogs with subheads: Old Time Singing, String Bands, Sacred, Fiddlin', Old Time Dance.

None of the other companies fell into line. As the music itself responded to change under the very impact of records and radio, the industry began a search for an ameliorative term to replace the stereotype. (That section of the industry that was quickest to loosen the hybrid's link with tradition eventually coined *country-western,* a combination beyond the scope of this paper.) The attitude of the music business toward *hillbilly* jelled soon after general acceptance of the term. In 1930, Bradley Kincaid, a fine Kentucky folksinger and early record and radio interpreter of traditional material, wrote to his own audience:

> There is a practice among recording companies, and those who are inclined to speak slightingly of the mountain songs, to call them Hilly Billy songs. When they say Hilly Billy songs they generally mean bum songs and jail songs. . . . [These] are not characteristic of mountain songs, and I hope . . . you will come to distinguish between these fine old folk songs of the mountains, and the so-called Hilly Billy songs.

Five years later John Lair, WLS impresario and himself a performer with the Cumberland Ridge Runners, stated, "Hill billies in radio? They ain't no such thing. Mountaineers and folk from the hill country, maybe, but no hill billies. 'Tin Pan Alley' hung this name on certain types of music and entertainers." By World War II, George D. Hay, "The Solemn Old Judge" who announced Grand Ole Opry's broadcasts, wrote, "We never use the word [*hillbilly*] because it was coined in derision. Furthermore, there is no such animal. Country people have a definite dignity of their own and a native shrewdness which enables them to hold their own in any company. Intolerance has no place in our organization and is not allowed." [62]

His championing of country people is noble and has been echoed by everyone who has profited from selling country music to the folk, as well as by academicians grimly intent on rescuing "true folk music" from engulfing waves of "hillbillyism." [63] It is left to Jean Thomas, Kentucky's "Traipsin' Woman," to marshal all the clichés of the defense in one pronunciamento. In her fictional biography of blind fiddler J. W. Day (renamed Jilson Setters), she portrays him upon return from a London concert before the English King and Queen. At home the learned Judge rebukes the crude Sheriff for having previously rejected the fiddler's old fogey songs. Mrs. Thomas ends her morality play scene with these words: "It would not be expected of all who hear Jilson's music to discriminate between his Elizabethan tunes and a hill-billy parody that so shamefully ridicules mountain minstrelsy."[64]

But why was such a shameful and demeaning term linked to folk-song in the first place? Ralph Peer saw it was a funny word; Tony Alderman as a fighting word. Both were right. It contained sufficient semantic elasticity to parallel the music industry's ambivalence, the scholar's distrust, and the public's acceptance of the new product. Only the individual consumer placing his quarters and half-dollars on record store counters seemed to ignore problems posed here in etymology and cultural history. High Society and the Academy frequently joined in their downgrading of Folk Art. The heroes and heroines—Henry Lee, Silly Bill, Floyd Collins, Fair Ellen, Sally Gooden, Omie Wise—all seemed much too uncouth when released on discs. Similarly, previous song variants circulated via broadsides, stall ballads, and pocket songsters had also been stigmatized.

It is unfair to the amorphous record buying public of the mid-1920s that so enthusiastically took the new hillbilly music to its heart to say precisely why it accepted a pejorative title for something it liked. Perhaps the folk sensed the larger community's antipathy to the discs that both commented on and documented traditional values. Out of the long process of American urbanization-industrialization there has evolved a joint pattern of rejection as well as sentimentalization of rural mores. We flee the eroded land with its rotting cabin; at the same time we cover it in rose vines of memory. This national dualism created the need for a handle of laughter and ridicule to unite under one rubric the songs and culture of the yeoman and the varmint, the pioneer and the poor white.

So long as we both exploit and revive hillbilly music, so long as we feel tension between rural and urban society, we are likely to continue to need Ralph Peer's and Al Hopkins's jest.[65]

APPENDIX I: INTERVIEWS 1960–1965 (SEE NOTE 19)

A. E. Alderman	Clayton McMichen
Charles Bowman	Callie Payne
Elbert Bowman	William Randle
Polk Brockman	Vance Randolph
Irene Futrelle	Charles Rey

Abel Green
Hattie Hader
Kemper Harreld
Otto Heineman
Bill Hopkins
John Hopkins
Lucy Hopkins
Walter Hughes
Rosa Lee Johnson
Lambdin Kay

Ernest Rogers
Carl T. Sprague
E. V. Stoneman
Colen Sutphin
Peter Tamony
Jimmie Tarlton
Dock Walsh
Jim Walsh
Byron Warner
Paul Whitter

APPENDIX 2: LOG (SEE NOTE 36)

Alonzo Elvis "Tony" Alderman
    b. Sept. 10, 1900, River Hill, Va.—
Charles Bowman
    b. July 30, 1889, Gray Station, Tenn., d. May 20, 1962, Union
    City, Ga.
Polk C. Brockman
    b. Oct. 2, 1898, Atlanta, Ga.—
"Fiddlin'" John Carson
    b. March 23, 1868, Fannin County, Ga., d. Dec. 11, 1949,
    Atlanta, Ga.
Vernon Dalhart (Marion Try Slaughter)
    b. April 6, 1883, Jefferson, Texas, d. Sept. 15, 1948, Bridgeport,
    Conn.
Albert Green Hopkins
    b. June 5, 1889, Gap Creek, N.C., d. Oct. 21, 1932, Washington,
    D.C.
Andrew Jenkins
    b. Nov. 26, 1885, Jenkinsburg, Ga., d. April 25, 1957,
    Thomaston, Ga.
"Uncle" Dave Macon
    b. Oct. 7, 1870, Smart Station, Tenn., d. March 22, 1952,
    Murfreesboro, Tenn.
Ken Maynard
    b. July 21, 1895, Mission, Texas—
Ralph Sylvester Peer
    b. May 22, 1892, Kansas City, Mo., d. Jan. 19, 1960, Los Angeles,
    Calif.

Carl T. Sprague

b. May 10, 1895, Manvel, Texas—

Ernest V. "Pop" Stoneman

b. May 25, 1893, Monarat, Va.—

Frank Buckley Walker

b. Oct. 24, 1889, Fly Summit, N.Y., d. Oct. 15, 1963, Little Neck, N.Y.

William Henry Whitter

b. April 6, 1892, Fries, Va., d. Nov. 17, 1941, Morganton, N.C.

APPENDIX 3: OKEH CHRONOLOGY (SEE NOTE 14)

December 4, 1914

Otto Heineman Phonograph Supply Company opens New York office: 45 Broadway. Firm imports Swiss phonograph motors and contracts with Garford Manufacturing Company, Elyria, Ohio, to produce its own motors.

June 1, 1918

Firm places first records (popular and standard music) on the market. They are double-faced and hill-and-dale (vertical cut). Labels and sleeves carry an Indian head design. The series begins with release of "Star Spangled Banner/American Patriotic Medley" by a Band (Okeh 1001) and continues through Okeh 1288 released in November, 1919.

October 1, 1919

Firm's name is changed to General Phonograph Corporation: 25 West 45th Street.

Ca. November 1919

Vertical cut Okeh records are replaced by lateral cut discs in a new series which begins with release of "The Vamp/My Cairo Love" by Rega Dance Orchestra/Green Brothers Xylophone Orchestra (Okeh 4000).

February 14, 1920

Mamie Smith records "first race disc" in New York, "That Thing Called Love/You Can't Keep a Good Man Down" (Okeh 4113) [7275/7276]. Record is placed in popular series and released July, 1920.

Ca. November 1920

Heineman begins to distribute Odeon and other foreign languages records in America. Classical music originally recorded in Europe is featured; however, some non-English popular and folk material is included.

Ca. June 1921

Firm begins a separate 8000 race series with release of "Play 'Em for Mama, Sing 'Em for Me/I Won't Be Back 'Till You Change Your Ways" by Daisy Martin (Okeh 8001) [7854/7855].

June 14, 1923

Fiddlin' John Carson records "first hillbilly disc" in Atlanta, "Little Old Log Cabin in the Lane/Old Hen Cackled and the Rooster's Going to Crow" (Okeh 4890) [8374/8375]. Record is placed in popular series and released July, 1923. The success of Okeh's first out-of-town expedition leads to many subsequent field trips particularly rich in recording early jazz, blues, hillbilly, and non-English folk material from ethnic groups in America.

Ca. January 1924

Okeh 4999 is released and popular series continues with a numerical jump to Okeh 40000.

Ca. October 1925

Firm begins a separate 45000 hillbilly (old time) series with release of "Run Along Home with Lindy/To Welcome the Travellers Home" by Fiddlin' John Carson (Okeh 45001).

October 22, 1926

General Phonograph Corporation purchased by Columbia Phonograph Company and renamed Okeh Phonograph Corporation: still at 25 West 45th Street. Otto Heineman continues as president of subsidiary to carry on sale of motors, needles, and parts as well as Okeh and Odeon records. Subsequent Okeh history integrated with Columbia's own complex development with some crossing of material between labels.

November 16, 1926

Okeh switches from accoustical (True Tone) to electrical recording process. First such race item to be released is "Candy Lips/Scatter Your Smiles" by Eva Taylor with Clarence Williams (Okeh 8414) [80214/80215] (rec. 11/16/26).

January 28, 1927

Earliest released electrical disc in hillbilly series is "West Virginia Rag/Coney Isle" by Frank Hutchinson (Okeh 45083) [80354/80356] (rec. 1/28/27).

March 31, 1931

Otto Heineman leaves firm. Okeh moves to Columbia office: 1776 Broadway.

Ca. December 1931

Columbia, beset by depression and buffeted by English owners, is purchased by Rigsby-Grunow (Majestic radios and refrigerators).

Ca. November 1933

Grigsby-Grunow goes bankrupt. Assets acquired, in February 1934, by Sacro Enterprises (banking syndicate). Columbia and Okeh labels are continued by a Sacro unit, American Record Corporation.

Ca. March 1934

Okeh hillbilly series thins out during depression years and is terminated with a release of "Going Down the Road Feeling Bad/Leaving on the New River Train" by the Crazy Hillbilly Band (Okeh 45579) [152680/152681] (rec. ca 1/15/34).

Ca. January 1935

Okeh race series also thins out in these years and is terminated with a release of "Little Green Slippers/Jug Band Quartette" by the Memphis Jug Band (Okeh 8966) [C-794/C-807] (rec. 11/7–8/34).

NOTE: Columbia has kept the Okeh label alive through the last three decades; however, I have closed my chronology with the termination of the 45000 and 8000 series. In these two sets, Otto Heineman and his staff inaugurated large-scale, serious recording of American folk music (albeit Okeh never made such a claim for its role during 1921–1931).

NOTES

1. *New York Journal* citation from Mitford Mathews, *A Dictionary of Americanisms* (Chicago, 1951), 808; Harben from William Craigie, *A Dictionary of American English* (Chicago, 1944), 1248; Hibler from James Masterson, *Tall Tales of Arkansaw* (Boston, 1943), 274–75; Carr from "A List of Words from Northwest Arkansas," *Dialect Notes* 2 (1904): 416–22.

2. Tobacco song reported by Nannie Fortson from her father's singing, Western Kentucky Folklore Archive, University of California, Los Angeles. Texas couplet from John and Alan Lomax, *American Ballads and Folk Songs* (New York, 1934), 51; these lines had previously appeared in Thomas Talley, *Negro Folk Rhymes* (New York, 1922), 43.

3. Alfred Holt, *Phrase Origins* (New York, 1936), 164.

4. Joseph Hendron, "The Scholar and the Ballad Singer," in *The Critics and the Ballad,* edited by MacEdward Leach and Tristram Coffin (Carbondale, Ill., 1961), 8.

5. A WNS feature by Margaret Anderson, *Champaign-Urbana Courier,* June 19, 1962.

6. Charles Seeger's comments in "Conference . . . on Folklore," *Journal of American Folklore* 59 (1946): 512; D. K. Wilgus, *Anglo-American Folksong Scholarship since 1898* (New Brunswick, N.J., 1959), 433.

7. "Folk Singing," *Time,* November 23, 1962, 60.

8. Academic inattention can be measured by: (1) contrast between bibliography on jazz-blues and hillbilly; (2) the first major compilation on *Mass Culture,* edited by Bernard Rosenberg and David White (Glencoe, Illinois, 1957), contains but one peripheral reference to hillbilly music; (3) no hillbilly records were reviewed in the *Journal of American Folklore* until April 1948, a quarter-century after they began to circulate.

9. David Riesman, *Individualism Reconsidered* (Glencoe, Ill., 1954), 185.

10. Kemble citation from A. N. J. Den Hollander, "The Tradition of 'Poor Whites,'" in *Culture in the South,* edited by W. T. Couch (Chapel Hill, N.C., 1934), 416. See also F. L. Owsley, *Plain Folk of the Old South* (Baton Rouge, La., 1949).

11. Shields McIlwaine, *The Southern Poor-White: From Lubberland to Tobacco Road* (Norman, Okla., 1939). The most comprehensive and valuable current work on Southern Highland literature is Cratis Deal Williams's unpublished New York University dissertation, "The Southern Mountaineer in Fact and Fiction" (1961).

12. McIlwaine's poor-white analogs are taken from Southern fiction. Ozark speech reveals two dozen additional terms, *acorn-cracker* to *weed-bender,* in Vance Randolph and George Wilson, *Down in the Holler* (Norman, Okla., 1953), 252. McIlwaine and Randolph, of course, do not exhaust the list!

13. Kyle Crichton, "That's Gold in Them Hillbillies," *Collier's* 101 (April 30, 1938): 24–25, reprinted in Linnell Gentry, *A History and Encyclopedia of Country, Western, and Gospel Music* (Nashville, 1961), 39–45.

14. In this paper I refer to record companies by their labels rather than full corporate names. Company genealogies are exceedingly complex and are developed elsewhere. See Oliver Read and Walter Welch, *From Tin Foil to Stereo* (Indianapolis, 1959), 399–407, 484–89. Generally race and jazz discographers fill in corporate genealogy in their compilations. See, for example, Dan Mahony, *The Columbia 13/14000-D Series: A Numerical Listing* (Stanhope, N.J., 1961). Because of the crucial importance of the Okeh label to my study I have outlined a brief chronology in Appendix 3.

15. Samuel Charters, *The Country Blues* (New York, 1959), is praiseworthy of Peer and makes a start at an appraisal of his role.

16. *Variety,* November 2, 1955, 52; letter to me, November 4, 1957.

17. No discography of this corpus is available. Scattered references to songs and singers can be found in Jim Walsh's biographical series on popular artists in *Hobbies* from 1942 to present.

18. Jim Walsh, "Late Carson Robison Pioneered Hillbilly Disc Biz 30 Years Ago," *Variety,* April 24, 1957, 45.

19. Much of the narrative in this paper comes from oral interviews listed in Appendix 1. The arrangement of material from Brockman and others interviewed is, of course, my own.

20. Fortunately, the *Atlanta Constitution* found its own station WGM newsworthy. Byron Warner's Seven Aces had come together in the spring of 1922 when the station was launched and the band was billed as the nation's second radio orchestra. *Constitution* stories on the Aces' radio programs are useful, today, to establish the chronology of Okeh's 1923 Atlanta expedition. See: (June 12), 18; (June 14), 16; (June 19), 7; (June 21), 18; (June 22), 16; (August 3), 9.

21. The *Atlanta Journal* gave even more coverage to its station WSB than the rival paper to WGM. *Journal* radio news for 1922–23 is particularly valuable, today, to document pioneer broadcasts of traditional folksong. The specific *Journal* story cited on the Okeh expedition is (June 15, 1923), 4.

22. The precise date of Carson's recording debut has long eluded discographers. (Okeh ledger files of the period are lost; letter to me from Helene Chmura, Columbia Records librarian, March 28, 1961.) However, hillbilly research can ride piggyback on jazz discography. Brian Rust, *Jazz Records A–Z 1897–01931* (Middlesex, Eng., 1962), lists master numbers for Warner's Seven Aces' first released record, "In a Tent/Eddie Steady" (Okeh 4888) 8376/8378. This disc can be compared to Carson's first record, "Log Cabin/Old Hen" 8374/8375. The *Constitution* stories cited in note 20 indicate that Warner finished recording on Thursday, June 14.

23. Brockman recalled Peer's initial response to Carson's singing in interviews. In Brockman's first letter to me, September 3, 1957, he wrote: [Carson's disc] "was recorded by the Okeh Company at my insistence with a 'fingers crossed' attitude."

24. In addition to interviews, three *Atlanta Journal Magazine* feature articles on Carson have been of particular value: (April 2, 1933), 1; (March 18, 1934), 9; (April 16, 1939), 7.

25. The date of Whitter's first recording is a real discographic mystery. Brockman clearly recalls that Hager recorded Whitter in New York before the Atlanta expedition. In Whitter's only folio, *Familiar Folk Songs* (Jefferson, N.C., ca. 1935), the author asserted a March 1, 1923, recording visit to New York City. However, his first released disc, "Lonesome/Wreck," bears master numbers 72168/72167, which indicate a December 1923 session. Either Whitter's March test pressings were not assigned master numbers until December, or he was called back to New York to re-record his own material.

26. All Okeh supplements, brochures, and catalogs quoted from or cited in this paper are from the private collection of Jim Walsh, Vinton, Virginia. A microfilm reel of these holdings is deposited at the John Edwards Memorial Foundation, University of California, Los Angeles.

27. The usage *old time* in a musical context is not cited in standard dictionaries.

28. The first use of the term *singing community* is unknown to me.

29. *A & R* man, the acronym or initialism for Artist and Repertoire man (talent scout-recording producer-studio factotum), does not appear in standard American references for alphabetic designations. The earliest usage I find is in *Talking Machine World* 20 (July 15, 1924): 106.

30. Letter to me, May 6, 1961. A photograph of the Victor studio in which the string-band recorded is found in Oliver Read, *The Recording and Reproduction of Sound* (Indianapolis, 1952), 15.

31. My treatment of this core anecdote comes from Tony Alderman. It is confirmed by Charlie Bowman (who recalled it from the telling of Al Hopkins). One "folk" variant by Clarence Ashley has already appeared in an educational film *The Roots of Hillbilly Music* in the "Lyrics and Legends" series produced in 1962 by WHYT-TV, Philadelphia.

32. As with Carson and Whitter, I lack documentary evidence for exact date of first recording by The Hill Billies. Again, jazz research is of great help. Albert McCarthy and Dave Carey, *Jazz Dictionary* (London, 1957), list a discography for The Goofus Five—a unit of a larger group, The California Ramblers. The unit recorded "Alabamy Bound/Deep Blue Sea Blues" (Okeh 40292) master 73099/73100 on January 14, 1925. This disc can be compared to The Hill Billies' first release, "Silly Bill/Old Time Cinda" master 73118/73122. Hence, the latter probably recorded on January 15, 1925.

33. Stoneman's recollection of his own role in the naming of the band differs from Alderman's in time sequence.

34. Alderman preserves a set of Hill Billies band photographs, including one of John and Joe Hopkins, John Rector, Uncle Am Stuart, John Carson, and himself at the May 8, 1925, Mountain City convention. After my first meeting with Alderman, he generously presented me with a full set of his pictures, and I have used them to supplement interviews. Many of the photos were taken by Alderman including the very first of the band in Galax about March 1925. It was sent to New York and used as the model for Okeh's publicity sketch. Alderman recalls photographing himself in the band by using his own delayed action camera.

35. My personal debt to the late Charlie Bowman is great. Although I began piecing data for this paper together in 1956 I had no direct lead to The Hill Billies until corresponding with Bowman following his letter-article to Joe Nicholas in *Disc Collector*, no. 16 (January 1961).

36. Because vital statistics for many persons named in this paper are not readily available I have included a log of such data in Appendix 2.

37. Just as The Hill Billies' name "got away" from the band (Alderman's phrase), a similar process took place three decades later when another band's name, Bill Monroe and His Blue Grass Boys, "got away" to become a generic musical term, *bluegrass.*

38. Unfortunately, records by most of the pioneer hillbilly performers are out of print and their reissues have not kept pace with jazz or blues reissues. A private LP disc by the Folksong Society of Minnesota, *Gid Tanner and His Skillet Lickers,* dubbed from early recordings, was pressed in limited quantity in 1962. It is an excellent sample of the music considered here. Frank Driggs, Columbia Records, has announced a three-part set of hillbilly reissues, including many artists named in this paper, for 1965 release.

39. To my knowledge only three pioneer hillbilly singers made the transition from pre-1925 discs to LP records: Samantha Bumgarner, *Banjo Songs of the Southern Mountains* (Riverside RLP 610) reissued (Washington WLP 712); Bascom Lamar Lunsford, *Smoky Mountain Ballads* (Folkways FA 2040), and *Minstrel of the Appalachians* (Riverside RLP 645) reissued (Washington VM 736); Ernest V. Stoneman, *The Stoneman Family* (Folkways FA 2315) as well as more recent Starday and World-Pacific albums.

40. *Talking Machine World* 20 (November 15, 1924): 51.

41. William Cobb, "Cousin Am and Cousin George," *American Mercury* 15 (October 1928): 207–14.

42. "Uncle" Dave Macon can be heard on a 1963 Folkways LP reissued from various labels (RBF 51).

43. W. C. Handy, *Blues: An Anthology* (New York, 1926), 42, 94. I am indebted to Bob Hyland for help in establishing "Hesitation Blues" history.

44. *Talking Machine World* 20 (May 15, 1924): 153; (June 15, 1924), 17, 66; (September 15, 1924), 58.

45. *Talking Machine World* 20 (November 15, 1924): 178.

46. John Cohen, "Fiddlin' Eck Robertson," *Sing Out!* 14 (April 1964): 55–59.

47. Jim Walsh, "Vernon Dalhart," *Hobbies* 65 (May 1960): 33–35, 45; continued in seven following issues.

48. George Kay, "Those Fabulous Gennetts," *Record Changer,* June 1953, 3–13, asserts for the Gennett label "the start of the hill-billy catalogue" in August, 1922, based on Wendell Hall's recording of "It Ain't Gonna Rain No Mo'" in Richmond, Indiana, prior to covering his own song for Victor in Camden, New Jersey. I find no evidence to support this claim for Hall or Gennett.

49. Jenkins's own account of the composition of "Floyd Collins" was sent by D. K. Wilgus to G. Malcolm Laws, Jr. for use in the revised edition of *Native American Balladry* (Philadelphia, 1964), 51.

50. Jim Walsh indicated to me that James Edward Richardson, Victor's sup-

plement writer between 1917–28, was the best in the business. It can be said, in retrospect, that he was ahead of folklorists by many decades in his sophisticated treatment of hillbilly ballads.

51. William Wooten, "An Index to the Films of John Ford," *Special Supplement to Sight and Sound,* Index Series 13 (February 1948), 5, lists *Hill Billy* as a five-reel Universal film. However, George Mitchell, "The Films of John Ford," *Films in Review* 14 (March 1963): 130, does not list this item. Correspondence from Mitchell, July 29, 1963, and Wooten, September 15, 1963, leads me to believe that *Hill Billy* was a working title for a film actually released in 1918 under the title *The Scarlet Drop.*

52. See George Fenin and William Everson, *The Western: From Silents to Cinerama* (New York, 1962), 193–225, for music in western movies.

53. Fenin and Everson, 181–90, for the cowboy's dress.

54. For the development of regional folk drama see Archibald Henderson, *Pioneering a People's Theatre* (Chapel Hill, N.C., 1945); Samuel Selden, *Frederick Koch: Pioneer Playmaker* (Chapel Hill, N.C., 1954). For hillbilly drama on Broadway see Arthur Quinn, "New Notes and Old in the Drama," *Scribner's* 76 (July 1924): 79–87.

55. Lane's book was one of a long line of mountain novels that used folklore themes; see Arthur Palmer Hudson, "The Singing South," *Sewanee Review* 44 (July 1936): 268–95. For an excellent criticism of Ozark dialect used by novelists and dramatists, as well as perceptive asides on the show business hillbilly, see Vance Randolph and George Wilson, *Down in the Holler* (Norman, Okla., 1953), 122–48.

56. This paper's focus is on record industry events after 1923. The combination *hillbilly music* could have been made earlier in time at any place where southern mountain or rural folksingers gathered to entertain. A study of the roots of hillbilly entertainment in all its professional forms is needed. The work of the Weaver Brothers and Elviry, a Missouri Ozark trio, needs particular attention. The group mixed country music and rural humor on the vaudeville stage before 1923.

57. "The Mountain Whippoorwill" has been widely reprinted since first publication in *Century Magazine* 87 (March 1925): 635–39. For commentary see Charles Fenton, *Stephen Vincent Benet* (New Haven, 1958), 143–49, 392. John Flanagan first directed my attention to this poem; see his "Folk Elements in John Brown's Body," *New York Folklore Quarterly* 20 (December 1964): 243–56.

58. Peter Tamony, "Jazz the Word," *Jazz* 1 (October 1958): 33–42.

59. *Talking Machine World* 20 (December 15, 1924): 207; 21 (April 15, 1925): 50; (November 15, 1925): 186; (December 15, 1925): 177.

60. "Heard on the Radio," *Ohio State Journal,* January 11, 1926, 6.

61. A significant facet of my interview with Green was his comment that in the 1920's he accepted race records as folksongs because he identified them with

Negro spirituals which were "folk," but nothing in his education or experience before 1923 had given him a base to which to relate hillbilly records. He did not place them in a folkloristic context until 1939 when records, including hillbilly items, were packaged in albums for sale to urban audiences who "enjoyed folksongs."

62. Bradley Kincaid, *Favorite Old-Time Songs and Mountain Ballads, Book 3* (Chicago, 1930), 6; John Lair, "No Hill Billies in Radio," *WLS Weekly,* March 16, 1935, 7; George Hay, *A Story of the Grand Ole Opry* (Nashville, 1945), 37.

63. Typical of academic criticism of hillbilly music is the view stated by West Virginia Professor Patrick Gainer when interviewed by G. C. McKown, *New York Times,* June 30, 1957, 2:7.

64. Jean Thomas, *The Singin' Fiddler of Lost Hope Hollow* (New York, 1938), 205.

65. In addition to participants whom I interviewed, collectors who shared tapes and records, and scholars whose works are cited in this paper and notes, I am indebted to Fred Hoeptner for his article which advanced some ideas presented here, "Folk and Hillbilly Music: The Background of Their Relation," *Caravan,* nos. 16, 17 (April, June 1959). The late John Edwards and I corresponded on many of the problems discussed in this paper. Gene Earle, D. K. Wilgus, and Ed Kahn helped me formulate ideas during 1961, 1962, and 1963 field trips. Harlan Daniel and Ronald Foreman helped "talk" the paper through its writing stage. The Modern Language Association (Washington, D.C., December 29, 1962) provided an opportunity to read a portion of this paper. Finally, I am indebted to my colleagues Mrs. Barbara Dennis and Mrs. Judy McCulloh for criticism and cheer.

Laborlore

From what experiences are labor traditions wrought? A robust picket line chant; a tool chest lid lined with faded dues slips; a secret hand clasp in a dim entry way; an echo of John Lewis's or Eugene Debs's oratory; a visit to a weathered stone marker at Homestead or Ludlow—all are part of the language, belief, and customs that comprise *laborlore*—the special folklore of American workers within trade unions.

At times laborlore reaches out as a force to touch persons far removed from unionism. When the Massachusetts Institute of Technology named Jerome B. Wiesner to its presidency on March 5, 1971, Wiesner, in a *New York Times* interview, attributed his "keen social awareness" to his childhood in Dearborn, Michigan. As a child, Wiesner would "run downtown after school to watch the pitched battles between automobile union men and Ford goon squads." Wiesner never became a unionist, but the image of the Dearborn beatings was etched on his mind. A part of labor folklore? Perhaps.

It is the ability to retain tension and emotion in memory linked to the need to project feelings into dramatic, musical, or linguistic form that turns everyday experience into folklore. Obviously, brutality at a plant gate is not folklore. But a mournful ballad or wry jest about the happening may enter tradition to be passed on among union men for generations.

Perhaps the best way to identify laborlore is to mention specific examples. There are well-known labor songs written and sung by such performers as Joe Glazer, Sarah Gunning, Utah Phillips, and Pete Seeger. Less well-known than the songs are short anecdotal tales told to reinforce philosophical positions and to build solidarity in times of stress. One such tale follows, a tale I heard from John Neuhaus, a

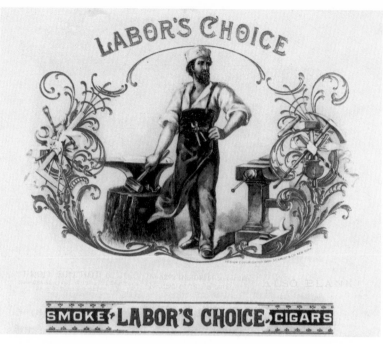

"Labor's Choice," cigar box lithograph (Schmidt and Co., New York, 1900).

San Francisco machinist and "double header" unionist (John held dual membership in the International Association of Machinists, AFL-CIO, and in the Industrial Workers of the World, "Wobblies"). It is called "The Striker's Wife."

The iron ore miners were on strike up in Minnesota. It was a long hard strike but the men held out pretty good. A lot of them were Finns; Finns believe in solidarity. One day a striker's wife was about out of money. She went to the butcher shop to try to buy some cheap cut of meat that might last the family for a week. She saw a calf's head in the case and figured it would make lots of soup. So she asked the butcher, "How much?"

He said, "One dollar."

That was too much so she started to leave. But just as she got to the door, she asked "Is this a union shop; is your meat union?"

He was surprised but replied, "Sure, I'm a member of the union (Amalgamated Meat Cutters and Butcher Workers of North America). I cut my meat by union rule—see my shop card in the window."

The lady said, "Well, I don't want any union meat. Don't you have a scab calf's head?"

The butcher was stumped but he was smart. So he said, "Just a minute, Ma'am," and he took the calf's head into the room back of the shop. Pretty soon the lady heard a lot of clatter. The butcher came out of the room and handed her the wrapped package. He said, "That'll be seventy-five cents, ma'am."

She was very pleased at the saving, paid up and started for the door. But she was curious, so she asked, "Isn't this scab calf's head the same as the union head you tried to sell me for a dollar?"

The butcher said, "Yes, Ma'am, it is. I just knocked out two bits worth of brains!"

A tale such as the one above can be told anywhere workers gather, and laborlore abounds with such stories. Ritual, however, is often confined to particular places and particular times. From my experience as a young shipwright in San Francisco on the eve of World War II, I recall, for example, the practice of the tool auction:

Shipwrights, marine joiners, boatbuilders, caulkers, and drydockers organized one of San Francisco's earliest trade unions, for they were there to dismantle ships for needed lumber and metal parts during the Gold Rush. When I joined Local 1149, United Brotherhood of Carpenters and Joiners of America, it was filled with immigrant mechanics from every shipbuilding center in the world: the Clyde, Belfast, Malta, Hamburg, Hong Kong. In the mid-thirties, our local was involved with the longshoremen and other maritime crafts in two waterfront strikes. Although the local was divided between radicals and conservatives, it was united on the need to preserve craft custom, to maintain solidarity, and to honor the dead. The tool auction was a unifying part of union tradition.

When an old-timer died, his tool chest was carried to the union hall. Chests were big and heavy, frequently ornate, and usually filled with handmade tools, including, perhaps, rosewood planes. (They were made of wood so that they would float if dropped overboard.) At the conclusion of the meeting, the union president would begin to auction the tools one by one and to gather a purse for the departed member's family. The chief function of the auction appeared to be to provide an unsophisticated form of social security, but there were other functions, as well. The local was small and the mechanics worked closely. When one of them purchased a dead colleagues tools, he kept some of his friend's skill alive. He also kept the tools out of skid-row pawnshops and, hence, out of the hands of strangers.

Laborlore 49

As is the case of much folklore, the tool auction ritual employed elements of sympathetic magic far older than unionism itself.

For lack of space, these two examples of tale and ritual must represent in this booklet the many kinds of literary genres and behavior patterns that constitute the large body of American laborlore. It grows with every day, but it still serves a fundamental purpose to the union men. It serves to bind people together and to give individuals a sense of dignity on the job and within their movement.

In the *Wall Street Journal* on March 4, 1971, Tom West, a member of the International Association of Bridge, Structural and Ornamental Iron Workers, described what it is like to be a top connector working three hundred feet above the Chicago Loop. (A connector bolts together the derrick-lifted structural steel units of a skyscraper under construction.) He also inadvertently revealed how much laborlore has become a part of his life.

In the article, West explained that incompetent ironworkers, or "Joe McGee's" as they are known, are recognizable by their mangled fingers and toes. Good workers are known by their stance aloft. Along with craft skills, Tom West had learned during his breaking-in period the essence of a journeyman's style—that it isn't enough just to walk the steel. To be fully esteemed by one's fellows, one must walk high steel with a "clump," hands and feet swinging normally, not rigid, and always ready to work.

In part, a worker like Tom West clumps along because he can "cut the mustard" on the job; in part, he holds his head because of a card in his wallet, a button on his cap, and an awareness—however dim—that he is in a movement, bigger and older than himself. When he expresses this awareness in traditional form, when he engages in "union talk," he forges a link in the chain of laborlore and contributes, as well, a tiny chip to the variegated mosaic of American tradition.

A Folklorist's Creed
and Folksinger's Gift

s a child I knew that miners worked in mountains, but the men of my imaginative realm dug gold, not coal. Teachers called them Argonauts, not yesterday's people; our miners amused themselves with jumping frog contests, not with Elizabethan ballads. In short, I was a Californian about as distant from the Appalachian Highlands as one could be and still remain within the continental United States. I did not venture east of the Sierras until World War II, when Navy service transported me from Pacific shore to Virginia tidewater. The trip from San Francisco by antiquated troop-train carried us into West Virginia's mountains, and I still recall my excitement in the rush through the C&O's Big Bend Tunnel. Although a young sailor, I had already been prepared by folksong to accept John Henry as a legendary hero, one who defied modernity and died tragically.

Even before this momentary glimpse of a dark tunnel and the Greenbriar River beyond the east portal, I had been pulled previously to another area in Appalachia and another set of heroes. Several months after my high school graduation, John L. Lewis had formed the Committee for Industrial Organization. Initially, I knew Lewis and the United Mine Workers of America only through radio and newspaper accounts, and from these I learned that the CIO had set a goal to organize Kentucky's Harlan County. In the 1930s I had been disposed to trade unionism by the values of my parents, by extensive reading, and, eventually, by tentative collegiate steps into New Deal politics. Never having seen Harlan County, still I knew its terrain as well as I knew the Berkeley campus. The towering campanile might have been a brooding tipple; the university president might have been a coal operator;

Appalachian Idyll *[Apple Butter]*,
by Clare Leighton, in Southern Harvest *(New York: Macmillan, 1942).*

Kentucky miners, in my mind's eye, resembled waterfront stevedores in jeans and hickory shirts.

It was characteristic of our generation that some students were drawn, as if by magnet, to industrial work—to the physical task itself, to the study of labor economics, or to union participation. Others sought employment in President Franklin Delano Roosevelt's alphabet agencies, such as the National Labor Relations Board. Still others went beyond the labor movement or public service to war in Spain. In apprenticeship as a shipwright, I learned old skills from proud immigrant craftsmen and was initiated into arcane traditions in Shipwrights' Local 1149 of the United Brotherhood of Carpenters and Joiners of America. After Navy duty, I resumed waterfront work in San Francisco, subsequently moving "uptown" to the building trades for years of work on decayed mansion and sterile high-rise, with Victorian gingerbread and plastic trim.

It was not until 1960 that I actually saw mountain coal miners in their own fields, heard the texture of their speech, and learned of their special concern for hazards and for solidarity. I visited coal camps in Harlan and neighboring counties, gathering material which is now spread out in *Only a Miner* (1972). The writing of this book, in turn, helped focus my thought on the connection of politics to culture, and on the special resonance in the term "insider"/"outsider."

We are all outsiders as America slips toward 1984. But to suggest that we are only a half-dozen years from Orwell's peak (or vale) is not to imply that we are doomed to a totalitarian end. Rather, we may use *1984* to focus on the polarities which rend national life and raise again the deepest issues of 1776; distant monarchy or self-ruled republic, arbitrary power or popular sovereignty. Even after American patriots rejected the crown in favor of independence, they divided internally on matters of distribution of wealth and direction of growth. It is not easy in the United States, today, to escape the tension generated in the conflict between Washington norms and parochial expression, between central power and marginal experience, between national goals and regional or ethnic identity. To be born in Harlan County, to sing old Baptist hymns, to dig coal, is at once to be quintessentially a red-white-and-blue insider as well as an outsider—a person of minority status, a member of folk society.

Thus, my purpose here is not to offer yet another document or an outsider's breathless discovery of Appalachia. Instead, in the manner of a blueprint, I trace a journey to the mountains—geographic and metaphysical. Many of us describe the flowering of consciousness in terms of actual movement—to school, to war, to the city, to a host of New Jerusalems. At times the travel is aimless like that of Jack Kerouac hurling himself, East to West, across the wide continent. At times it is channeled like that of Thomas Wolfe riding trains, South to North, from Asheville and Chapel Hill to Cambridge and Manhattan. Often these journeys in growth are joined with a metaphoric quest for heroes (in modern parlance, "role models"). My early personal hero, a legendary black steel driller in West Virginia's Big Bend Tunnel, was supplanted, in time, by living brave coal miners in Kentucky. Within this community of heroic work, I met Sarah Ogan Gunning, a magnificent Appalachian folksinger able to couple militant rhetoric and traditional tunes. Her pairing of seeming opposite expressions has helped me and many others to clarify perceptions of mountain life; in this paper I comment on her gifts in order to frame my creed.

We have heard of youngsters in England coming of age on "the playing fields of Eton." Some of us in the 1930s sensed that Harlan was our Eton—a field of tension in the form of class turmoil. The actual struggle was miner versus operator; the struggle in our minds was over choice of tactical position: labor organization and New Deal reform versus left activism and revolutionary cause. If the symbol Harlan is still applicable to industrial warfare and ideological stance, it was also, in an earlier day, an emblem of maturation for a handful of youngsters remote from mountain life. To complete the inside/outside linkage, coal miners helped bring me from the Pacific to Appalachia—truly from periphery to heart. Also, Harlan County helped open my mind to the notion that this highland area, in some senses, formed "a nation" located outside mainstream America.

My interest in Appalachia has thus stretched from student years in Berkeley to the publication of *Only a Miner,* and continues to this day. Writing compelled me to identify myself as one both close to and distant from the mountain. Also, the book's reception encouraged me to articulate my understanding of what it means for anyone to be an enclaved American: highland, lowland, rural, urban, farm, factory. I had conceived the book mainly as a form of dues, a return to working people whose values I shared, and a return to academic colleagues with whom I shared commitment to the discipline of folklore. I had never intended it to be a mountain tract, nor an explication of the political-cultural link in Appalachia. Yet books escape their writers and mine is now found on various Appalachian studies lists—a guide in folklore and history.

This paper, then, traces philosophic travel—the shaping of a particular folklorist's values against a background touching the intersection of folklore and ideology in the United States.

The American Folklore Society was established in 1888, bringing together Harvard philologists, Smithsonian Institution ethnologists, established writers, and private antiquarians. Many of these pioneers were deeply concerned with minority cultural forms such as Indian myth or Negro song. Some folklorists were satisfied to gather art, artifact, custom, and belief, while others, beyond the academy, became partisans of rights and reforms. On the whole, folklorists were content to collect and classify, and hence avoided overt political formulas. Nevertheless, they addressed themselves to the most controversial concerns of nationhood. Was our culture American or European? Whether new, old, or actually shaped between, was American expressive life a unitary whole or an unstable conglomerate? Beyond the nature of the lore itself, how did folklorists see tradition carriers—the folk? Did scholars accept any special obligations to the subjects of their study? Were we to take our stand for cultural pluralism or for continued stirring of the melting pot, for untrammeled development or for the retention of community?

Until the Great Depression, most American folklorists accepted consensual values from the broad pool of ideology which shores the State: empiricism, pragmatism, parliamentary democracy, free-market economics, individualism. In the 1930s, a few folklorists such as Charles Seeger and Alan Lomax turned either to formal Marxism or to its special manifestation in anti-fascist and popular-front strategies. Today, in looking back at the left's use of folk culture, we tend to reduce commentary to notes on specific mining songs, dust-bowl ballads, and Jim Crow blues, or to their composers and interpreters. This preoccupation with "protest song" neglects an appraisal of the sweep as well as the limitation within radical esthetic theory. Regardless of past positions, the conceptual challenge of Seeger and his peers was largely dissipated after World War II in the commercial folksong revival. Within the discipline of folklore, the surviving residue of radical analysis was ultimately displaced in Cold War years by a return to standards of pure scholarship and value-free science, or by an advance to new schools such as structuralism and semiotics.

These brief paragraphs on ideology can be made specific by reference to the most noted collector to visit Appalachia. When Cecil J.

Sharp traveled in 1916, 1917, and 1918 to the Southern Highlands, he sought English folksongs which had been carried to the New World. Although he avoided American politics, he was aware of the large forces which framed his own work. At home in England, Sharp had been touched by both Fabian Socialism and British cultural nationalism.

During the nineteenth century, some European folklore had been used to assist subject people in freeing themselves from alien domination. For example, Elias Lonnrot's *Kalevala* (1835), composed out of locally-gathered folk poetry, helped stave off the Russification of Finnish culture and helped prepare for the emergence of Finland as a sovereign state. England in this same century also was receptive to the formal use of national lore, but at a level of intensity far below that of a subjugated nation. In the United States, the mix of folklore and nationalism was complicated by the subordinate roles of tradition bearers such as Indians, Negroes, and immigrants. Conversely, not only did we lack an overarching national lore, but it was virtually impossible to impose notions of Elizabethan survivals and Anglo-Saxon relics on a heterogeneous population.

Contrary to some recent misreadings of his mission, Sharp was not lost in romanticism, antiquarianism, or chauvinism. Henry Shapiro, in *Appalachia on Our Mind* (1978), presents Sharp as a myth maker—both a creator of mountain symbols and himself a symbol to Americans of Merrie Olde England. This denies the collector's monumental contribution—a massive gathering of traditional Appalachian songlore, an unending scroll in cultural understanding. Putting to one side his rich songbag, I view Sharp as a full-hearted human being, a talented musician, and a cultural evangelist aware of the challenge in advocacy and activism. Some of his hosts in the mountains were settlement school builders—part of the broad American uplift/progressive movement, represented by exemplary figures such as Jane Addams. Actually, Sharp had already observed English settlement schoolteachers ambivalent in their purposes—teaching beloved folksong but modifying traditional style. Needless to say, he broke with those who let down "pure" standards.

To revise history is the prerogative of each generation, but to reduce Sharp to an enthusiast for "the inherent value of the naif culture of Appalachia" (Shapiro, p. 255) is to do an injustice. For the record, Sharp's collection is unparalleled; it can not be whittled down in magni-

Appalachian Coal Camp, *by John A. Spelman, in* At Home in the Hills
(Pine Mountain, Ky.: Pine Mountain Settlement School, 1939).

tude or power. Sharp is hardly discussed today as an ideological person, but in terms of my paper's bent, I can report that, paradoxically, even his gathering of non-political lore had a political dimension. Sharp's aspirations for mountain children were as high as those he held for English working-class youth familiar to him. In 1905, Miss Mary Neal of the Esperance Working Girls' Club, St. Pancras, had asked him to help teach folksong and dance to young seamstresses. Sharp introduced to the club William Kimber, a bricklayer and traditional performer of Morris Dance, in order to bridge rural and industrial modes and consciously to help working people revive national folk expression.

In my first discovery of the wealth of coal mining song, I had decried Cecil Sharp's neglect of this lode in favor of early song. It is part of my growth that I have been able to penetrate to his real achievement and see that his educational mission in Appalachia was threaded to his experience in Britain by a belief that rural or isolated folk could use traditional music both to retain personal strength and to contribute to national well-being. Sharp's life work affirmed that the folk, whether in English countryside, London slum, or Blue Ridge Mountains, could make complex choices about its sense of autonomy and community and could ultimately use its lore to shape reality.

The list of folklorists drawn to mountain life before and after Cecil Sharp is endless, and guides to their findings are available. Here, I cite but two collectors: Alan Lomax in the 1930s and Roger Abrahams in the 1960s. Not only is each a superb collector, but together they are examples of activism appropriate to separate decades. Lomax championed left formulations in the New Deal period and contributed considerably to the shift of militant songs from mountain to city. In part, we know "Which Side Are You On" because of his efforts. Abraham held fast to liberal values in the Cold War years, seeking to accommodate sophisticated anthropological and literary theory to problem solving in race relations and ghetto education.

However, the main connection today between the discipline of folklore and Appalachian studies comes not from within the academy, but from the public sector. The Smithsonian Institution's Festival of American Folklife from 1967, the National Endowment for the Arts's Folk Arts Program from 1974, and the Library of Congress's American Folklife Center from 1976 have all funded Appalachian fieldwork or participated in mountain projects. Here I shall not detail the work of these three federal units, except to say that their administrative heads (Ralph Rinzler, Bess Hawes, Alan Jabbour) have assimilated manifold positions which run from that of ballad scholar Francis James Child to that of sociolinguist and ethnographer Dell Hymes. Despite some differences in personal position, Washington's new folklorists represent a long-overdue commitment by government to cultural equity for the folk.

From the sketch of the politics of other folklorists, I turn to mine. Our public positions can be tagged as "mainstream," "engaged," or "esoteric"; I have tried to wear some of each silk. Further, I have not avoided facing the external consequences of scholarly investigation. At times, we seem to be agents of large society mechanically pursuing assimilative strategies; at times, we seem to be advocates of artistic resistance, best labeled as "cultural Luddites." In two decades of commentary on labor lore I have attempted to use research tools to describe material intrinsically dynamic, but also I have used this scholarship to certify value inherent within blue collar society.

Parallel to my teaching and writing, in the mid-1960s I began to lobby for the American Folklife Preservation Act (signed into law January 2, 1976). In these Washington years, I had occasion to talk to most Appalachian congressmen about folk culture. I found myself partial to those like Carl Perkins (Kentucky) who supported the folklife bill, and critical of those like James Quillen (Tennessee) who opposed it. The fact that some mountain representatives could vote against a bill which many Appalachians judged to be in their best interest forced me to examine my understanding of America's complex values. Was it presumptuous on my part to assert that a particular piece of legislation was good for people in the mountains? What made me so certain that Perkins was "right," Quillen "wrong," and Green the judge? Did I have the right to speak for constituents within Appalachian districts? This is, again, the nettlesome problem of outsiders intruding into mountain life. No matter how mechanically one states the inside/outside dichotomy, nor how it is frequently simplified, Washington experience told me that these oppositions are real and must be understood by all Americans facing change.

Beginning in the 1930s with the view that coal miners ought to be free to organize unions of their own choosing, I had gone in the 1960s to a belief that Appalachians ought to be free to perpetuate their cultural differences: dialect, music, crafts, worship, ritual. On Capitol Hill, rather than in the Cumberlands or the Alleghenies, I had affirmed the cause of ecology and pluralism and had moved from the rhetoric of Eugene V. Debs and John L. Lewis to that of John Muir and Horace Kallen. Also, while lobbying I began to explore the parallels among natural, historic, and cultural preservation, and to sense that eagles and snail darters had much in common with fiddle tunes and quilt designs. Beyond groping for fresh connections, I came to believe that no members of folk society could be free in work or in identity if they allowed themselves to be pitted against environmental visions.

No single term has emerged to unite a Sierra Club ethic with a commitment to autonomous regional or ethnic expression. While waiting for a label to combine interest in studying vernacular language and literature with interest in slowing change in land use and life style, I see my present-day actions as contributing to this desired unity. Scholarship and citizenship should ride in tandem; "ideology" need not be a pejorative term. With others, I search for means to link the conservative values in conservation movements and the radical values in movements of self-determination. In a metaphoric sense, I wish to see John Henry emerge from tunnel tomb, not to die once more defying new augers and shovels which scar his land, but this time to harness technology to human scale.

This paper serves to describe intertwined journeys: one, from San Francisco to Harlan County; another, from labor partisanship to pluralism and ecology; still another, from social democracy to libertarian freedom. Along the path I was fortunate to meet Sarah Ogan Gunning, a Kentucky folksinger. Ironically, I met her not at home in a coal camp, but rather at home in a Detroit ghetto, whence she had been taken by her own journey. Something of her story is found in brochure notes accompanying two LPs: *Girl of Constant Sorrow* (Folk-Legacy 26) and *The Silver Dagger* (Rounder 0051). These record notes are available; here, I shall offer but a few details on her role in Appalachian political and cultural events.

Sarah Elizabeth Garland was born June 28, 1910, in a mine camp on Ely Branch, Knox County, Kentucky. Her father, a sharecropper and Missionary Baptist preacher, turned to coal mining when his region shifted from frontier farming to extractive industry. Upon the death of his first wife, he married Elizabeth Lucas at Little Goose Creek, Clay County. Three of Oliver Perry Garland's children—Aunt Molly Jackson, Jim Garland, and Sarah—were destined to fame as folksingers. Each grew by absorbing a wide repertoire: classic ballads, love lyrics, banjo frolics, comic ditties, local broadsides, religious hymns. Each was a master at Appalachia's high lonesome song style.

During 1931, Kentucky coal fields were at their nadir, and the AFL United Mine Workers of America was in disarray. Some miners responded by joining the communist-led National Miners Union, when the Communist party was mired in sectarianism and isolated from allies on the left. The NMU, a dual union, disappeared after John L. Lewis revitalized the UMWA in Blue Eagle days, 1933–34. Historians, left and right, have continued to argue crisis and failure in Harlan County. Whether or not the NMU was "correct" in its line, it did not live beyond the New Deal, and its partisans who could not rebuild their lives in home coal-camps migrated north.

NMU stalwart Jim Garland, as well as Molly and Sarah, both married to NMU members, were all three affected by this shift in labor position and shift out of region. During 1935, ballad collector Mary Elizabeth Barnicle helped Sarah and her family move to New York City's lower East Side. Ghetto life was as debilitating as mountain poverty, and in a few years Sarah's husband, Andrew Ogan, was dead. In 1941, Sarah married Joseph Gunning, a Brooklyn metal polisher who found wartime shipyard employment on the distant Columbia River. Eventually, the Gunnings put down roots in Detroit, and when Joe was no longer employable, Sarah moved to Hart, Michigan, to be near her son and grandchildren.

At the surface, we see a mountain girl, widowed young, remarried, and migrating with husband in search of work. However, Sarah never permitted herself to be uprooted from mountain culture; she carried it proudly wherever she lived. Sustaining herself by clinging to old songs and still older performing styles, she sang occasionally to Professor Barnicle's classes at New York University, as well as to left-wing hootenannies. On these stages, she met the stars of the then-developing urban folksong revival: Pete Seeger, Burl Ives, Huddie Ledbetter, Josh White, Woody Guthrie, Earl Robinson, Lee Hays, Will Geer. Alan Lomax collected a dozen of Sarah's songs in 1937 for the Library of Congress, but after the Gunnings left New York, she dropped away from folksong activity. I first visited her in Detroit in 1963 while gathering material for *Only a Miner*. She was known to me through her field recordings as well as through the stories of her sister Aunt Molly Jackson, whom I had visited in Sacramento, California, some years before.

After editing Sarah's first LP, I had the opportunity to invite her to festivals (among others, Carnegie Hall, Smithsonian Institution, University of Chicago), and to a few labor education meetings. On these dual platforms she has been not only a great teacher but has renewed early commitments. Sarah accepted her sharing of a stage with the president of the United Auto Workers, Walter Reuther, as a natural reward for holding the faith. While observing her in seminars, I was struck by her ability to synthesize contrastive values and by her towering personal honesty. Synthesis for her did not mean flaccid compromise nor mealy rhetoric. Her values were expressed quietly but with conviction and often were infused with wry humor. She was incapable of dissimulation, exaggeration, or self-pity.

Sarah's ability to integrate divergent positions within her own cultural frame was rare indeed. A clash of Marxian and Lockean ideologies developed in the early 1930s, when a handful of northern organizers— radicals and intellectuals—met great numbers of rural-based, conservative folk in Cumberland coal camps. For many mountaineers, this tension was disorienting and, hence, to be avoided. Nevertheless, a few individuals were able to weld radical expression to traditional values, at times in lasting forms. Sarah's labor compositions were folk-like songs, holding polemical texts set to poignant melodies. Not only did she pull together the realms of militancy and antiquity, but she performed with stubborn integrity in the oldest style at her command. When song content featured sorrow or hardship, she transcended the message of despair by using a stylistic delivery as natural as the flowering redbud at her earliest home. In singing to students in the 1960s, she projected neither a narrow vision nor a sense of personal alienation. In her most sorrowful songs, she retained the wholeness of belief that all of us can endure.

I lack the skill to probe Sarah's inner strength, but I have observed that she was strong enough to deal with conflict springing from the rift between fundamental religion and radical creed, between a Kentucky childhood in coves still fresh and an adult life in drab slums. For many, this tension destroys the possibility of artistic statement. For Sarah, seemingly, it has fueled song composition and performance. In a sense, hard times have girded her poetic power, enhanced her esthetic gift.

Those outside Sarah's experience have many choices in listening to her. We can hear her either as another mountain singer with an antique songbag or as a polemical fanning flames of discontent. I have tried to listen not to two Sarahs but to the whole Sarah. Over the years, she has represented for me the very best within Appalachian folklife — cultural integrity and physical survival. That she now lives far away from her native mountain is a disturbing symbol of cultural and political tragedy.

Why must so many Appalachians leave home to seek new work? Is the process of demographic destabilization fixed in the American psyche or economy? Are we too restless or too grasping a people to knit together our third century of nationhood? Is the kind of synthesis which Sarah made in her songlore an appropriate model for fellow Appalachians who are uprooted or powerless? Song performance obviously has sustained her and given personal strength, but can this creative gift be translated into power for others of her sex, class, and region? These rhetorical queries are answered from left and right by slogans: power to all, power to few. Answers can flow, as well, from the center: power is dangerous — diffuse it by accommodation, balance, synthesis. Centrists lack the incandescent glow of left and right. Partisans at the spectrum's ends flaunt their uncompromising purity in position. Centrists move by murky indirection and blurred rhetoric.

In her songbag Sarah has treasured, equally, material that is both revolutionary and conservative in content. One must hear her move readily from "Christ Was a Wayworn Traveler" to "I Hate the Capitalist System" to appreciate her light-year span in ideas, all modulated by constant mountain style. I have never known her to use the word "synthesis." She has had to remember old ballads and compose new ones, but not to employ scholarly terminology in self-description.

I have not attempted to achieve symmetrical balance here by weighing my journey against Sarah's. I was called to folklore before we met; she enlarged my understanding of its complexity. Her repertoire was formed before we met; I helped place a selection of her songs on LP, enlarging her audience. Fifteen years have elapsed since *Girl of Constant Sorrow* appeared, and I have returned to Sarah in this paper, not to explicate a given song, but to reflect on her role as an exponent of Appalachian achievement. In creatively balancing rival modes, she has made a large enough statement, but I feel also that she has something to teach us beyond this notion of mediation.

The Southern Highlands have in the past decade become an economic battlefield in the energy war, and it has been difficult for students and teachers to focus on cultural matters. Especially neglected is Appalachian folk esthetics. I am drawn to Sarah because she has been buffeted long by divergent concepts of artistic purpose. Figuratively, she has been a self-propelled Chautauqua troupe with esthetic discourse as its subject. Over the years she has internalized a half-dozen norms. In her father's Baptist culture, old hymns, prophetic in content and sung in drawn-out tone, were valued. Her mother retained haunting lyrical songs which helped project harsh frontier experience into fantasy. When NMU organizers came to Kentucky, Sarah learned that art was a weapon in the class struggle. Before she left New York, her hootenanny friends had begun to flatten folk style on the pop culture anvil. At recent festivals, Sarah's polemical songs have been hailed variously as reflectors of a romanticized radical past or as novel tools to alter present-day consciousness.

This paper does not afford the compass to extend these many positions; all require further exploration. But demanding attention here is one specific dogma which complicates the serious study of Appalachian folk esthetics. It states that culture is a decorative latticework built on top of an underlying concrete structure. At one level, we hear formulas which describe basic means of economic production and reflexive artistic superstructures. At another, we are told that if we solve the problem of absentee ownership of resources, secondary matters such as hill dialect, child-rearing practice, and denominational identity will be resolved. I have never heard Sarah lecture on cultural imperatives, but beyond the mountain esthetic code which came to her in childhood, she did hear Marxist organizers in the early 1930s. Absorbing some of their views, she placed their chips into her Kentucky mosaic. Although it was exciting to compose picket line songs, Sarah never abandoned "Loving Nancy."

In a curious way, she inverted the notion of culture as projection of a politico-economic base. By hanging onto her time-tested ballad style, mountain speech, and local humor, she found her way to appropriate radical positions. In Harlan's time of terror, she possessed the inner strength to stand up to coal operators' gun thugs because she was secure in all her feelings. Her expressive life held an intrinsic power based on continuities in tradition. Essentially, Sarah's skill in integrating American polarities was complemented by a supple esthetic philosophy. Characteristically, after meeting Joan Baez at the Newport Festival (1964), Sarah summed up her own views in a laconic comment. She observed that Miss Baez was a nice young woman who hadn't learned to sing mountain music properly.

Sarah Ogan Gunning, like other Appalachians, lived through the deepest change in the region's economy and the most devastating accommodation to such change. Unlike many of her peers, she compressed experience into a handful of memorable new songs and reshaped an old esthetic sense to frame them. From the outside, I bring paradigms of mediation and inversion to Sarah's contribution. These technical terms are not in her vocabulary, but their absence in no way diminishes her power. She has joined modernity to tradition; she treasures a great variety of song; she is conscious of external hardships as well as of internal gifts.

Folklorists are not usually comfortable with questions of political philosophy, their own or that of the folk. My personal turn from song collecting to a volunteer stint as a Washington lobbyist, and to an active setting for reformulating notions of freedom, has not been typical of choices made by my peers. Nevertheless, I have been able to collect in the mountains, to write *Only a Miner,* and to find my book useful in Appalachian studies. The opportunity to turn congressional offices into seminar rooms on folk culture was highly rewarding.

In my endeavors as scholar and citizen, I have been helped by diverse model figures. Of the four named in this paper—John Henry, Cecil Sharp, John L. Lewis, Sarah Ogan Gunning—two exemplified the best within mountain life; two came from outside to add to mountain life. John Henry, if he ever lived in reality, now lives only in heroic legend. Cecil Sharp is known chiefly to ballad scholars. John L. Lewis's story, revised as the fortunes of organized miners shift, is nevertheless central in labor history. Sarah Ogan Gunning, sustained by traditional values, is hardly known to large society. Even in the mountains she is known chiefly by a few folksong fans and by tiny groups of student-activists. In a nation where tens of millions see and hear country stars Loretta Lynn and Dolly Parton, Linda Ronstadt and Emmylou Harris, Sarah's voice is virtually silent. Yet, better than leaders in high place, better than Nashville queens, better than outside interpreters of folk culture, Sarah, in my view, serves as exemplar for Appalachian citizens at home as well as in America's countless byways.

BIBLIOGRAPHY

In revising this paper I benefited from talks with Loyal Jones, Herbert Reid, David Walls, and David Whisnant. For further reading see:

Ardery, Julie, editor. An autobiographical manuscript by Jim Garland completed before his death, September 6, 1978. Forthcoming in 1980.

Green, Archie. Brochure notes to LP, *Sarah Ogan Gunning: Girl of Constant Sorrow* (Folk-Legacy 26) 1965.

———. "Industrial Lore: A Bibliographic-Semantic Query," *Western Folklore* 37 (July 1978): 213–44.

———. Introduction to *Folklife and the Federal Government,* by Linda C. Coe. Washington: American Folklife Center, Library of Congress, 1977.

Hevener, John W. *Which Side Are You On?: The Harlan County Coal Miners, 1931–1939.* Urbana: University of Illinois Press, 1978.

Karpeles, Maud. *Cecil Sharp: His Life and Work.* Chicago: University of Chicago Press, 1967.

Seeger, Charles. *Studies in Musicology 1935–1975.* Berkeley: University of California Press, 1977.

William, John A. "Radicalism and Professionalism in Folklore Studies." *Journal of the Folklore Institute* 11 (1975): 211–39.

Wilson, Mark. Brochure notes to LP, *Sarah Ogan Gunning: The Silver Dagger* (Rounder 0051) 1976.

Austin's Cosmic Cowboys
WORDS IN COLLISION

aving reached the eighties, we are conscious that much of the new vocabulary of the sixties and seventies, psyche-delic or apocalyptic, is already dated. The very technology which extends language into space through computer-ized rocket travel also renders many neologisms obsolete before they take hold widely. Nonce words have a partial life, fluid and catchy; they live furtively, grasping at sub-stance. The combination "cosmic cowboy" surfaced during the seven-ties, caught on to describe a new stylistic synthesis within the ferment of American music, and fell from favor by the decade's end. Words hardly receive formal burial or marble headstones; they merely fade out of usage, unlamented except by lexicographers. When *Newsweek* featured Willie Nelson in a cover photo as "King of Country Music," reporter Pete Axthelm (1978) managed a concise article without once using "cosmic." As this qualifier descended, others arose. At the end of 1979, Robert Redford and Jane Fonda appeared in a call-to-the-wild film about a wasted cowboy, *The Electric Horseman;* today, we use a re-lated cinematic phrase, "urban cowboy" (Latham 1978:21).[1]

These references put me at the end, not the beginning, of an ety-mological study. The American cowboy's name has long been potent throughout the world. Responding to and reflecting upon cowboy imagery, many folklorists—among them John Lomax, J. Frank Dobie, Moody Boatright, and Américo Paredes—have helped explicate his language and lore. Following their trail, I focus on a short-lived term, tangential to cowboy reality, used to describe country rock music and its audience in Austin, Texas, during the seventies.

Austin's eclectic composer/performers, in the past decade, drew upon folk or popular expression to mark contemporary social colli-

"*Willie Nelson and Michael Murphey Together,*" *Armadillo World Headquarters concert, September 15–16, 1972, poster by Michael Priest. (Courtesy Michael Priest)*

sion and convergence. Some conflict is endemic within any community—ethnic, regional, occupational, or social. Even as loosely defined a coterie as the fans of "low-brow" music (folk/country/blues/rock) includes individuals of different esthetic preference and linguistic behavior. Musical enthusiasts can mark such dissonance, or consonance, in arenas from honkytonk to recording studio, by their use of certain words. "Cosmic cowboy" reveals such tension and resolution; it commented upon the considerable degree of interaction among vernacular and popular forms—musical, graphic, and literary. Moreover, like other discrete verbal tags, it demonstrated the clash of large values in American life.

It has taken "cowboy" three centuries to draw to itself a rainbow of meaning, supplanting the earlier terms "herder" and "drover."[2] Jonathan Swift used the new word in 1725, in a poem for Stella, to refer to Irish lads who tended cattle. During our Revolutionary War, however, the then-novel "cowboy" developed a pejorative connotation. It was used to describe Tory guerrillas who, by tinkling cowbells, beguiled patriotic Americans into the brush. Such King George loyalists—bushwhackers and cattle skinners—also ambushed and savaged George Washington's men.

After the Texas Revolution, this villainous connotation appeared along the Rio Grande, where *vaquero* met cowboy. The former had little use for the latter, who rustled Mexican longhorns. In 1847, Mirabeau Lamar—soldier, poet, historian, and second president of the Texas Republic—noted in his papers (1978:99) that Anglo "Cow-Boys" were marauders, thieves who rounded up "wild cattle" between the Nueces and the Colorado. In this predatory border region (*El Desierto Muerto*), a "cow driver" was often a robber and, at times, a murderer (Nance 1963:45–67).

It was not until the Civil War's close that "cowboy" again changed in value. When Texas cattle started to be driven north to market, the word lost its opprobrious color. Cowboys at the Chisholm Trail's end did raise Cain, but there was little need to stigmatize them as violent raiders. The food needs of a growing industrial nation thus established a social setting in which "cowboy" gained a positive connotation. In economic terms, cowboys were the cousins of all other food handlers, earlier and later: of dusty millers, sweaty butchers, wheat threshers, fruit tramps, salmon fishermen, airplane-flying crop-dusters, bracero crop-pickers, and supermarket stackers. Glenn Ohrlin (1974), an Ozark rancher and traditional singer, has tagged cowboy workers neither tough nor mean but rather plain and regular. To labor endlessly at hard, rough, unglamorous jobs precludes being a cruel gunslinger or mythic hero.

In short, "cowboy" is a semantically elastic marker. It has denoted variously a Tory guerrilla, a Western outlaw, a skilled rider, or a puritanical worker. To this array we can add the cowboy as a carouser, a

FIGURE I. Drunken Cow-Boy on the "War-Path," *by Henry Worrall. From
Joseph G. McCoy,* Historic Sketches of the Cattle Trade of the West and
Southwest *(Kansas City, Mo.: Ramsey, 1874).*

prankster, a man full of raw vitality, a brother of Puck and Falstaff. Two
early humorous images are found in Joseph G. McCoy's *Historic Sketches
of the Cattle Trade of the West and Southwest* (1874). This classic, illustrated
by Henry Worrall, offers an important eye-witness account of the Texas
drives to Kansas boomtowns, where herds were held for rail shipment
to Chicago. Worrall's engravings include the earliest visual portrait I
have found of the shoot-'em-up, hell-raising cowboy—the figurative
ancestor of many recent country and rock singers (fig. 1). McCoy high-
lighted this character at play in a "vortex of dissipation" at an Abilene
dance hall (fig. 2):

> A more odd, not to say comical, sight is not often seen than the
> dancing cow-boy; with the front of his sombrero lifted at an angle
> of fully forty-five degrees, his huge spurs jingling at every step or
> motion; his revolvers flapping up and down like a retreating sheep's
> tail; his eyes lit up with excitement, liquor and lust; he plunges in and
> "hoes it down" at a terrible rate, in the most approved yet awkward
> country style; often swinging "his partner" clear off of the floor for
> an entire circle, "then balance all" with an occasional demoniacal
> yell, near akin to the war whoop of the savage Indian (1874:139).

Cowboy literature includes autobiographies, histories, critical essays, picture books, and fiction. Such reports make it clear that the cow-

FIGURE 2. Dance-House, *by Henry Worrall. From Joseph G. McCoy,*
Historic Sketches of the Cattle Trade of the West and Southwest
(Kansas City, Mo.: Ramsey, 1874).

boy remained both a working and a comic figure through the closing
decades of the last century. He also became a legendary figure, coura-
geous and formidable, who could ride even under the weight of distorted rhetorical comparisons such as "Pegasus of the Plains."

Although folklorists generally distinguish legend from myth, most
writers on the West treat these genres as interchange. While old trail
drivers and ranchers romanticized their callings in memoirs, others—
dime novelists, pulp journalists, tent showmen—also sought to create
a new folk hero, a Rousseauian nobleman. The legend makers often
borrowed attributes from predecessors of the cowboy: mountain trappers, Indian scouts, explorers of the prairie and plain. Retrospectively,
one does not marvel that some workers in the cattle trade were enshrined both in folk imagination and in popular literature, only that
this process began so early. John Baumann, a British traveler, wrote:

> The cowboy has at the present time become a personage; nay, more,
> he is rapidly becoming a mythical one. Distance is doing for him
> what lapse of time did for the heroes of antiquity. His admirers are
> investing him with all manner of romantic qualities; they descant
> upon his manifold virtues and his pardonable weaknesses as if he
> were a demi-god, and I have no doubt that before long there will
> be ample material for any philosophic inquirer who may wish to en-

lighten the world as to the cause and meaning of the cowboy myth (1887:516).

After the turn of the century, movie producers joined the myth makers. *The Great Train Robbery*'s Western outlaw sequence was made in 1903; a three-reel presentation of Buffalo Bill's touring Wild West Show was released in 1910. Also, in this year, the Essanay Company began a long series of Bronco Billy miracle plays for Saturday matinees. These formulaic productions, based on countless dime-novel and tent-show predecessors, set cinematic patterns still visible on television. During the twenties Tom Mix replaced Billy, but Mix, too, was frozen in contrived and romantic plots. Many adults reacted ambivalently to film hokum: it was trash to spoil youthful minds, harmless escape, or dangerous fantasy. Because the cowboy as an American exemplar emerged dually as a normal worker and a mythical hero, he simultaneously attracted defenders and detractors. While pulp writers and screen directors featured guns, guitars, and bravado, realistic ethnographers stressed thorns, fleas, and grit. Often it proved difficult to judge the symbolic role of either gun or grit.

Popular images of the cowboy engendered criticism. Although some riders embellished their own lives, modeling themselves after their fictional incarnation, most wranglers objected to such theatrical portraits. Meanwhile, writers sympathetic to reality noted or ridiculed the (self-)caricatures. For example, Isabelle Randall, traveling from England to Montana, wrote of her train trip on the Plains: "In swaggered two men, dressed to the highest pitch of cowboy dandyism" (1887:6). Humorist George Ade depicted Teddy Roosevelt's Rough Riders as players "cavortin' around town here in their cowboy hats and gassin' in front of every store" (1903:251).

During the twenties the swaggering dandy cavorted in a very specific place—the drugstore. By definition, the "drugstore cowboy" was a braggart, loafer, or good-for-nothing poseur dressed like a Westerner. Credit for bringing him to life artistically belongs to Thomas Aloysius Dorgan ("Tad"), cartoonist, sports writer, and shaper of much American slang. His "Indoor Sports" cartoon for *The San Francisco Call and Post* (July 5, 1923) first presented three drugstore cowboys in the saddle, dressed sharply but not in cowpoke costume. Tad saw them as ladies' men, flappers' foils, or collegiate sheiks, and equated the sexual euphemism "cake eater" with "drugstore cowboy" (fig. 3).

FIGURE 3. *"Indoor Sports," by Thomas Aloysius Dorgan [Tad],*
in San Francisco Call and Post, *July 5, 1923.*

In February 1925, *College Humor* used the new term generically, and
soon John Held, Jr., and his many imitators, began to draw Jazz Age
cowboys in exaggerated bell-bottoms, with or without chaps, lounging
at soda counters and ice-cream parlors. Youngsters kidded them: "A
drugstore cowboy is quick on the straw!" One target was Will Rogers.
Corey Ford wrote the following uncomplimentary caption for Miguel
Covarrubias's caricature of Rogers (fig. 4):

> In his familiar chaps and two-gallon hat, America's Drug Store
> Cowboy loiters as usual at the corner of Main Street and Park Ave-
> nue, his long lariat mouth uncoiling slowly as he drawls a few homely
> observations for the *Times* (each in a little worse taste than the last),
> calls all the passing celebrities by their first names, offers his advice
> to every one free for what it is worth, and pursues his daily racket of
> "jes' bein' common folks" (1930:84).

The mocking term lives. Pat Frank described a character in *Seven
Days to Never* as marrying "a marijuana-smoking drugstore cowboy"
(1957:102). Frank's novel added a new dimension to the locution. In
Tad's America the drugstore had been the milieu for adolescent bravado — an innocent place for hanging-out. Now, adult drug hangups
have intensified the overtones of "drugstore cowboy."

FIGURE 4. *"Will Rogers," by Miguel Covarrubias. From Corey Ford,*
The John Riddell Murder Case *(New York: Scribner's, 1930).*

Hollywood, Nashville, and Austin have combined to delineate a new breed of "cowboy"—neither ordinary worker with cattle, wild renegade, nor national mythic figure, but rather a bittersweet antihero. The movie *Midnight Cowboy,* released in May 1969, centered not on a brave rider but on a callow bus rider, one who reversed Horace Greeley's dictum by going East to hustle fame and fortune. From a small-town café in Texas ranch country, the dishwashing cowboy plunged into a surrealistic Manhattan of perversion and poverty. The film resonated powerfully in a cosmos populated by Tim Leary, Ken Kesey, and their camp followers; it also managed to invert the time-tested message of writers like Ned Buntline, Owen Wister, and Zane Grey, and of painters like Frederic Remington, Charles Russell, and Will James.

Subsequent to this film, the midnight cowboy's many buddies within song texts became mysterious, rebellious, nostalgic, lonely, gypsy, hip, or cosmic. The noun "cowboy," when used to describe country rock musicians, functions as a badge of distinction. In a sense, these latterday buckaroos have recycled "cowboy" to hitch themselves to a romantic past, as well as to explain to each other something of their troubled present.

One contemporary nuance surfaced in Peter Rowan's composition "Lonesome L.A. Cowboy." The song appeared on *The Adventures of Panama Red* (1973), an LP by the New Riders of the Purple Sage. Rowan's hero proclaims: "I been smokin' dope, snortin' coke, tryin' to write a song, forgettin' everything I know 'til the next line comes along." This passage is striking not because of the reference to drugs, but rather because the cowboy has been removed completely from his traditional range. Neither rescuing a companion nor trailing cattle, he is transformed into a writer trailing an elusive refrain. Not only is this Angeleno lonely and frightened, but he finds himself an alienated intellectual distanced from life. Pens and guitars may or may not be superior as tools to lariats and saddles, but the accoutrements of the muses are the only tools available to modern musical cowboys.

How did the cowboy emerge, within scores of country songs, as a tattered hippy under a Stetson? Record liner notes, as well as interviews and concert reviews, offer widespread answers. Waylon Jennings, a "bad boy in leather," talking with *Rolling Stone* reporter Chet Flippo, used "cowboy" to signify oppositions: an El Paso honkytonk, where Jennings had performed, housed "some pretty wild old cowboys. . . . You walk in there, like last night, and they say, 'He's a cowboy singer, let's whup his ass' " (1973b:28). In this tightly compressed statement the El Paso beer drinkers (old cowboys) are booted hellions, died-in-the-wool conservatives ready to pounce on any alienated, long-haired stud (cowboy singer), who, seemingly, represents creative freedom. Thus, the cowboy becomes a Janus figure, for he is at once redneck audience and isolated artist, straight and freak, hunter and hunted.

A drugs-drugstore connection underlies the country music establishment's first emotional reactions in the sixties to "turned on" or "hippy" songwriters such as John Hartford. Does it not now seem strange to recall that in 1967 "Gentle on My Mind" was perceived by many country stalwarts as a "far out" or "high" composition? When Glen Campbell first presented "Gentle" to television audiences he made it an instant hit. In Nashville at that time, I can recall no critic who equated the word "hippy" with "cowboy"; but only a few years later, enthusiasts were using the latter to describe the country music's rebellious fringe. On October 14, 1970, the Country Music Association presented an annual award to Kris Kristofferson for "Sunday Morning Coming Down," a somber drugs song. The composer, appearing on prime-time television, offended his hosts by his offbeat conduct. Symbolically, Kris helped transform the road-weary musician into a trail-weary cowhand. It was after the CMA broadcast that I first heard Nashville people class Kris as a "cowboy"—light years removed from Gene Autry and Roy Rogers.

While Kristofferson's conduct nettled Nashville's brass, Paul Hemphill commented on the CMA awards program for the *New York Times:*

> You could sense Tex Ritter and Roy Acuff and all the rest hunkering down in their seats as [Kris] floated to the stage of the Grand Ole Opry House to accept the award: suede bell-bottoms, shoulder-length hair, strange deep-set Jack Palance eyes; weaving back and forth with his back to the audience for nearly 10 seconds like a cowboy who had lost his way. . . . Nashville's Music Row is still seething. "I mean, hell, he didn't even wear a tux" (1970:54).

Hemphill, a superb reporter, grasped at once the irony of a tuxless cowboy, who nonetheless was not so wasted that he could not rope a Nashville prize.

Kristofferson's appearance has become an oft-told anecdote in the shop-talk which clusters around the country music industry. David Allan Coe, self-billed as the "Mysterious Rhinestone Cowboy," in *Pick-*

ing Up the Tempo paid tribute to Kris as a leader who opened Nashville's doors to other underground artists:

> [Kris] snuck right by 'em. And the next thing you know he was being nominated for awards and worse, he was winning them. Then the truth came out when he appeared at the awards show wearing levis (heaven forbid). Nashville was in a tizzy. . . . Here was this goddam hippy, right in front for the world to see, staggering around, drunk as shit, insulting dignitaries with his uncouth mouth and setting a bad example for national television (1975:1).

These vivid accounts of cowboys in suedes or hippies in levis shrewdly prodded at the industry's real weakness—its inability to accept the talented outsiders who were forging new country sounds. Dave Hickey, a Texan from Fort Worth and a former graduate student at Austin, reported scornfully from Tennessee that his "favorite low riders, lonesome pickers, and telecaster cowboys" were "just about the only folks in Nashville who will walk into a room where there's a guitar and a *Wall Street Journal* and pick up the guitar" (1974:90).

By the mid-seventies, "cowboy" for an outsider or outlaw had assimilated into country music language. The word that had previously connoted romance in group names such as Hank Williams and the Drifting Cowboys or Pee Wee King and his Golden West Cowboys now bespoke marginality. Country fans during the early seventies also used "cowboy" for performers like Waylon Jennings and Willie Nelson. These two stars had earned their spurs by being Texans; more importantly, they were willing to flaunt openly their break with Nashville's sounds and codes. Their music also earned the sobriquet "outlaw." Michael Bane, in his book, *The Outlaws: Revolution in Country Music,* relates how the term arose. Hazel Smith at the Glaser Studios ("Hillbilly Central") received a phone call "one day in 1973" from a disc jockey in Asheboro, North Carolina, who wanted to feature the then-new music of Kris, Waylon, and Willie and "needed a hook, something to give the show an image." Hazel obliged: "Call it 'Outlaw Music.'" Later she explained that she had been influenced in her choice by Lee Clayton's "Ladies Love Outlaws," the title song of a Jennings LP released in 1972 (Bane 1978:4–10).

Significantly, Dave Hickey called his report for *Country Music* on the new trend in Nashville "In Defense of the Telecaster Cowboy Outlaws." The words "cowboy" and "outlaw" couple naturally. But the latter term had built-in limitations. How can "outlaw" be applied to popular culture heroes who decorate their dens with platinum records and jet around the world for lucrative concert tours? An irreverent reporter for the *Village Voice,* Nick Tosches, made fun of such "outlaws," picturing them as "oligarchs" who hung high only in the hit charts, not the gallows tree (1976:142).

AUSTIN IN THE SEVENTIES

"Cowboy," the recent generic term for country music's tricksters and gypsies, achieved currency not only in Nashville but also in Austin, Texas, during the early seventies. It served to describe many writer/ performers: for example, Waylon Jennings, Doug Sahm, Jerry Jeff Walker, Guy Clark, David Allan Coe, Ray Wylie Hubbard, Michael Murphey, Kinky Friedman, and Willie Nelson—not all of whom were comfortable thus linked with each other: The music they played was variously labeled "redneck rock," "outlaw music," "progressive country," and "country rock."

Jan Reid coined the first term for his book, *The Improbable Rise of Redneck Rock* (1974), a report on Austin's bizarre cowboy musicians. Coming from a blue-collar family in Wichita Falls, Texas, Reid was familiar with Southern vernacular speech and had seen country customs carried to city centers. He picked "redneck," a two-century old synonym for "clod" to describe Austin's exciting fusion of orthodox country and high-energy rock music. Reid, with Don Roth (1973), had employed the accurate but less dramatic "country rock" in their earlier article "The Coming of Redneck Hip." Also seeking a catchy name, Austin radio station KOKE-FM introduced "progressive country," which achieved a limited currency beyond Texas (Carr 1973:D9).

A dynamic process of change, not yet fully explained by musicologist or historian, has driven many American country musicians to reach to blues, jazz, and rock expression. Conversely, "uptown" musicians have turned "down" and "back" to rural or folk roots. This reach "across the tracks" has moved some individual creators from mainstream to marginal life, and others in the reverse direction. Country rock did not originate in any single community nor with a special set of creators. In 1968 audiences from Sunset Strip to Harvard Square enthusiastically received The Byrds' *Sweetheart of the Rodeo,* an LP which anticipated Bob Dylan's *Nashville Skyline.* Gram Parsons from Waycross, Georgia, sought to play white soul music and pioneered in fusing genres before his untimely death in 1973. Emmylou Harris and Linda Ronstadt, both from urban settings, are present-day country-music queens. The Allman Brothers, beginning in a Muscle Shoals, Alabama, studio in 1969, pulled country blues and hard rock together and, incidentally, used the new music to raise funds for Jimmy Carter in 1976.

Despite this spread in site, style, personality, and nomenclature, the richest single setting for musical convergence was Austin. A puzzling combination of influences fused not only the styles of country music and rock, but also the social identities of "hippy" and "cowboy." It became hip to be a hick. Why did this happen initially not in Nashville, San Francisco, or Manhattan, but deep in the heart of Texas?

I will not compress Austin music into a history capsule, but rather will describe the setting in which both rednecks and rockers began to portray themselves in dress and song as cowboys. The common conflict between those from opposite sides of the track—rich/poor, worldly/parochial, mainstream/minority, "straight"/"freak"—received a special expression in Austin. "Cowboy" or "kicker" were synonyms for "straight" and essentially designated a youth from a poor, rural, and outspokenly patriotic family. By contrast, "freak," "long-hair" and "head" suggested a well-to-do or urban background. Throughout this century, parents of Austin "cowboys in blue jeans" were locally called "cedar choppers." This term identified hill folk who cleared timber for ranchers, burned charcoal for city dwellers, and hacked ties for railroad construction crews. With Austin's urbanization, "cedar chopper" was carried to the schoolyard, along with a similarly derogatory ruralism, "goat roper."

Many members of Austin's music audience were students directly out of rural homes, or only a generation removed. The ambivalence they felt about their origins was not a new phenomenon. John Avery Lomax had labored in Austin itself long ago to help Texans appreciate their frontier roots. J. Frank Dobie, the "Cowboy Professor," while teaching Southwestern life and literature, had opened the eyes of students to previously overlooked regional values. Kris Kristofferson had found fans among Austinites ready for a rock philosopher in shaggy denim. And long before any hippies rocked in Austin's black bars, Jimmie Rodgers, a white Mississippi railroad boomer, had pulled together Anglo and Afro expressions. In his Kerrville mansion near Austin, the singing brakeman had also donned a Stetson and play-acted the cowboy. The crossbreeding of music in Texas (black and white, rural and urban) moved ahead after World War II in Buddy Holly's and Roy Orbison's rockabilly innovations. We sense the pained pleasure of the response of young Texans to their rural roots in Roxy Gordon's *Some Things I Did* (1971) as well as in his literate criticism of "new music" in *Picking Up the Tempo,* a "half-savage" country Western tabloid published from 1974 to 1978.

References to certain musical styles or movies frequently reflect youthful tension. For example, reporter Pat Lewis in Prince Georges County, Maryland, noted that student "dropouts" or "grits" borrowed Kung Fu film techniques to fight "niggers" and "freaks." What is important about Austin—indeed, almost mysterious—is that the early seventies seemed to bring a local inversion in style. Young cedar choppers/cowboys/goat ropers had regularly enjoyed country music and Western swing, often blaring it from pickup truck radios. Their antagonists had lived on rock and roll and revival folksong. Yet, in time, some Austin rock freaks borrowed elements of kicker style and perceived themselves as cowboys.

In breaking these identity barriers or, more properly, internalizing these dual artistic forms, young Austinites were commenting upon a complicated dialectic between Southern and national norms as well as between black and white expressions. In a time of civil-rights strife, dissent about Vietnam, and altered moral codes, all played out against the backdrop of an unrelenting industrialization of the South, it proved impossible for musical or social taste and style to remain compartmentalized.

The meeting of partisans from Austin's two separate sectors created new performers and audiences. Native Texans and strangers drawn to the open Austin community experimented by integrating the sounds of Bob Wills and Mick Jagger. This mix crossed lines of race, residence, and status. In their patter, musicians asserted that "small-town" Austin was "laid-back," or relaxed. The pressure of conforming to business demands was less rigid in Austin than in Nashville or Hollywood. To depart these "hype" and "jive" centers asserted freedom. Also, students in great numbers, touched by Haight-Ashbury's and Berkeley's liberating breezes, formed ready and paying audiences. Finally, Texas regionalism (and chauvinism) shored up moves toward independent creativity. It was as much fun to trumpet musical experimentation as it was to flaunt that Texas could go it alone with gas and oil: Let them freeze in the dark listening to moldy fig music!

New sounds and styles demand new locutions. Austin's young red-necks and schoolyard goat ropers extended their names and dress to Texas rock musicians returning home from both coasts, as well as to thousands of college students who grooved and boogied to post-Beatles rhythm-and-blues tunes. Hip musicians were drawn to the image of the cowboy-as-rebel breaking with Nashville and other established institutions. The genuine range-rider was seen as a loner—perhaps he could double as a cultural radical or displaced intellectual. These musicians, strong enough to feel comfortable with psychedelic light shows as well as with screen cowpokes riding down the canyon, helped Austinites bridge past and present. A University of Texas student at a Willie Nelson picnic could be loyal to parents and peers simultaneously. In collegiate terms, it was fun to seek the traditional highs of beer and the innovative highs of dope, while listening to music that spoke to both pleasures.

Attractive as it was to Nashville expatriates, Austin had little need to import musical talent. Local performers and club owners had prepared well the way for cultural synthesis in the early seventies. While the Kingston Trio defined folksong for most American students, a handful of Austin dissidents turned to mountain ballads and frolics or to bluegrass, often hootenanny flavored. Local folk buffs performed in off-campus pads, at the University of Texas Union, and at the now legendary gas station/hillbilly beer joint, Threadgill's. The Waller Creek Boys —Janis Joplin, Lanny Wiggins, Powell St. John—played there, meeting uncompromising country musicians out of blue-collar life. In the din of a Wednesday-night picking session at Threadgill's bar, St. John (1974) recalled later he met Bill Neely in "tailored Western shirt, starched jeans, and gleaming Tony Lamas," playing "a big red Gibson Hummingbird guitar." Powell liked Bill and his personal country songs which reflected farm, Depression, and work experience. The two played together for several years at barbecues, parties, and rallies until St. John went on to rock with Austin's Conqueroo and San Francisco's Mother Earth.[3]

Marcia Mouton Ball, a young pianist and sure-voiced singer from a Vinton, Louisiana, Cajun family, had tried her hand in a "folk trio" while attending LSU in 1968. After college she turned to "Joplin-screaming" in Baton Rouge rock clubs. In Austin, in February 1972, she and Bobby Earl Smith formed Freda and the Firedogs, one of the first long-haired country bands to meet rural fans on their own turf. At the

FIGURE 5. *"John Clay, Janis Joplin, and beer drinker,"* by Hal Normand, in Texas Ranger, *December 1962.*

Split Rail, Austin's downhome honkytonk, Marcia handled with ease blues, boogie, and soul, winning short-haired "ultra-conservative" audiences by her infectious "Cotton-Eyed Joe" and her yodeling "Cowboy's Sweetheart."

Janis Joplin had been drawn to folksong while she was attending the University of Texas during 1962 (fig. 5), but forged success a few years later in San Francisco's cauldron. She and Haight-Ashbury rapidly drew Austin musicians; in this new setting, Texas blues and rockabilly fed into California electronic music. Like a compelling light show, rock turned off and on, bathing its victors in gold and punishing its failures with base colors. A few Austin musicians resisted San Francisco and remained at home; some, broken there, returned to form and reform local bands; others tripped back and forth unscathed. Three of the best Austin rock bands were the Thirteenth Floor Elevators, Conqueroo, and Shiva's Headband.

Bob Brown recalled for Jan Reid the Conqueroo's performance at the IL, a run-down Negro bar in Austin's East side: "It was the kind of place where older black people gathered in the afternoon to play dominoes. But here a bunch of cracker hippies marches down and starts playing so loud that food is flying off forks all over the neighborhood" (1974:34). Brown's account is highly significant, for it catches the double incongruity of white youngsters performing unconventionally in a Southern black setting and of collegiate rock-and-rollers ("acid heads") marching under the old poor-white trash banner, "cracker." Brown bridged the linguistic polarity built into the then-discrete categories, separated by color or esthetic taste. Both "cracker" and "hippy" were pejorative terms, but they were seldom joined in ordinary speech in 1967. Interestingly, proprietor Ira Littlefield advertised the IL as featuring Austin's "best beatnik bands." The claim shows a wry sense of humor—for the word "beatnik" was already dated—or else a keen prescience in anticipating the cultural explosion on the horizon.

I read considerable meaning into the act of a black owner renting his Austin bar to a white college-based rock group in the sixties. Before random behavior can become situated or patterned to symbolize large social events, it must begin in time and place and be repeated. The participants in any new cultural enactment must sense both the fragility of their debut and the possibility for reward in repetition. The usual term in musical vocabularies to mark black/white (as well as folk/pop) hybridization is "crossover," which resembles "creole" as used of speech or cooking. No two Texans agree on what single act marked the crossover in Austin, although all agree that it denoted a musical and communal ambience alike. The IL Club happening is a tiny, now obscure, chip in a panoramic mosaic—one that shows starry cosmic cowboys, some riding ethereal broncos and others mounted on mystical little armadillos.

Some of the young Texan musicians in the Elevators and Conqueroo knew and played country music, but none was ready to go beyond exciting and liberating rock to country. However, a few members of Shiva's Headband helped nudge Austin toward recognizing its own crossover music. In 1969 this band had performed in the Vulcan Gas Company—a "hippy spot," tolerant of dope—which closed down after conservative criticism. Homeless, Eddie Wilson and Spencer Perskin, both associated with the Vulcan and Shiva, opened the Armadillo World Headquarters in August 1970. Originally conceived as a rock club, the 'Dillo soon turned to other musics and community arts. In one of the first attempts to explain the Armadillo to a political audience, *Texas Observer* reporter Henry Staten noted that Wilson wished to avoid the Vulcan's insularity and consciously sought to "break down some of the barriers between hip and straight in Austin" (1971:19).

Wilson had seen this process in action when he accompanied artist Jim Franklin to the Cactus Club. Wilson recalled for Chet Flippo in a report to *Rolling Stone:* "It was a smoky little joint that had discovered what hippie music could do for beer sales. Hippies and rednecks were forced into the same bar—the hippies because the music [rock] was there and the rednecks because the beer was there" (1972:18). The Cactus Club no longer exists, but it served to link the Vulcan's followers to the Armadillo's dreams. There is a logical progression from cracker hippies at the IL, to hippies and rednecks sharing at the Cactus, to large new audiences at the Armadillo hearing the best of America's musicians—Willie Nelson, Bill Monroe, Earl Scruggs, Gram Parsons, Ry Cooder, Commander Cody, Mance Lipscomb, Lightning Hopkins, Clifton Chenier, Jimmy Cliff, Randy Newman, and countless others.

In covering the anomalous reach across social barriers, as well as the emotional shift from hostility to accommodation, nearly all Austin reporters remarked on the amazingly disparate types who gathered to hear the music. Wayne Oakes, a sponsor of the Kenneth Threadgill Jubilee (July 10, 1970) wrote that this "most improbable social event to occur in a decade" brought together "thousands of Texans ranging from insurance salesmen to hippies to cedar choppers." Janis Joplin flew in from Honolulu to honor patriarch Threadgill, who had befriended her in her college days. She was cheered by "women in beehive hairdos and gold lamé western pants [who] mingled congenially with long haired hippie chicks in Mexican blouses and bluejeans" (Oakes 1970:17–19). Janis's death three months later inspired pundits to explain the role of her Austin "mentor." Threadgill, they said, had the power to suspend generational and class distrust because listeners from all backgrounds recognized his country ballads and Nazarene hymns as real.

An attempt by Austin's liberated community to stage an out-of-town rock festival in Bastrop during 1970, on the heels of the Threadgill Jubilee, fell flat when "straight" citizens expressed displeasure. The rumor that Bastrop dwellers had set up a new firing range within gunshot of the festival site discouraged participation. Two years later, however, the Dripping Springs Reunion dissipated considerable tension. This festival, billed as both a "Country-Western Woodstock" and a

"Redneck Olympiad," was simultaneously an esthetic success and a commercial washout. Commentator Dean Rindy, who had made the hegira from a Houston John Birch Society journal to campaigning in Austin for George McGovern, was present at Dripping Springs and understood its dichotomy: "The Reunion was an amiable encounter between two rival civilizations—Middle America meets the Freaks. About 30 percent of the audience was Austin hippies . . . barefoot, long-haired, dangerous radical ideas, the slavering mad dogs of Wallace and Agnew's fantasies. But everybody got along fine." Rindy also witnessed some sartorial crossover: "There were lots of flunkies and Dallas PR smoothies affecting a kind of mountebank chic (double-knit suits and silk ties, cowboy boots and velvet pants)" (1972:17–19). After Dripping Springs in 1972, only a very obtuse reporter in or near Austin could fail to see the dramatic juxtaposition within audiences, as well as the glaring examples of mountebank chic displayed by urban saddlebums and ersatz cowboys.

One of the Nashville performers at Dripping Springs was Willie Nelson, who sensed considerable potential in his then-new barefoot audience. A year later he returned to this site to stage his first Texas Fourth of July picnic. Building Austin pride, Nelson moved there from Nashville shortly after the original Reunion. Townsend Miller, country commentator in the *Austin American-Statesman,* had been a keen fan since Nelson used to sing on road tours to small "cowboy" audiences at local Austin dance clubs like the Broken Spoke and the Big G's. On August 12, 1972, the born-again Nelson played at the Armadillo World Headquarters. Miller was struck particularly by the incongruity of seeing Willie on psychedelic posters, possibly the first such depiction of a country star. Knowing that students and street people—regulars at the 'Dillo—would surely turn out, Miller appealed to "conservative, traditional fans" to join the "young liberal fans" at the concert. Miller decried self-segregated audiences for country music, and used his column deliberately to narrow such esthetic and generational gaps (1972a:37).

ADVENT OF THE COSMIC COWBOY

Out of all the names and descriptions applied to Austin's fusion of contradictory cultural modes, one phrase caught on as the symbol of the style and the era. Michael Murphey supplied it with the release in the summer of 1973 of his LP *Cosmic Cowboy Souvenir* (see fig. 6). The lyrics of the title song are, like those of much rock composition, rather

FIGURE 6. Cosmic Cowboy Souvenir, *jacket cover by Bill Holloway*
(A&M LP album, 1973).

vapid. We have come to expect strong patterns and familiar structures
when reading traditional folksong as poetry. Because "Cosmic Cowboy" is not cast in a conventional ballad mold it is diffuse. Nostalgically,
it projects open-ended images away from New York and California
toward Texas — the land of cattle-in-mesquite and home-on-the-range.
The text follows:

Burial grounds and merry-go-rounds
Are all the same to me;
Horses on posts and kids and ghosts
Are spirits we ought to set free.
Them city slicker pickers got a lot of slicker licks than you and me —
But riding the range and acting strange
Is where I want to be —
At.

I just want to be a Cosmic Cowboy;
I just want to ride and rope and hoot.
I just want to be a Cosmic Cowboy;
A supernatural country rockin' galoot.

Lone Star sippin' and skinny dippin' and steel guitars and stars
Are just as good as Hollywood and them boogie-woogie bars.
Gonna buy me a vest and head out West
my little woman and my Self;
When they come to town they're gonna gather round
And marvel at my little baby's health.

Now big raccoons and harvest moons keep rollin' through my mind.
Home on the range where the antelope play is very hard to find.
Don't bury me on the lone prairie; I'd rather play there live.
I'm doin' my best to keep my little pony in overdrive.

Murphey composed "Cosmic Cowboy" while he was singing at the Bitter End in New York's Greenwich Village in August 1972. Born in Dallas, Murphey had turned from Baptist orthodoxy to Albert Schweitzer, and from a job as a Hollywood Screen Gems tunesmith to the free life of a composer/performer of rock poetry. Although some of his material, recorded by the Monkees and other pop figures, was highly successful, Murphey became dissatisfied with glitter. Raising his flag high, he set out to emulate the poetry recitals of Vachel Lindsay and the folksong concerts of Carl Sandburg. He left California for Texas in 1971 and took the hard road of cross-country performance.

Murphey's 1972 LP *Geronimo's Cadillac,* whose title song criticized the white exploitation of Indian life and land, had been well received by folk and rock fans alike. Hence, Nashville producer Bob Johnston, aware of Music City's grudging but accommodating acceptance of the cowboy/outlaw figure, selected "Cosmic Cowboy" as the title number for Murphey's 1973 LP *Cosmic Cowboy Souvenir.* Murphey had wanted the name "Souvenir," to suggest the variety of his compositions. However, Johnston, and his associates, sensed the potential of "Cosmic Cowboy" and added it to the LP title after the jacket's art work had been prepared by Bill Holloway in Austin.

One can never satisfactorily explain what makes a song a hit— provocative title, simple melody, instant humor, haunting sadness, memorable poetry, ready symbolism. "Cosmic Cowboy" was for a brief period a country rock favorite, yet when it dropped from the charts its title still remained in public consciousness as a generic label, both positive and pejorative. Its value as a naming term exceeded its worth as a song, for no better label surfaced in the seventies to encompass cracker hippies, beer-drinking or dope-smoking rednecks, collegiate faddists, and folk-like musicians in levis.

The chronology of Murphey's song reveals the movement of his catchy title into general Austin speech. After its composition in New York, he recorded "Cosmic Cowboy" on January 17, 1973, for Herb Alpert's A&M label, during a four-day session in Ray Steven's Nashville studio. Murphey premiered the song for Austin audiences on February 23–24 at the Armadillo World Headquarters, a setting of great exuberance. On March 16 the new song was copyrighted, and on May 1 the LP on which it appeared was also copyrighted. Murphey displayed the album in a concert at the Armadillo on June 29–30, and on August 30 *Rolling Stone* reviewed it favorably. A year later the Nashville-based Nitty Gritty Dirt Band recorded "Cosmic Cowboy" on their album *Stars and Stripes Forever.*

Austin's provocative blend of country and rock music found no sign more striking than "cosmic cowboy," and even this term was never appreciated unequivocally. No artist—musical, literary, or graphic—working within a cultural greenhouse can arbitrarily select a name for an era. Words like "jazz," "blues," "funk," and "rock" emerged slowly from Afro-American experience to identify musics and periods. A similarly lengthy process extended the Anglo-American words "hillbilly," "country," "Western," and "bluegrass" to musical forms. No Austin neologism ever underwent such a basic evolution.

Early in 1972 Ray Wylie Hubbard, a young Dallas performer who had moved from folk rock to honkytonk music, introduced a tongue-in-cheek piece both at Austin's Castle Creek and the Saxon Pub. "Up against the Wall, Redneck Mother" was at once irreverent, perverse, and vulgar. It put down kickers and ropers, yet with enough raucous humor to appeal to a few of them. Hubbard had composed "Redneck Mother" in 1969 after a "real American mother" had hassled him about his long hair in Red River, New Mexico. Eventually, Jerry Jeff Walker brought this "albatross song" to national audiences with his *Viva Terlingua* LP—yet neither Hubbard nor Walker could pin the word "redneck" to Austin's vigorous music. Neither was it in Eddie Wilson's power to label Austin's music "dillo."

In Austin's honkytonks I heard "cowboy" constantly, both as a derisive and appreciative tag, but I never heard "outlaw" in ordinary speech in any musical setting. During the mid-seventies Austin fans tied "cowboy" directly to long hair, dope, revival folksong, cliché-laden poetry, and pop astrology. Yet Michael Murphey's phrase "cosmic cowboy" finally caught Austin's imagination. It helped pull country musicians and rock fans into one milieu by giving them at last a label both could use.

"Cosmic" has its antecedents, too. Steve Miller's composition "Space Cowboy" (1969) and Sly and the Family Stone's "Spaced Cowboy" (1971), formed part of the referential frame for Murphey's catchy title. Sly, Miller, and Murphey, of course, all performed for audiences who had grown up in post-Sputnik America. Some saw cosmic life as a series of *Star Trek* dramas, while others related cosmic creeds to the revival of astrological belief by counter-culture converts. *Hooka,* a Dallas underground paper, appeared briefly to trumpet the Human Order of Kosmic Consciousness. Before and after Murphey wrote his piece, dozens of other songs had joined the word "cosmic" to "boy," "Charlie," "chicken," "dancer," "debris," "funk," "overload," "ray," "street," "vortex," and "wheels." None was as influential as "cosmic cowboy"; none served to specify a wide social need.

The first printing known to me of "cosmic cowboy" as a discrete word combination was on Michael Priest's Armadillo World Headquarters poster (February 23–24, 1973). The shift from poster to naming device was immediate. That March Al Reinert's "So Long, Cosmic Cowboys," which dealt not with music but with the Houston-based space program, appeared in *Texas Monthly*. Reinert's prose was colorful: "Astronauts, tight-lipped, square-jawed and blue-eyed, dedicated patriots . . . a species of Cosmic Cowboy storing up energy to blaze a trail to the Moon" (1973:39).

Reinert's borrowing was complimentary to Murphey's coinage, but when "Cosmic Cowboy" began to bother some listeners, satiric versions materialized. David Hisbrook and Gary Wilcox offered "Too Much Cosmic (Not Enough Cowboy)" (United Recording Artists 921) on a 45-rpm disc. Before this record was issued, John Clay, a dedicated performer of old-time music, composed and sang another parody. From Stamford, Texas, Clay had come to Austin in 1960 and had turned to the campus "folksong revival" at its beginning. He has experienced a variety of Austin's musical scenes and has observed closely most of the city's musicians—famous or obscure, original or derivative. The text of his "Plastic Plowboy" appeared in *The Rag,* Austin's radical tabloid (on September 4, 1973), and more recently on the 1980 LP *Drifting through the Seventies.* Two stanzas follow:

And where has Psychedelic America gone?
All those swinging days and nights of yesteryear,
When we'd trip out for hours on dreams of fruit and flowers,
But the kids nowadays are drinking wine and beer.

Where have my psychedelic posters gone?
Did the landlord burn 'em where we used to live?
My memory has lapsed, and it used to be a steep trap,
But nowadays it's much more like a sieve.

So I wanna be a plastic plowboy. . . .

Three typical deprecatory uses of "cosmic cowboy" appeared in *Texas Monthly.* Larry King, Texas-born novelist and political essayist who abhors romanticized rurality, stated in "Redneck":

Now, the Rednecks I'm talking about are not those counterfeit numbers who hang around Austin digging the Cosmic Cowboy scene, sucking up to Jerry Jeff Walker and Willie Nelson, wearing bleached color-patched overalls and rolling their own dope, saying how they hanker to go live off the land and then stay six weeks in a Taos commune before flying back on daddy's credit card (1974:50).

William Martin, Rice University sociologist, also reported sourly on thirty-six hours of progressive country music in "Growing Old at Willie Nelson's Picnic":

I had expected thousands of cosmic cowboys and assorted freaks, but I had also expected fairly large numbers of authentic rednecks, and I knew if I got uncomfortable with the freaks I could go sit with the kickers. . . . There were some kickers there, all right. About six. The other 25,000 were freaks or freakish, all under 25 (1974:94).

Finally, Bill Porterfield, Texas newspaperman and radio commentator, took a swipe at cosmic brethren riding "In Search of the Modern Cowboy":

The new musical romanticism has [the cowboy as] a gentle knight, repulsed by arms and armor and aggression and refinery air, returning to a pastoral West. . . . It is a curious hallucination. Cosmic cowboys around counterfeit campfires, breathing burning grass and drinking longnecks, listening to the lowing of Darrell Royal's Longhorns (1975:59).

Although, I feel, Murphey had composed "Cosmic Cowboy" seriously, intending it to be relevant to a wide audience, and recorded it without a hint at parody, he backed away once the song became a subject of ridicule. In hindsight, Murphey averred that "he had written the song tongue-in-cheek, never intending it to be taken seriously." Further, he came to despise his Austin fans as "hooting hippies who fancied themselves goat roping cosmic cowboys" (quoted in Reid 1974:264). When Jan Reid's publisher put a color photo of Murphey on the dust wrapper of *Redneck Rock,* Murphey was distressed at being associated with this alliterative book title. Partly he was sensitive to the gimmickry of the title and partly he questioned Reid's credentials.

In an interview with Chet Flippo for *Texas Parade,* Murphey distanced himself from "Cosmic Cowboy," asserting that he had been misunderstood:

I never intended that it be taken seriously. I wrote that one night at the Bitter End in New York. Jerry Jeff and I were there, playing cowboy . . . and I just kinda made it up and sang it that night as a joke. We cracked up—look at us, we're the cosmic cowboys. . . . It gets under my skin a little bit. Somehow that phrase caught on and people said, yeah, that's what we are and they started wearing boots and huge cowboy hats. It went too far. It's fun to have fun but we came off as Clint Eastwood all the time, Clint Eastwood with hair (1974a:20).

It is futile to dispute, retrospectively, whether or not "Cosmic Cowboy" arose as a joke. Murphey perceived himself as a poet/philosopher for the seventies, and his songs were too precious to him to let others reinterpret them. He was not the first composer to be made uneasy by success. Ironically, his hit was anchored to the very ambivalence felt by so many Americans about the shift from rural to urban society. Whether he liked it or not, Murphey's song title took hold in speech and helped label a cultural amalgam that had been building for decades. Cedar-chopping/goat-roping youngsters in the Texas hill country were born into Western life codes. They may have been pained when hippy school rivals took up their levis and downhome music, but it was also a conquest for the rural life, a vindication of good horse-sense in clothes and musical taste.

In retrospect, the counter-culture of the sixties was almost as much sartorial as it was moral or political. A. R. Gunter, in the University of Texas' student newspaper, the *Daily Texan,* saw country rock as bringing together "two social factions . . . flower children and cowboys" (1972:14). Gunter stressed the disappearance of visual and aural barriers as these factions came together, and lauded Murphey as a boundary-breaker—who pulled the barbed wire down instead of keeping it taught. Austin fans liked the euphony of "cosmic cowboy." More significantly, the semantic overlap of "cosmetic" and "cosmic" helped the former word cover the incongruity of well-to-do youngsters dressing down in cowboy make-up—urban dudes for the seventies.

Interestingly, Murphey's sidemen give a more detailed account of the song's composition than does the composer himself. Herb Steiner and Craig Hillis were playing in Murphey's band when he composed "Cosmic Cowboy" in New York and when he recorded it in Nashville. Steiner had studied anthropology at UCLA, and had been influenced by the folksong boom before he turned to rock in Hollywood clubs. Hillis, an "Air Force brat," had attended the University of Texas, when acid rock surfaced, and had made the pilgrimage to California, where he met and played with Steiner. Both toured with Murphey: Herb on steel pedal guitar, Craig on lead guitar.

Steiner and Hillis recalled for me the specific circumstance of Murphey's composition of "Cosmic Cowboy," literally at the edge of a Manhattan Holiday Inn's roof swimming pool (above 57th Street). (The notes on the album give this credit to the Bitter End's dressing room.) From Steiner and Hillis, I learned that the song was inspired directly by the antics of Bob Livingston, a Texan musician from Lubbock. While at the Bitter End, Livingston had met Cosmic Suzanne, a lost Austinite in Manhattan. Livingston served as the butt for much band humor, and Suzanne, temporarily on the scene, brought the word "cosmic," connoting drugs, into constant group usage by the band members. Livingston's special contribution was eventually credited in the liner notes for *Cosmic Cowboy Souvenir,* where he was identified with background vocals, electric rhythm guitar, bass, and "funky energy."

Murphey literally taught the new song to his sidemen at the pool's edge; it helped them trip back from the skyscrapers rimming the Holiday Inn to the open range. Hillis immediately sensed the contradiction in the song's title: cowboys then were not usually expected to experience altered states of consciousness. However, Steiner liked very much the alliteration of the title. Both sidemen, of course, caught the phrase's verbal charge; they saw themselves as participants in a high drama of musical linkage.

Not all country rock stars enjoyed this drama or proved prophetic of its power. Doug Sahm, an eclectic San Antonio musician, sourly told Chet Flippo that the cowboy music era had ended: "This cosmic cowboy shit has had it" (1973a:30). What had gone wrong? A rather mild and opaque portrait of a spaced-out cowboy, a dopey rider from outer space, had become for Sahm a dubious symbol. Why? Part of the answer lies within Murphey's song, and part in the Austin scene. On first hearing the lyric, I was uncertain whether Murphey thought his cowboy was a hero or antihero, redneck kicker or liberated philosopher. He, too, may have been uncertain. Yet, despite the song's fuzzy nature, the word "cowboy," whether linked with "cosmic" or standing alone, has fantastic strength. It holds always in bond the multiple images of guerrilla, buckaroo, wrangler, stoic, dude, braggart, hustler, rebel, mystic.

Not all of Austin's actors on the stage of convergence performed music; the cultural meld also released other artistic energies. An early visual image of the new order emerged when Austin's KOKE-FM settled into a progressive-country format. The station released a magazine ad by Kerry Awn (Kerry Fitzgerald) featuring a super-roper cowgirl lassoing an out-of-date radio. Next, a bumper sticker (and an ad) appeared showing a lean cowboy, his rope taut around the neck of a reluctant goat. In 1975, KOKE sold mail-order "Super Roper T-Shirts" with the goat logo (fig. 7). Perhaps the most succinct application of "goat roper" to musical expression occurred in the summer of 1974 when the entertainment guide *Free & Easy* featured a full-page bar-club guide called "Austin Bands from Dopers to Ropers." These incongruous twins, dissolute satyr and spirited dude, have been depicted endlessly in Austin graphics; Kerry Awn's series of monthly calendars for the Soap Creek Saloon has, over the years, been especially abundant in dopers and ropers (often indistinguishable from each other).

Michael Priest's wonderful graphics best extended the meaning of

FIGURE 7. *Super Roper logo, drawn by Kerry Fitzgerald (Kerry Awn), used as* KOKE-FM *ad in 1975.*

Professor Worrall's carousing cowboys (1874), Tad Dorgan's cake eating cowboys (1923), and Miguel Covarrubias's drugstore cowboy (1930). Priest, a self-taught artist, came to Austin in 1969 and was caught up immediately by the laid-back community. By 1971 he was trying his hand at commercial work for the Armadillo World Headquarters and other musical clubs. The major artist associated with the Armadillo is Jim Franklin, but it was Priest's sardonic cowboys rather than Franklin's droll armadillos which gave a visual dimension to cosmic cowboy music.

For a concert on September 15–16, 1972, shortly after "Cosmic Cowboy" was composed but before it was sung in Austin, Priest portrayed Willie Nelson and Michael Murphey as two relaxed cowboy musicians (see p. 67). In this commentary, I have not detailed Nelson's fabulous story, for it has been well told by others. By any measure, he is a giant in country music, at once soulful and oracular. His travels from Texas to Tennessee and back to Texas form a rich saga appropriate to a Dos Passos trilogy. Priest's first linkage of Murphey and Nelson as tipsy comrades, arm-in-arm, was itself a visual emblem which said that straights and freaks were ready to ramble together. Significantly, Murphey, the college-educated citybilly, is shaggy and bearded, while Nelson, the Texas country boy, is cleanshaven. This contrast reflects very accurately the "pre-cosmic" notion that country musicians were straight while city folksingers were freakish.

Priest has told me that he chose cowboy costume as a symbol to bridge town and country. Alabama-born, he had come to Austin by way of small-town Texas, and had known the word "cowboy" as a derogatory equivalent for "cedar chopper" and "goat roper." Because he liked kicker music but lived mainly within the open Austin community, he desired to bring his dual worlds together. In short, Priest had not foreseen Murphey's specific song, but had already observed and welcomed the mixing of styles. Priest was ready to draw a mustang rider in space lassoing a comet (fig. 8) as soon as Murphey was ready to sing "Cosmic Cowboy" in Austin. One detail in this poster (February 23–24, 1973) is important historically, for it credits Stan Alexander as "The Original Cosmic Cowboy." Professor Alexander, now at Stephen F. Austin State University, Nacogdoches, had first introduced Murphey to folksong in the early sixties, when Murphey was a student at North Texas State University, Denton. Alexander, while himself a student in Austin, had been a regular at Threadgill's, and was a pioneer in bringing Texas country music and urban folksong into conjunction.

Priest also helped advertise "A Tribute to the Cosmic Cowboy," a benefit concert for Houston's non-commercial FM station, KPFT (February 10, 1974) (fig. 9). For this occasion Priest outdid himself with a poster cowboy, stars on chaps and fat joint in hand. This little imp was later reincarnated when Lone Star beer emblazoned him on Texas T-shirts. Chet Flippo reported on the Houston event for Rolling Stone in "The Day the Kickers Ruled," noting that the concert included, among others, Michael Murphey and some eight thousand fans in cowboy hats and boots: "Big doggin'-heel jobs caked with the remains of dusty trails and cowflop-clearings. Between the headgear and footwear, a snappy parade of cowboy shirts and pants floated by" (1974b: 24).

One of the fascinating aspects of Murphey's composition was that it helped many Austinites deal with plasticity and reality, with long hair and country roots. His song touched liminal existence itself—did one live at home, away from home, or perhaps in the doorway? The Rag raised these concerns in a reflective story on KPFT's benefit concert.

FIGURE 8. *"Cosmic Cowboy Concert," Armadillo World Headquarters, February 23–24, 1973, poster by Michael Priest. (Courtesy of Michael Priest)*

FIGURE 9. *"A Tribute to the Cosmic Cowboys," benefit concert for* KPFT,
February 10, 1974, poster by Michael Priest. (Courtesy of Michael Priest)

In "The Kosmic Kowboys," reviewer "Danny" (1974) confessed that
he had previously been unimpressed by cosmic cowboys' time-wasting
and bullshit. But he came over at the crazy concert when everybody
joined Murphey in his chorus line. Danny noted: "Everyone onstage
was swapping hats. Doug Sahm had come back out and was dancing
around Jim Franklin, who wore possibly the biggest white Stetson this
side of the moon. I must've sung along too, the whole thing felt that
good. The image finally made sense."

The Rag's iconoclastic reporter was conscious that the new portrait of hip Texans held contradictions (long hair and longhorns)—that the country rock colony did not include Negroes or Chicanos and flaunted its male machismo. Critically, he could reject the false values in Murphey's construct, but at the concert Danny, too, was caught up in the song and dance. Intellectuals and radicals who live outside also need to come inside, to swap hats, to sing along, to savor communitas.

Cowboys never were given to bunking entirely in one place: they have moved from home ranch to town flophouse to rodeo motel to neon honkytonk. Precisely because we Americans wanted a folk hero who could express our hidden liminality, who could live in many doorways, who could be orderly lawman and disorderly brawler, we stretched the elastic word "cowboy" to its limits. It is easy to find cowboy portraits in sketches and songs frozen within ethical frames, positive or negative; it is difficult to find them poised between sets of values. Murphey's "Cosmic Cowboy," at best, struggles to carry loads we all share.

To close my comments on the negative valence engendered by Murphey's song, I offer two views. *Cosmic Cowboy Souvenir* evoked from a *Creem* reviewer this squib: "Lobotomy music, one cliche after another" (1973:71). By far the most thoughtful criticism of the composition as a symbol was penned by editor Jeff Nightbyrd (1975) for the *Austin Sun,* an alternative community newspaper. In "Cosmo Cowboys" he distinguished Murphey, the sensitive composer, from his song, which had come to personify collegiate "nerds" (who wore embroidered cowboy shirts and simulated-alligator boots). Nightbyrd despised Austin's fake cowboys (dopers) for their cosmetic finery as well as straight cowboys (ropers) for their previous trashing of hippies. Taking a dim view of these two groups, even when they coexisted at Willie Nelson's picnics, the writer pointed out that such celebrations had spread stench and trash over the Texas countryside. Nightbyrd, a veteran of SDS activism in the sixties, felt that the cosmic cowboy phenomenon not only masked political realities, but, worse, held back people in their need to remove masks.[4]

Jack Jaxon offers the last picture of the "Cozmic Cowboy"—a cartoon with running text published in the *Austin Sun* (March 11, 1976) as a "handy guide for out-of-staters" (fig. 10). A "genuine bad-ass redneck Texas cowpoke" stares down a hairy, "austintatious," jewelry-bedecked dude, while the artist explains their sartorial contrast. A two-

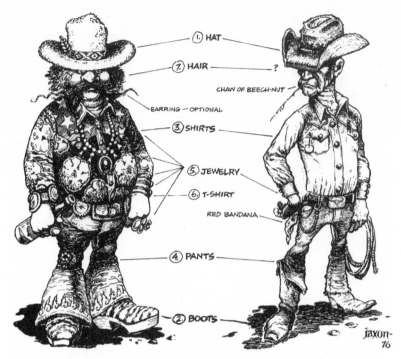

FIGURE 10. *"Cozmic Cowboy Identification Chart,"* by *Jack Jaxon, in* Austin Sun, *March 11, 1976, and* National Lampoon, *December 1977.*

page comic-strip sequence on pickups, dancehalls, and other earthy pleasures elaborated the differences. *National Lampoon* reprinted Jaxon's cowboy pair at year's end 1977 in an "Identification Chart" (without the accompanying comic strip). Depending on one's point of view, one can either say that the *Lampoon*'s use marked the cosmic cowboy's coming of age in national consciousness or else the end of the phrase's utility.

PERSPECTIVE

I have shaped this study largely in terms of dated references to a song title, some contextual background, and the reproduction of several graphics. A brief discussion of two Texas musicians, Kinky Friedman (the "Texas Jewboy") and Guy Clark ("Old No. 1"), who used new cowboy music to explicate ethical issues, can add perspective. Kinky has gone to great pains to reject labels, but he has deliberately juxtaposed cedar-chopper and freak values in his compositions. Dressed in Western garb he is an irreverent practitioner of guerrilla theater. His painful social commentaries ("They Don't Make Jews Like Jesus Anymore") invoke the searing moral conflict of modern times, while his flamboyant choreography recalls the high drama of cowboys on an end-of-the-trail spree. To see him use his stage-prop Star of David as a hat rack for a Stetson is to be outraged.

Nashville, in the mid-seventies, adapted to some Austin country music, but Kinky pushed beyond both sites to extraordinary limits. His "Sold American" delineates a faded cowboy star whose sequins have fallen from his jeans. He is not just a country music has-been; he is Everyman—fleeced, flawed, fallen. "Ride 'Em Jewboy" employs the waltz-like lilt of a traditional nightherding song, but its biting message attacks the scourge of fascism. At a concert at the Armadillo World Headquarters (September 20, 1975), I observed that this song moved some of its auditors to dreamy dancing and others to troubled introspection. Yet Kinky, in bold chaps, held the divergent audience together.

Guy Clark soaked up cowboy and oil-field lore during his childhood at Monahans, West Texas. Like a magnet, this flat and arid land drew boomers and roustabouts, many bringing tales of work in fields as far as Venezuela or Saudi Arabia. When Guy took to wandering as a minstrel he fell back on his early memories to compose a set of fine songs. One is "Desperados Waiting for a Train," the story of a driller whose wells have run dry. Guy recalled Jack Prigg playing dominoes in his grandmother's kitchen and was pained that his friend had grown old. Using poetry to transcend age, he transformed old Prigg into the archetypal outsider, a desperado.

My favorite Clark song is "L.A. Freeway," recorded initially by Jerry Jeff Walker in 1973. Guy used to commute from a straight job in Long Beach to Hollywood to try to sell his pieces. His anxiety about surviving the freeway, a steel and concrete spider web, spilled over into "L.A. Freeway." It is nominally a song about a nostalgic trip back home to Texas. When I heard Guy sing it at Castle Creek (January 15, 1976), his sidemen literally stood aside to let him spin the ballad of travel and death alone. Clark posed for his auditors a set of metaphoric questions: Is the open road still the symbol of freedom, or the site of deathly wrecks? Shall we ever escape modernity's steel and concrete? Guy in concert is flashy in neither dress nor mannerism; his denim shirt is more appropriate to a drilling platform than to a collegiate bar. But his powerful songs span seminar room and rotary rig, while his queries are central to our times.

For many years, Nashville composers have inflicted countless cloying songs upon America's blue-collar workers and rural poor. Understandably, a Tom Joad or a Flem Snopes became a social object for Tin Pan Valley—recipients of packaged country banality. But Kinky Friedman, an Austin misfit, and Guy Clark, a young West Texas good ol' boy, have been able to make old workers and fallen cowboys sympathetic subjects in song. This is a real achievement within an industry geared to unraveling emotion on sanitized discs.

Not all Austin fans in the seventies perceived Guy or Kinky as filling their musical cornucopia. Nashville patriots, jazz buffs, rock diehards, reggae cultists, and new wave pioneers all rejected the cosmic cowboy as an unadulterated disaster. We need to document the views of these naysayers as well as those of the "holdout" performers. We must also explore the tense relationship which young Western swing performers such as Alvin Crow and his Pleasant Valley Boys established with the progressive scene. In the thirties Bob Wills had been truly progressive—an exponent of heady cultural syncretism. An exemplary Wills stylist, Crow, based in Austin, had been influenced deeply by rock and boogie, yet he found it most difficult to describe his music as convergent in style.

In exploring the various responses to cosmic cowboy music, we need to look at one of its early influence, the "folksong revival" at the University of Texas. Pete Seeger, Joan Baez, Bob Dylan, and their companions inspired many campus followers. Some sought out local old-time musicians in order to learn their traditional styles, and some used folksong as grist for the popular mill. Many other paths opened. For example, Segle Fry, after a Kingston Trio concert (December 17, 1958), was caught up by folksong. He went on to perform, to manage the Chequered Flag coffee house, and to help aspiring stars move to the cactus circuit. Looking back to Austin days, Fry's fellow student Bill Malone recalls encountering esoteric "folksingers" who knew militant Spanish Civil War ballads but none of his beloved country music classics (1976:243–57). Ultimately, participants and audience members together must detail Austin's full musical history.[5]

Hopefully, in treating the rise and fall of a seventies phrase I have enlarged our understanding of the cowboy as hero and antihero, as dweller in bunkhouse and honkytonk. However, no word study really ends until its referent has from speech. Looking back at his hit from the vantage point of a half-decade, Michael Murphey stated: "the cosmic cowboy myth is dead" (Zibart 1978:D15). But even for Murphey the mythic figure is not really dead, for his Epic album, *Peaks Valleys Honky-Tonks and Alleys* (1979) includes a reborn "Cosmic Cowboy," recorded live at Hollywood's Palomino club and still questing for the Texas range. The term "cosmic cowboy" caught on because it helped us understand crossover music—music that meant not only tunes listed on folk, country, or rock charts, but also texts signifying deep social change. We need a language able to describe those expressions which comment on the constant meeting of rural and urban, black and white, and innovative and conservative forces in America. A pluralistic society, with or without a transcended national ethos, must find words to mark a people's travel across borders of class, ethnicity, and region.

Finally, when "cosmic cowboy" vanishes, other terms will arise to describe hyphenated music growing from folk and pop roots. In the twenties, "hillbilly" was extended from the name of a rural bumpkin to a music which bridged mountain sounds and city performance. The progression of the phrase "rhythm and blues" to "rock and roll" comments not only on musical styles, but on processes of synthesis in Anglo- and Afro-American cultures alike. The combination "Western swing" holds white and black tension in balance. In Texas, parallels occur as performers from French- and Spanish-language communities play "zydeco" and "norteño"—adding blues to Cajun music or polkas to Mexican music. Many words like "rockabilly" developed from the fifties term "rock." Other words such as "folk," "hard," "acid," "raga," "swamp," "glitter," and "punk" have all joined "rock" to mark special musical forms. The pairing "country rock," ultimately, seems best to cover Austin's cosmic cowboys and their lore; its emergence deserves a discrete study.

Austin's creators, and their fellow composer/performers throughout America, have been superb artists. They have balanced extremes of cloying sentiment and frightening dissonance, mediated much of the polarity built into modern life, and articulated the need to get off the freeway. I treasure the union in companionship of goat ropers and liberated freaks, of superkickers and isolated intellectuals, much more than I fret about the sham of romantic rednecks or their myopia. In short, I lack any anxiety over rhinestone-decorated, cosmic cowboys—Austin's centaurs. Sensitive to cosmetic portraits and plastic packaging, I am chiefly concerned about our fragmented polity, about Americans in collision with each other. Is there any way to pull our society together into a sane future if disparate cultural expressions cannot be respected and shared?[6]

NOTES

1. I include in my bibliography all items which are cited by page within my article, select items which are referred to without page citation, and some general background material. However, the bibliography does not list every song, book, film, sound recording, review, and lexicographical allusion mentioned in my article.

2. I have in progress a study on the cowboy in English-language dictionaries.

3. Neely's story is forthcoming in a monograph by Nicholas Spitzer. The many articles on Threadgill form a source for anecdotes and photos of Austin music. See M. Dreyer (1972), Langham (1973), Mays (1973), Miller (1972b), Oakes (1970), Olds (1970), Smith (1979).

4. For additional evaluations and reconsiderations see Burnett and Titley (1978), Flippo (1979), Frink et al. (1974), Johnson and Lightfoot (1973), Morton and Conway (1977), Perry (1979), Reid (1976a, 1976b), Tucker (1976), E. Ward (1979).

5. University of Texas students wrote papers which hold rich details on Austin music. For example, Cecil Jordan has made available to me a typescript on his experiences as a Soap Creek Saloon bartender (1977). Some needed papers are: (1) an interview with Burton Wilson to supplement his *Book of the Blues* (1971, 1977), a superb collection of photographs; (2) a study of radio station KOKE-FM's introduction of the phrase "progressive country music"; (3) a report on public television station KLRN's show "Austin City Limits," which beamed such music to national viewers; (4) an account of the filming in Austin of the movie *Outlaw Blues* (1976).

6. I owe thanks to Austin performers, commentators, and enthusiasts who I have made vibrant for me their music. Special thanks go to Roger Abrahams, Richard Bauman, and Nicholas Spitzer for reading drafts of this paper. Peter Tamony prepared me to listen to words about music; Michael Priest helped me to see Austin music. I am grateful to staff members in three libraries: the Travis County Collection of the Austin Public Library; The University of Texas Writings Collection; and the Barker Texas History Center of the University of Texas. Finally, I want to thank Michael Murphey for permission to quote "Cosmic Cowboy" and A&M Records, Inc., for permission to reproduce the cover of *Cosmic Cowboy Souvenir*.

BIBLIOGRAPHY

Ade, George. 1903. "Mr. Lindsay on 'San Jewan.'" In *In Babel: Stories of Chicago*. New York: McClure, Phillips.

Adkins, Lieuen. 1962. "What to Do til the Cops Arrive." *Texas Ranger* 77 (December): 19–22.

Allen, Bob. 1979. *Waylon and Willie.* New York: Quick Fox.

Allen, Nelson. 1975. "KOKE-FM." *Picking Up the Tempo* 6:7–8.

Anonymous. 1973a. " 'Cosmic Cowboy' Orbits Murphey." *Dallas Iconoclast* (June 15): 8.

———. 1973b. Review of *Cosmic Cowboy Souvenir. Creem* (September): 71.

———. 1976. "Ray Wylie Hubbard Haunted by His Hit 'Redneck Mother.' " *Country Style* (October): 31.

Axthelm, Pete. 1978. "King of Country Music." *Newsweek* (August 14): 52–57.

Bane, Michael. 1978. *The Outlaws: Revolution in Country Music.* New York: Country Music Magazine Press.

Baumann, John. 1887. "On a Western Ranche." *Fortnightly Review* 47:516–33.

Bentley, Bill. 1976. "Austin's Favorite Honky-Tonk Songstress, Marcia Ball." *Austin Sun* (March 11): 13, 17.

Brammer, Bill. 1974. Review of *The Improbable Rise of Redneck Rock. Austin Sun* (October 17): 18–19.

Burnett, John, and Bob Titley. 1978. "Putting Up a Front: The Truth about Austin's Music Scene." *Austin Sun* (January 20): 12–13.

Carr, Patrick. 1973. "It's So 'Progressive' in Texas." *New York Times* (July 22): D9, D16.

Clay, John. 1962. "The Folkmusic Revival." *Texas Ranger* 77 (October): 30–31.

Coe, David Allan. 1975. "Kountry Muzak." *Picking Up the Tempo* 9:1–2.

Cusic, Don. 1976. "Neil Reshen: Riding Herd on the New Breed." *Record World* (March 6): 6ff.

"Danny." 1974. "The Kosmic Kowboys." *The Rag* (February 18): 10–11.

Dreyer, Martin. 1972. "In the Shadow of Greatness." *Houston Chronicle, Texas Magazine* (August 13): 18–23.

Dreyer, Thorne. 1975. "Who Are We to Say the Boy's Insane?" *Austin Sun* (May 1): 13, 20–22.

Endres, Clifford. 1974. "Jaxon Returns: The Long Road Back to Austin." *Austin Sun* (November 7): 13, 20–23.

Flippo, Chet. 1972. "Uncle Zeke's Rock Emporium." *Rolling Stone* (October 12): 18.

———. 1973a. "Random Notes: Doug Sahm." *Rolling Stone* (December 6): 30.

———. 1973b. "Waylon Jennings Gets Off the Grind-'Em-Out Circuit." *Rolling Stone* (December 6): 28.

———. 1974a. "Hill Country Sound." *Texas Parade* 45:16–23.

———. 1974b. "The Day the Kickers Ruled." *Rolling Stone* (April 11): 24.

———. 1978. "The Saga of Willie Nelson: A Reconsideration." *Rolling Stone* (July 13): 45–49.

———. 1979. "The Austin Scene and Willie Nelson: A Reconsideration."
   Popular Music and Society 6:280–83.

Ford, Corey. 1930. *The John Riddell Murder Case.* New York: Scribner's.

Frank, Pat. 1957. *Seven Days to Never.* London: Constable.

Frink, Clayton, et al. 1974. "Austin Music: Progressive Country." *Austin
   American-Statesman, Show World* (July 14), 1–28.

Gordon, Roxy. 1971. *Some Things I Did.* Austin: Encino Press.

———. 1975. "Stars." *Picking Up the Tempo* 8:1–7.

Greco, Mike. 1979. " 'Honeysuckle Rose': Something 'bout a Cowboy." *Los
   Angeles Times, Calendar* (December 23): 47–48.

Green, Archie. 1965. "Hillbilly Music: Source and Symbol." *Journal of American
   Folklore* 78:204–28.

———. 1975. "Midnight and Other Cowboys." *JEMF Quarterly* 11:137–52.

Green, Douglas B. 1978. "The Singing Cowboy: An American Dream."
   Journal of Country Music 7:4–61.

Gunter, A. R. 1972. "Musical 'Boundaries' Disappearing as Country-Rock
   Stirs Social Mix." *Daily Texan* (December 7): 14 and (December 8): 15.

Hemphill, Paul. 1970. "Kris Kristofferson Is the New Nashville Sound." *New
   York Times Magazine* (December 6): 54–55 et seq.

Herschorn, Connie. 1973. "Austin Builds Country Rock Base." *Billboard*
   (September 8): T-13.

Hickey, Dave. 1974. "In Defense of the Telecaster Cowboy Outlaws." *Country
   Music* 2:90–95.

Holden, Stephen. 1973. Review of *Cosmic Cowboy Souvenir. Rolling Stone*
   (August 30): 86.

Ivins, Molly. 1974. "The University Universe." *New York Times Magazine*
   (November 10): 36–58.

Jaxon, Jack. 1976. *Comanche Moon.* San Francisco: Rip Off Press/Last Gasp.

Johnson, J. J., and J. E. Lightfoot. 1973. "Death and the Armadillo: A
   Rediscovery of the Southwestern Soul." *Journal of the American Studies
   Association of Texas* 5:73–78.

Jordan, Cecil. 1977. "Requiem for a Scene." Unpublished MS.

King, Ben. 1972. "Threadgill Unifies Cultures with Yodels, Rodgers Style."
   Daily Texan (September 21): 14.

King, Larry L. 1974. "Redneck." *Texas Monthly* 2 (August): 50–55 et seq.

———. 1976. "David Allan Coe's Greatest Hits." *Esquire* 86 (July): 71–73,
   142–44.

Lamar, M. B. 1968. *The Papers of Mirabeau Buonaparte Lamar,* vol. 6. Austin:
   Pemberton Press.

Langham, Barbara. 1973. "Late Train to Nashville." *Texas Parade* 33 (April):
   42–45.

Latham, Aaron. 1978. "The Ballad of the Urban Cowboy." *Esquire* 90
(September 12): 21–30.

Lewis, Pat. 1975. "Fear and Loathing in P. G. County." *Washington Star*
(April 25): B1, B3.

Malone, Bill C. 1976. "Growing Up with Texas Country Music." In *What's
Going On? (in Modern Texas Folklore)*. Francis Abernethy, ed. Austin: Encino
Press.

Martin, William C. 1974. "Growing Old at Willie Nelson's Picnic." *Texas
Monthly* 2 (October): 94–98, 116–24.

Mays, Prissy. 1973. "Old Is Beautiful—in Music or on Threadgill." *Alcalde*
(May): 13–15.

McCoy, Joseph G. 1874. *Historic Sketches of the Cattle Trade of the West and
Southwest*. Kansas City, Mo.: Ramsey.

McKenzie, Marty, and Clifford Endres. 1976. "Austin City Limits." *Austin Sun*
(March 25): 1, 20.

Middleton, Russell. 1973. "Progressive Country in Austin." *Advent* 1
(November): 20–21, 30.

Miller, Townsend. 1972a. "Willie Nelson Bringing 'Em All Together (and
Ain't It Wonderful)." *Austin American-Statesman* (August 12): 37.

———. 1972b. "At 62 Ken Threadgill Gets His Big Break." *Country Music* 1
(October): 19–22.

———. 1974. "Austin Combines Traditional and Progressive Sounds to
Become Nashville II." *Billboard* (July 9): T-4.

———. 1975. "Time for an Official Song." *Austin American-Statesman*
(December 5): 55.

Milner, Jay. 1976. "Outlaws Love Texas." *Texas Music* 1 (May): 17–21, 45–47.

Morthland, John. 1975. "Country-Rockers: Takin' the Hard Beat Down
Home." In *Sound, the Sony Guide to Music 1975/1976*. Knoxville: Approach
13-30 Corporation.

Morton, Marian J., and William P. Conway. 1977. "Cowboy without a Cause:
His Image in Today's Popular Music." *Antioch Review* 35:193–204.

Mudon, Bill. 1976. "*Cisco Pike, Outlaw Blues,* and *Convoy*." *Picking Up the Tempo*
19:8–10.

Nance, Joseph Milton. 1963. *After San Jacinto*. Austin: University of Texas
Press.

Nightbyrd, Jeff. 1975. "Cosmo Cowboys: Too Much Cowboy and Not
Enough Cosmic." *Austin Sun* (April 3): 13, 19.

Northcott, Kaye. 1973. "Kinky Friedman's First Roundup." *Texas Monthly* 1
(May): 95–96.

Oakes, Wayne. 1970. "Thousands Turn Out for Threadgill." *Texas Observer* 62
(August 7): 17–19.

Ohrlin, Glenn. 1974. *The Hell-Bound Train*. Urbana: University of Illinois Press.

Olds, Greg. 1970. "Threadgill." *Austin American-Statesman, Show World* (July 5): T26–T29.

O'Malley, Suzanne. 1972. "Austin—a Nice Place for Music." *Daily Texan, Pearl* (December): 11–13.

Patoski, Joe Nick. 1974. Review of *The Improbable Rise of Redneck Rock. Daily Texan, Pearl* (November): 6.

———. 1976. "Guy Clark—Desperado Waiting for His Fame. *Austin Sun* (January 16): 13.

Perry, David. 1979. "Cosmic Cowboys and Cosmetic Politics." *JEMF Quarterly* 15:38–43.

Porterfield, Bill. 1975. "In Search of the Modern Cowboy." *Texas Monthly* 3 (October): 58–64, 88–96.

Randall, Isabelle. 1887. *A Lady's Ranche Life in Montana*. London: Allen.

Reid, Jan. 1974. *The Improbable Rise of Redneck Rock*. Austin: Heidelberg.

———. 1976a. "Postscript: The Improbable Rise of Redneck Rock." In *What's Going On? (in Modern Texas Folklore)*. Francis Abernethy, ed. Austin: Encino Press.

———. 1976b. "Who Killed Redneck Rock?" *Texas Monthly* 4 (December): 112–13, 209–16.

Reinert, Al. 1973. "So Long, Cosmic Cowboys." *Texas Monthly* 1 (March): 38–42.

———. 1978. "King of Country Music." *New York Times Magazine* (March 26): 20–28, 50–53.

Rindy, Dean. 1972. "Country Karma." *Texas Observer* 64 (April 14): 17–19.

Roth, Don, and Jan Reid. 1973. "The Coming of Redneck Hip." *Texas Monthly* 1 (November): 70–76.

St. John, Powell. 1974. Liner notes for Bill Neely's *Blackland Farm Boy* (Arhoolie 5014).

Savage, William A., Jr. 1979. *The Cowboy Hero: His Image in American History and Culture*. Norman: University of Oklahoma Press.

Smith, Rick. 1979. "A Musical Oasis." *Austin American-Statesman* (February 25): B1, B11.

Spitzer, Nicholas. 1975. "Bob Willis Is Still the King." *JEMF Quarterly* 11:191–96.

———. 1979. "Bill Neely: Life and Lyrics of a Texas Songster." Unpublished MS.

Staten, Henry. 1971. "Armadillo World Headquarters." *Texas Observer* 63 (February 12): 18–19.

Tamony, Peter. 1958. "Jazz, the Word." *Jazz* 1 (October): 33–42.

Thorsen, Karen. 1976. "Has Austin Upstaged Nashville?" *Oui* 5 (March): 77–78, 125–26.

Tosches, Nick. 1976. "Outlaws as Oligarchs." *Village Voice* (May 31): 142.

Tucker, Stephen Ray. 1976. "The Western Image in Country Music." Unpublished M.A. thesis, Southern Methodist University.

Van Zandt, Townes. 1977. *For the Sake of a Song*. Houston: Wings Press.

Ventura, Michael. 1977. "Queen of the Honky-Tonks, Marcia Ball." *Texas Sun* (May 27): 12–13, 20.

Ward, Ed. 1974. "There's a Little Bit of Everything in Texas." *Creem* (April): 46–48, 76–77.

———. 1979. "'70s the Decade/Music." *Austin American-Statesman* (December 21): G1, G7.

Ward, Robert. 1976. "Redneck Rock." *New Times* 6 (June 25): 55–62.

West, Richard. 1974. "So You Want to Be a Redneck." *Texas Monthly* 2 (August): 57–59.

Wiemers, Carl. 1973. "Austin Next Nashville." *Daily Texan* (July 24): 13.

Wilson, Burton. 1971. *Burton's Book of the Blues*. Austin: Speleo Press.

———. 1977. *Burton's Book of the Blues,* rev. ed. Austin: Edentata Press.

Worley, Barbara. 1970. "How Bastrop '70 Got Offed." *Texas Observer* 62 (September 18): 15–16.

Zibart, Eve. 1978. "The Cosmic Cowboy's New Dimension." *Washington Post* (May 3): D15.

Tom Benton's
Folk Depictions

uring George Orwell's year, Americans struggle for precise terms to define their present-day corporate and technocratic polity. However far we have come from agrarian origins, and however bewildering this new state seems, our President reassures that the nation stands tall. The latter ambiguous metaphor holds positive and negative charges depending upon users' perspectives. Grappling with pulsing modernity, imperial power, deindustrialization jitters, and corrosive self-doubt, we fall back upon time-tested Jeffersonian ideals: individualism, democracy, freedom.

We have no alternative but to root the present in familiar rhetoric. With need to cloak the home computer as well as the nuclear missile in comfortable garb, we take up the sounds and sights of folk society. We continue to search for prairie grass at the launching pad's edge; we perceive the astronaut as a pathfinding Natty Bumppo who has exchanged coonskin cap for space helmet. These transformations, both personal and national, invoke the talismanic tag "folk" in a thousand guises. Press, screen, cassette, disc, and tube combine to restate the power of homespun, the pleasure of handicraft, the promise of everyday life.

In film, Sissy Spacek helps us see Loretta Lynn's childhood home in a bleak Appalachian coal camp. Are we to retain a picture of poverty, or sense a mountain woman's exemplary strength? Arlo Guthrie uses his father's "This Land Is Your Land" to call forth Whitmanesque vistas in 1984's campaign rallies. Do we say that Woody's song is now dated? Interior decorators select patchwork quilts to soften executive boardrooms. Are such muted wall hangings out of place? The Library of Congress circulates a cowboy exhibit which juxtaposes everyday work artifact and mythic portrait. Buffalo Bill, Lone Ranger, and Marlboro Man ride the range together. Do we reject this trio as unauthentic?

Such questions append themselves endlessly to presentations as well as representations of folk art and event. Jesse Jackson carries the black preacher's down-home prose to national pulpits. What is the proper query: Why does this particular oratory lift audiences, or is it useful in the White House? Willie Nelson moves listeners with both "Red-Headed Stranger" and "Amazing Grace." One song is new; the other, old; are they equally significant? In museums, Thomas Hart Benton still helps us ponder the meaning of country fiddler and hymn singer, tale teller and sorghum maker. What are the best questions to carry away from gallery wall or exhibit catalog?

In his lifetime, Tom Benton never labeled himself a "folk artist," nor did he gather a prize collection of folk art, but for a half-century he served as a folklorist without an academic diploma. Figuratively, his portfolio of prints and paintings made him an art minister to the realm of folklore/ethnology/ethnography. Historians generally wall off genre painters (for example, Mount and Bingham) from anthropological painters (for example, Catlin or Reiss). The former are defined as elegiac; the latter, scientific. Although unconcerned with photo-realism, Benton, too, contributed strongly to American documentation as he "studied" in schools of genre and ethnography.

Charles Seeger, folklorist/musicologist, and Benton explored together trails leading back from modernity to traditionality. Like Seeger, Benton enjoyed his place within the company of learned delineators of folk experience: Washington Irving, William Faulkner, William Sidney Mount, George Caleb Bingham, John Lomax, Vance Randolph.

This running together of writers, painters, and collectors is deliberate. All combined ethnographic strategies with creative expression. Irving savored one folk tale's maple sugar; Faulkner, another tale's sour mash; Benton, sugar and mash. Both authors, as did Benton, moved easily from prosaic description to visionary projection. Mount's music makers and Bingham's river folk rose to life again in Benton's verdant fields and coves. Lomax and Randolph, in their song hunting, combined documentation and imagination; each was linked to Benton by deep conceptual ties. The America of these interpreters revealed itself by plowed earth patterns as well as coal-mine scars, by patterned figures within ballads and blues, by facial patterns of dust and sweat, and by templates (patterns in mind) of belief in democracy.

I Got a Gal on Sourwood Mountain, *by Thomas Hart Benton, 1938.*
In Creekmore Fath, The Lithographs of Thomas Hart Benton
(Austin: University of Texas Press, 1979). (Courtesy Creekmore Fath)

Tom Benton wrote two autobiographies: one anecdotal, the other professional. Additionally, he offered numerous articles, popular and technical. Lecturing frequently, he occasionally livened public discourse by brawling with opponents. Despite his ease with spoken and written words, he felt no need to assert credentials as an academic folklorist. Nevertheless, when we dip into his writing, sophistication in folk matters becomes obvious. Two brief citations suffice to encompass Benton's awareness and affection:

> There is much traditional music in the hills, profane as well as sacred. This is no discovery of mine. Interested people, better equipped than I, have been ferreting it out for years (1937, 112). I like their [hill musicians'] plaintive, slightly nasal voices and their way of short bowing the violin. I like the modal tunes of the old people and the odd interludes, improvisations, often in a different key, which they set between a dance tune and its repetition. I've played with, and for, the hill folks on a harmonica and have picked up unwritten tunes and odd variants of those which have found their way into music books (1937, 113).

Benton was generous in acknowledging debts to folksong collectors, but, more importantly, he enjoyed the music enough to perform it. Beyond performance he caught its modality in sketch, watercolor, lithograph, easel painting, and mural. Along with depictions of mountain musicians, he presented bygone occupational practices as well as those in smoke-stack industry. Finally, in art, he linked folk music and work lore to native legend and myth. Literally, no major American painter took up as many folk subjects as did Benton. This long concern with ballad narrative and performance, buckskin-clad heroes, and populist symbols forces Benton to seek an explanatory keyword, "folk patterns."

Looking back in 1951 to his relationship with John Steuart Curry and Grant Wood, Benton wrote:

> We believed that only by our own participation in the reality of American life—and that very definitely included the *folk patterns* which sparked it and largely directed its assumptions—could we come to forms in which Americans could find an opportunity for genuine spectator participation (1971, 108). [italics mine]

Earlier, in 1934, while addressing a John Reed Club meeting, he had groped to explain the substance of American nationality. He called up the then-conventional formula of interplay of inheritance and environment among inhabitants. A people's psychological attitudes/national ideals flowed out of such interplay, and, as well, constituted "the *folk patterns* which determine the direction and nature of everyday action and thought" (1971, 51). [italics mine]

These usages of "folk pattern" are heavily coded and require amplification. I have already suggested that the best documentarians of folk experience saw land lines resonant in facial expression, and heard these same configurations externalized in song and tale. Benton carried this special notion of a patterned plow line or guitar run (as a self-contained structured entity) to a conceptual level: the guiding assumptions of nationhood: egalitarianism, beckoning frontier, a citizenry both autonomous and autochthonous.

With pencil and brush, he captured field and stream, hill and dale. Beyond such specifics of place, he sought the pennants, literal and ideational, with which the folk decorated its barns and mills. Benton knew the look of men and women who liked to break new soil. Not only was it important to place their turmoil on canvas, but it was necessary to affirm their guiding values. Rejecting elitism before New Deal years, Benton related folk themes within his art to the underlying belief in participatory politics in the United States. Hence, we must cope with the duality built into his keyword, "folk patterns"—folkways rooted in time and place, overarching philosophies.

Elsewhere in this catalog, Matthew Baigell and Alan Buechner comment upon Benton's art and music. Here, I marshall biographical details which focus current attention upon the continuing vitality of his musicians and artisans.

Born in Neosho, Missouri, on April 15, 1889, Benton knew frontier life, but not from within folk society's confines. His great uncle, Thomas Hart Benton, was Missouri's first Senator, a Jacksonian champion of western expansionism. Tom's father, a vigorous Democratic Congressman, brought the family to Washington where his son became intrigued by the elegant murals in the Library of Congress and the Capitol Building.

At home, Tom had known "ridge runners and bottom scrapers," who looked like the backwoodsmen in historical paintings. Indians in murals, also, seemed familiar. But sixteen miles from "The Nations"

(Oklahoma), hometown Neosha had attracted Seneca green-corn dancers and drummers to Fourth of July days. Seneca music complemented Ozark country sounds. Accompanying his father on the campaign trail, Tom heard camp-meeting shouts and frolic music alike; in Washington, a far different salon music. Clearly, Benton developed ease within folk and high society, slipping naturally from Huck Finn's to Mark Twain's domain.

As an art student in Paris (1908–11), Benton struggled to assimilate the full range of modernist expression. Back home, his move from European-influenced experimentation to a romance with the American Scene did not occur in a magic day, but progressed slowly through a decade. During Navy Service in Norfolk, (1918), he sketched shipmates, articulating roots, personal and artistic:

> Down there in Virginia, I was thrown among boys who had never been subjected to any aesthetic virus. They were boys from the hinterlands of the Carolinas, from the Tennessee country, from all over the South, in whom I discovered, despite all the differences in our experience, bonds of sympathy (1937), 45).

In March 1924, Benton returned to Missouri to be with his father:

> After his death . . . I was moved by a great desire to know more of the American which I had glimpsed in the . . . words of his old cronies, who, seeing him at the end of his tether, had tried to jerk him back with reminiscent talk and suggestive anecdote. . . . I started going places, but I sought those which would present best the background out of which my people and I had come and I left the main traveled roads, the highways, and plowed around in back countries . . . where old manners persisted and old prejudices were sustained (1937, 77).

Although Benton traveled these back roads extensively, he summered regularly at Chilmark, a Martha's Vineyard village. Hence, his life journey triangulates by references to Neosho, Paris, Chilmark. At home, he could and did step from family mansion to cabin; in Paris, the swirl of the cabin hoedown faded; at Chilmark, he could again hear gaunt fiddlers and admire garrulous storytellers. In choice of artistic subject, not only did he trust his experience, but he fashioned a populist compass for his art. About 1915, he became acquainted with anarchists, socialists, and communists. Initially pulled to their polemical creeds, he accepted broad notions of social justice, but, in time, was repelled by Marxism. Rejecting academic and abstract art norms, as well as socialist-realism formula and party-line didacticism, he articulated a mid-ground esthetic—one tied intimately to governing paradigms in folkloric studies.

In an October 1929 show at New York's Delphic Gallery, Benton grouped his drawings in four sets: King Cotton, Lumber Camp, Holy Roller Camp Meeting, Coal Mines. Literally, the artist had carried sketch books to these four settings. Presciently, by this classificatory presentation, he anticipated a litany of New Deal concerns for marginal Americans: forgotten workers, sharecropper, Indians, Negroes. Benton, like John Dos Passos in fiction, shared Franklin Delano Roosevelt's concern for citizens ill-fed, ill-housed, ill-clad.

Benton's favorite political anecdote came from his father's description of the Missouri cow "which had its head in the west where it ate, and its teats in Wall Street where it was milked" (1969, 167). To complete the metaphor, I suggest that Benton's most tranquil and bucolic characters—hill farmers, ballad singers, country dancers—still telegraph messages. Each print or painting with a folk theme asserts that the cow must be turned around. Needless to say, Congressman Benton had relished a traditional anecdote long used in protest circles. His cow lives, today, but within a pasture of terminal screens.

Americans enjoy investing streets and strips, beasts and birds, with symbolic power. We see bald eagle and buffalo, log cabin and coonskin cap, as national icons. The Statue of Liberty is one kind of unifying site: Arlington Cemetery, another. Pictures of young George chopping down the cherry tree and young Abe reading by firelight guide patriotic endeavor. Would Benton have placed these canonical markers under the rubric, "folk"? At times, "folk" signifies *all* Americans—singular, central, wholesome. At times, this same word stands for *some* Americans—plural, peripheral, less than whole. Under one light, we see a Washington portrait as uniting a total citizenry. Under another light, this same picture distorts and loses power.

Puzzled by actual present-day adversity, a few Americans seek folk forms which challenge complacent assumptions of singularity. Museum galleries, local festivals, and Charles Kuralt's TV tours, present an infinite variety of expressions or constructs, regularly tagged as "folk": birch bark canoe, desert rain dance, Amish hat, Cajun fais-do-do; voodoo conjuration, corn stalk doll, scrimshaw, fishing fleet blessing, soul food feast, snake handling ritual, Saint's Day processional, barn hex sign, animated gospel sing, Santa Fe Santos, Missouri string band.

We can use Benton's words to suggest the projection of item into sign. Reflecting on his Neosho childhood and the "horrible decorative monstrosities" his parents had purchased to mark "advanced status," Tom wrote:

The shrewd and narrow practicality of the dominant classes . . . was enough to kill even the simple home arts, and, under the influence of mercantile persuasion, the fine old patchwork quilts and hooked rugs of the grandmothers and the solid hickory chair and benches of the grandfathers were thrown out of home after home in favor of cheap, jerry-made, but showy manufacturers (1937, 28).

While objecting to non-representational art, in 1954, Benton quali-fied his remarks by observing: "Mere patterns can get along by them-selves quite easily. Our grandmothers made them with quilts, highly abstract patterns, and nobody hired a highbrow to find special mean-ings for them" (1971, 125). In Tom's realm, where *he* found meaning in quilts, they stood easily for both old ways and proper abstraction. Quilts commented eloquently on change in community and in esthetic code.

At this juncture, I select a grab-bag of Benton's works for special attention, and treat his depiction of folk emblem and enactment under three rubrics: Rural music, Occupational lore, Bonding legend.

Long before Benton grounded art experientially, he had known folk music in traditional settings. As a child, while visiting grandfather "Pappy Wise" at Waxahachie, Texas, he heard the cotton farmer-fiddler play old tunes. Also, in childhood, on Ozark river "floats" (fishing from skiffs), he heard river guides sing the old ballads. During adult walk-ing adventures, Benton might swap a sketch for a tune, adding to his personal songbag.

When Benton began to offer paintings and lithographs for sale, he reached a public that already knew John Lomax's *Cowboy Songs* (1910) and Carl Sandburg's *American Songbag* (1927). Unlike these collectors, Benton worked from pencil sketch pad, watercolor, and clay model to easel painting and public wall mural. Turning to lithography in 1929, he used such drawings-on-stone for work which he then might repeat on canvas. As well, he often followed a painting or mural by reducing its subject to print size.

"Country Dance" remains an American folk archetype in three in-carnations. In 1928, Benton finished the original painting in oil. This dramatic work catches a set of dancers poised at abandon's border. A lean fiddler saws away while clustered figures fill a bare room, lit only by a hanging lantern. These dancers seem "real," but not "clear" as in an FSA photo. We are left to speculate whether Benton intended these men and women to signify all hoedowners, or only a set particular to a given Ozark community. In 1937, the artist returned to this subject, painting it in tempera under the title "Sourwood Mountain." In its third mode, a 1938 lithograph, he named it "I Got a Gal on Sourwood Mountain," a familiar Appalachian frolic piece. The title change may be coinciden-tal, or it may speak to the artist's heightened attention to classificatory norms.

In 1931, Benton moved "his" fiddler outside, adding a guitarist and an accordionist to form a string band, "Missouri Musicians." To com-ment on Anglo-American folk music, this bright painting has been widely reproduced with various labels: "old-time," "mountain," "hill-billy," "country," "western." Some years ago, Wilbur Leveritt (1975) identified the trio's members: Wilbur (g), brother Homer (f), cousin Neville Oatman (a). Tom had met the young men while they played at a summer party held by Benton's brother, Nat, near Republic.

Benton posed Neville seated on the running board of a Model-T Ford—probably because it was there, part of the "natural" landscape. Yet, in 1931, "tin lizzies" had already been invested with symbolic value as they broke the rhythms of rural life and shackles of puritanical morality. Ambivalent about his creation, Henry Ford, in the mid-1920s, subsidized old-time fiddlers and square dancers. In musical perfor-mance, the arch-progressive industrialist found a balm evocative of the past, and appropriate to the politics of his friend Calvin Coolidge. Benton's accordionist literally sat on a machine's running board while fiddler and guitarist faced the machine. Today, we see "Missouri Mu-sicians" variously: the Ford, in 1931, already an everyday prop in tradi-tional society; the same new Ford symbolizing cultural clash. By 1984, the Model-T is itself so distant that it seems more antiquated than Ozark string-band music.

With the painting fresh in mind, Benton placed the trio in a litho-graph, also titled "Missouri Musicians" (1931), but this time, comple-menting music by dancers, log cabin, horse-drawn buggy, and rooster (and without the Ford). In 1934, the Century of Progress International

Exhibition invited the artist to send a print to Chicago. Some sixty copies were sold during the fair and at the Art Institute. Strangely, the Institute did not buy a copy of this now highly valued work. Were the curators put off by dissonant music, or by a vernacular form defined outside high culture's realm?

After the Chicago showing, Benton re-named the lithograph, "Coming 'Round the Mountain," his first work to bear a folksong title. The print serves well to pose large problems in comprehension of the never-facile switch from music to art, or art to music. A narrative song or painting can offer sequential events as it focuses upon one. A non-narrative song or painting must work with tone and texture. A viewer who has not heard "Coming 'Round the Mountain" finds it impossible to fathom the story of careening horses and serene rooster. That viewer who knows the song understands instantly that Benton's performers offer a traditionally exaggerated piece — one which inverts the ordered world, and lightens daily burden with parody and play. The Leverett Brothers knew a nonsense song did not have to make sense; Benton placed such folk wisdom in "Coming 'Round the Mountain."

Among Benton's musical adventures is his unusual Decca album, *Saturday Night at Tom Benton's,* recorded in 1941. The artist designed its sprightly cover and penned its informative brochure. Three ten-inch 78-rpm discs held three traditional folksongs, a southern dance in-strumental, and the "Chilmark Suite," named after Benton's summer studio. There, perhaps as early as 1929, Tom on harmonica and Rita (Mrs. Benton) on guitar pulled together an informal band of visiting art students and country folk — farmers, fishermen, mechanics. Gale Huntington, a local folksinger and collector of maritime lore, made an especially strong contribution to the band, known locally as Tom Benton and His Harmonica Boys. Gale, a fiddler and guitarist, and his daughter Emily became the subjects in one of Tom's most popular paintings, "The Music Lesson" (1943).

The story of *Saturday Night at Tom Benton's* requires full treatment else-where; here, I note only that Tom enjoyed the harmonica at his Green-wich Village studio, as well as at Martha's Vineyard. In Manhattan, he gathered a crew of artists and musicians to form an urban hillbilly band. Frank Luther and Carson Robison came fresh from their roles as old-time recording stars, and Charles Seeger, Carl Ruggles, and Henry Cowell, from avant-garde musical chambers. By far the most famous band member turned out to be Tom's pupil, Jackson Pollock. After

Benton accepted a mural commission at the Missouri State Capitol, Tom, Rita, and their son TP continued to play Saturday night music with new friends in Kansas City. In 1941, Jack Kapp arranged a New York recording session in Decca's studios. By the time of the album's release, we were at war, and Tom concluded his brochure: "real American made music" will be needed "in the days to come."

Benton's choice in 1920 of a summer home at Martha's Vineyard had drawn him from mountain to maritime folk. Something in the weather-beaten countenance of sailors and fishermen, with their distinct folk dialect, and in New England's ever-present antiquities, reinforced the artist's plan for an extensive series, "American Historic Epic." Ten of sixty projected mural panels were completed, but never placed on walls. Benton's first installed set at the New School for Social Research, New York (1930), included scenes of taxi-dance and burlesque-hall musicians. Soon the artist found an opportunity to place folk musicians in similar murals.

In 1932, for "The Arts of Life in America" panels at the Whitney Museum library, Benton included a country trio—fiddle, harmonica, guitar—and paired dancers. His subtitle for this Western aggregation employed the square-dance call, "Swing 'em Round and Come Down the Middle." For the Southern panel he included a fiddler, guitarist, and preacher exhorting a church gathering, as well as a separate trio of unaccompanied black singers.

In 1973, the Country Music Foundation commissioned "The Sources of Country Music," Benton's final mural. The artist painted it, acrylic on canvas, in his Kansas City home studio to avoid on-site climbing at Nashville. Not surprisingly, Benton returned to hymn singers, square dancers, and familiar string-band instruments, as well as a dulcimer. The guitarist, a larger-than-life singing cowboy (resembling Tex Ritter), spoke to the convergence of Tin Pan Alley and Lone Green Valley. A paddle-wheel riverboat and a steam engine suggested the transformational role of industry and commerce in Anglo- and Afro-American folk music.

Implying stylistic fusion, the mural did not specify the particular artistry of Jimmie Rodgers or Hank Williams, Kitty Wells or Dolly Parton. As a collector, performer, and delineator, Benton, better than most of his peers, knew country music's alterations. By stressing roots, Benton satisfied traditionalists and innovators at Nashville's marts. After his death on January 19, 1975, the mural was shown first at the Smithsonian's Hirshhorn Museum, and subsequently installed permanently in its Foundation home. Here, countless fans see it, incorporating its colorful imagery into their own statements of country identity.

We have no trouble in accepting an Ozark or Chilmark fiddler as a folk figure, but become uncertain in defining this person similarly when cultivating a field or commuting to a factory. Benton never formally denominated any subjects as members of folk society. A musician made music, a farmer plowed, a roustabout loaded cotton, a steel worker guided a ladle—this sufficed. However, scholars who gather and comment on workers' lore have no choice but to use norms from folklore, the discipline.

John Lomax understood cowboy songs to be folksongs because the native ballads of ranch and range, in form and purpose, resembled antique English and Scottish models. George Korson, encountering immigrant Irish miners in Pennsylvania's anthracite fields, responded to their isolation and solidarity. He sensed that mining songs, and parallel forms, functioned to soften toil's edge. Today's ethnographers stress the interaction of either job skill or repetitive process with lore itself. Specifically, contemporary students seek expression which marks, alternatively, workers' bonding or alienating forces at the work place.

We need not pause too long with arcane formulas as we look again at Benton's workers. From Navy days at Norfolk until his death, he sketched laboring men and women preparatory to memorializing them in more permanent form. From a variety of radical mentors, Benton learned that workers might play a special role in changing society. Accordingly, about 1931, he offered "Strike." In this somber oil painting, an armed guard takes aim at a coal-mine striker who holds high a union sign. A dead miner lies between the contenders. The colliery continues to belch smoke, suggesting, ambiguously, either that the guards have kept the mine open, or that the strikers have set it afire. Benton returned to this scene in a 1933 lithograph, again titled "Strike."

It was not unusual for intellectuals in Depression and New Deal years to identify with labor strife. Before and after Benton, artists as diverse as John Sloan, Ben Shahn, William Gropper, Palmer Hayden, and Ralph Fasanella portrayed labor in multiple dimensions. Some painters favored close descriptive reporting; others dwarfed or magnified workers on their jobs; still others flaunted revolutionary banners. Perhaps the most unusual work places were Charles Sheeler's geometric factories devoid of living things.

Breaking with leftist friends during the mid-1930s, Benton engaged in heavy polemics with communists from the magazines *Art Front* and *New Masses*. In sectarian days these critics had blasted Tom's "flag-waving" Americanism. When they embraced a similar popular-front chauvinism, Benton scorned their propaganda. This turbulent ideological debate—the province of historians—also concerns today's labor educators and activists. Do workers empower themselves best by collaborating with employers, or conversely, by stressing their separate consciousness and discrete culture?

Some artists, touched by radical politics in this century, have viewed workers as a collectivity, an enlarged folk society: enclaved, joined internally, encoding key traditions. Conservative scholars pulled to occupational culture have not always walked in step with leftist partisans similarly interested in such culture. Fortunately, when Benton rejected governing notions of class struggle, he did not leave behind his infatuation with work experience. I would suggest that he understood, experientially, the views held by Lomax and Korson that cowboys and coal miners constituted enclaved communities. We are challenged to see Benton's workers as folk figures.

As early as 1921, Benton began to paint representative workers. "The Drillers" idealized jackhammer men—"construction stiffs" or "hard hats" in today's parlance. This painting, harking back to Tom's fling in the Synchronist school, pairs two workers. These twins could well have been sculpted out of the very stone they had cut. Arched backs, swirling wall, and sinewy air hose stress sensuous design over meticulous detail. A decade later, Benton returned to a single black jackhammer man in the panel "City Building" at the New School for Social Research. This worker, anonymous only in name, is angular in frame and bone-weary in stance. His highly detailed air drill, strangely, floats above him as a kind of proletarian scepter.

In my view, Benton's strongest industrial scene is "Steel," also a New School panel. It celebrates our then-dominant industry, by focusing upon key processes—hearth, ladle, furnace—with only six intent men in action. Molten steel lights up dark machines. Benton's mills are neither romantic nor satanic. Essentially, they do not consume their hands—a view often held by outsiders. Somehow, Benton learned that Vulcan's sons had captured their old god's vitality.

Benton's autobiography includes several steel mill scenes: we should know where these preparatory drawings were made, and to whom Tom

"Pouring Steel," by Thomas Hart Benton. In Thomas Hart Benton, Benton's Drawings
(Columbia: University of Missouri Press, 1968).

talked about steel for the New School project. Surely, in 1930, few artists saw steel workers as folk. Today, with television documentaries on
Youngstown and Monongahela Valley obsolescence, we are able to see
Benton's furnace men as brothers to ox team drivers, ship figurehead
carvers, and country sorghum makers. Such crafts are now relegated to
folk festivals from the National Mall to the Golden Gate. Will "quaint"
steel laborers, as symbols of lost power, be invited to future festivals?

Benton's best work scenes touch rural life or extractive industries (where mine or mill remain part of an outdoor landscape). Generally, he made no hard distinction between farm and factory. In numerous vignettes about cotton, he documented transitions from the soil to vessel's hold. Benton captured planting, chopping, picking, ginning, weighing, and river loading.

In the painting "Cotton Loading" (1928), black laborers manhandle cotton bales while two idlers rest on the bank above the river boat. A white man—plantation owner or gin boss—watches all. The river is wide; the work, endless. Cotton farming is now heavily mechanized and ginning, automated. Hence, Benton's painting reminds viewers either of a forgotten work practice, or of a net which captured black and white, cropper and planter, roustabout and pilot. "Cotton Loading" does not alter by use of the word "folk." Rather, we enlarge vocabularies when we open ourselves to this scene's full significance.

One can dip randomly into any Benton anthology and find memorable work depictions, pastoral to mechanical. In his 1939 lithograph "Planting," a black man and woman plow an Arkansas hill field with a solitary mule. He guides the wooden hand plow; she scatters seeds from a bucket. To Creekmore Fath, in 1966, Benton noted that such old scenes might still be found in remote areas: "Old ways don't die easily." Perhaps a census statistician knows how many cotton farmers plow and sow by hand. Such quantification has its use in measuring the persistence of traditional practices. Beyond establishing time lines, we must underscore questions of meaning in the folkloric record. What does the woman in "Planting" sow—cotton, corn, anger, hope, gain?

Benton could not treat occupational culture without having absorbed considerable rail lore during his wide travels. In 1903, brakeman Thomas W. Jackson had cleaned up a batch of smoking-car jokes (some dating back for centuries) for pulp publication, *"On a Slow Train through Arkansaw."* In print for half-a-century, this train-butcher book sold millions of copies. Benton, recalling it from his youth, placed a humorous anecdote—cattle on the track—in a 1929 painting. In 1941, he returned to this subject for a popular lithograph, "Slow Train Through Arkansas." The artist, of course, added longevity to an already hoary anecdote, and exposed new audiences to American legendry.

The familiar folksong "Wreck of the Ol' 97" served Benton both as a painting subject (1943) and a lithograph (1949). He painted "Engi-

"Loading Cotton," by Thomas Hart Benton. In *Thomas Hart Benton,*
Benton's Drawings *(Columbia: University of Missouri Press, 1968).*

neer's Dream" in 1970, based on an obscure 78-rpm disc by Vernon
Dalhart, and "Casey Jones" in 1968, widely known in hundreds of variants. Benton, fascinated by steam trains since childhood, drew them as
soon as he could grasp pencil and crayon. The affection never ended,
for a glorious engine runs in his final mural.

One of Benton's painting (1967) as well as a lithograph (1967) of black
tie spikers at work ahead of an engine, "Ten Pound Hammer," carries
an important association: "Old story of my youth—before the steam
hammer beat John Henry." Did Tom really hear a construction narrative dating before John Henry's exploits at the Big Bend Tunnel? We
shall never explicate all the sources of Benton's knowledge.

Planting, *by Thomas Hart Benton. In Creekmore Fath,* The Lithographs
of Thomas Hart Benton *(Austin: University of Texas Press, 1979).*
(Courtesy Creekmore Fath)

A little known "cartoon" series closes these comments on Benton's
workers, rural and urban. In the mid-1930s, sit-down strikers achieved
high visibility as did CIO leader John L. Lewis. In Michigan's embattled
auto industry, several near-Fascist and Nazi cults arose to counter local
communists. *Life* deployed Benton to Detroit on the Fourth of July
holiday, 1937, to sketch labor-political conflict. The magazine on July 26
ran a marvelous photo of Tom sketching in Schwaben Park, while a
curious youngster in lederhosen observed the artist at work.

Life featured seventeen drawings, all captioned by Benton. Finding
nothing more sinister than picnic red-hots and mustard, beer and pret-
zels, youngsters on pony rides, a hillbilly wedding, and similar rites,
the artist summed up "Battle Front of Revolutionary Michigan" with
a loafer seated in a tilted chair, feet on desk, dozing in his UAW union
hall. Perhaps Tom's most esoteric caption remains, "The Revolution in
Pengelly Hall. Flint's Smolny Institute." How many American workers,
today, are secure in the knowledge that one of their labor temples, during 1937, was likened to Leningrad's nursery of the Russian Revolution?

Benton, of course, could handle allusion at the barricades, in the

Bible, or from classical mythology. His checklist includes "The Prodigal Son," "Susannah and the Elders," "Achelous and Hercules," and "Persephone," but it is the artist's feel for modern legendry that establishes his hold as the prime painter of American folklore. He credited Jesse Ames Spencer's tome, *History of the United States* (1866), with its many old-fashioned engravings, for inspiring his turn to pictorial history. Tom had plowed through Spenser's pages while in the Navy. Karal Ann Marling suggests that Tom also drew upon Zane Grey and William S. Hart for mythic pictures.

Actually, Benton shared with many writers and artists a two-century task of decolonizing American art and letters, affirming the worth of local expression, and extending the rubric "native" to include red and black creativity. Folklorists in and out of the academy—Henry Rowe Schoolcraft, John Wesley Powell, Lucy McKim, Joel Chandler Harris, George Lyman Kittredge, Constance Rourke, Carl Sandburg, Zora Neale Hurston—labored in this unending cause.

One sees Benton's early turn to folk material in the completed panels for the "American Historical Epic" which stressed discovery, settlement, and retribution. Epic themes regularly came down to individual portraits. "King Philip," the Massachusetts chief (1922) is as bright and sculptural as Benton's jackhammer "Drillers." "The Pathfinder" (1926) in buckskins, with powder horn and long rifle, is a romantic brother both to the Indian chief and the construction twins. "Pathfinder" also reminds viewers of Daniel Boone and Davy Crockett—Indianized white men able to call upon dual totems for their success. Needless to say, scouts, trailblazers, trappers, and hunters—all garbed in coonskin caps and moccasins—appeared in Benton murals for decades.

I select these three paintings as representative Bentonesque heroes, and I invite the comparison of chief, drillers, and pioneer with the folk performers in "Missouri Musicians" and "Coming 'Round the Mountain." The lesson to be drawn from this comparison, I feel, is not one of jolting polarity—sensuous beauty versus rawboned homeliness—but, rather, one of continuity. In the American imagination, King Philip, Natty Bumppo, Daniel Boone, Davy Crockett, Buffalo Bill, Uncle Remus, John Henry, and Paul Bunyan, merge into the songlore of Benton's string-band music makers. His folk musicians could and did sing about their past from defeated chief to tunnel stiff. Not only did Benton comprehend continuity within American folk tradition, but he linked performance to song content.

For his Missouri State Capitol murals (1936), Benton presented a panorama of local history, everyday custom, social protest, and revered literature. Over three doorways he placed Huck Finn and Jim, Frankie and Johnnie, and Jesse James. The latter outlaw, of course, figures in formal history, folksong, and oral tale. Frankie and Johnnie are known largely through song, both popular and folk. Huck and Jim remain literary figures, nevertheless perceived by many to be folk archetypes. Benton selected stories from his state's "mythology," and, by doing so, forced scholars, if not public viewers, to search again the arena in which Mark Twain's characters continue to meet ballad heroes.

Teachers tend to believe that most Americans are familiar with ballad subjects from Barbara Allen and Nomie Wise to Lord Lovell and Floyd Collins. However, we have never tested this assumption. We cannot, with certainty, compare ballad giants to Scarlett O'Hara or J. R. Ewing. This matter points to a strength inherent in Benton's "Jesse James" and "Frankie and Johnnie." In both these panels, the narrative is obvious even to one who has not heard the referential song or tale. Frankie catches her man with a rival in a bar; she shoots him down. Jesse and his gang rob a bank, hold up a train, and leave dead on the ground. Benton counted on familiarity with these ballad events to stimulate public attention to his murals.

Following the Missouri assignment, Benton selected his three "doorway" scenes and a sorghum-mill detail for a set of four Capitol lithographs. Creekmore Fath's book on Benton's prints includes song texts for "Frankie and Johnnie" and "Jesse James" — texts dating back to the editor's student days at Austin, where J. Frank Dobie and other teachers, encouraged Fath's gathering of songs and prints. We need many similar ties of texts, well-known and hidden, to Benton's art.

The published research, during Benton's lifetime, on "The Ballad of the Jealous Lover of Lone Green Valley," is found in an article by Ray Lawless — a study supplemented by Marilyn Stokstad. Here, I touch only the matter of the painting's composition which twines musical performance and narrative exposition. The artist balances dual sets of central figures: a girl fatally stabbed by her knife-in-hand lover; three mountain musicians with a jug on their table. The fiddler and one harmonicist (or, does he finger a jew's harp?) play music, while a third musician holds a harmonica and sings. The painting's flowing lines suggest music's movement from performers to ballad actors. Benton's title names the song of tragic confrontation.

We move readily from this ballad painting to a concluding over-view of Benton's folkloric contribution. In a 1961 letter to Professor Lawless, Tom placed "Jealous Lover" in a "folksong series" (planned in the 1920s and executed in the 1930s and beyond) "part of the general plan of American myth and history at which . . . I'm still working." We have no record, today, of such a discrete, sequential series. Instead, we have Benton's lifetime attention to folk artifact and practice. Perhaps, a scholar will wish to identify all such subject matter. Gale Hunting-ton, Benton's neighbor at Chilmark, could help in this project. He and Tom swapped song, jest, and unresolved questions about lore.

The challenge to retrace Benton's path to folklore is great. In Janu-ary, 1942, John Lomax visited with Tom in Kansas City. The artist had known the ballad hunter's books, but this was their first meeting. Tom revealed his interest in recording traditional Ozark fiddlers for the Library of Congress (a project in which Vance Randolph was then engaged). Writing to Alan Lomax at the Library about the plan, Tom observed "The tire shortage makes me a little fearful of the roads down there." From our vantage point, it seems incredible that Benton could have been put off at any time by worn tires or bad roads. It is our loss that we have no Benton-gathered field recordings.

To explore Benton's views from a friend's perspective, I queried the late Charles Seeger (1975). He had met the artist about 1921 in the com-pany of musical modernists, Carl Ruggles and Edgar Varesi. Seeger contrasted his own slow turn from abstract composition to folksong collecting/analysis with Tom's seemingly quick and decisive shift in this same direction. Seeger confessed "swiping" the notion of "the raw and the cooked" from Benton years before either man had encountered the anthropological formula of Lévi-Strauss. Artist and musicologist relished the raw after early diets in art school and conservatory (Green 1979; Reuss 1979).

The two friends had joined together in spirited old-time music in Benton's Greenwich Village ensemble. Charles accorded Tom the dis-tinction of being the world's most original interpreter of Bach, twist-ing the latter's music into Arkansas hillbilly sounds. Despite such ca-cophony, Seeger recalled with pleasure performing in the band at the dedication of Benton's and Jose Clemente Orozco's murals at the New School for Social Research. This happening (January 19, 1931) lodged in Seeger's memory as a marker in his personal odyssey to folk-music study.

In trumpeting Benton's worth, his close friend Thomas Craven used the term "folk art": "His painting is a complex instrument; in popular appeal a folk art, but fundamentally an intellectual performance—a folk art, incorporated with a structural mechanism from the Renaissance." A half-century's reflection modifies this view. Benton made his art accessible to vast numbers of citizens, and, accordingly, reached many folks. However, he never was a "folk artist" even by that term's most fluid definitions. Craven hit the mark in stressing "intellectual performance." Essentially, Benton—like Lomax, Korson, Randolph—returned some folk culture to its own carriers, while directing collected songs or song pictures to a public beyond enclaved society.

Indifferent or hostile commentators, less friendly than Craven, have long denigrated Benton's portraits as brutish. In 1933, one critic had asserted that Tom placed his city racketeers and burlesque queens, hillbillies and cornfield Negroes, in a parade of contempt (Rosenfeld). Fifty years later, another critic continued with this cry: the American Scene paintings of Benton, Grant, and Curry remain a "bad art historical joke" (Allright). When Tom lived, he smote such opponents hip and thigh. The distancing of invective—theirs and his—refocuses sight on Benton's work in gallery and anthology.

We ask: How did Benton's rank-and-file Americans see his delineations, never entirely realistic, but neither overtly sentimental nor grotesque? Painting from outside of folk society, he knew its heart as well as did any previous interpreter. Unfortunately, we have few direct reports from those who saw themselves mirrored in Benton's paintings. One of Tom's students described his teacher's addiction to "hollow-and-bump muscularity"—no polish, no cosmetics. Some viewers winced at portraits so caricatured, at characters eternally seedy. Despite the strictures of others, Wilbur Leverett, the guitarist in "Missouri Musicians," remained proud of "his picture," neither feeling that it denigrated him nor that it ridiculed his culture.

Two of Benton's early Chilmark paintings have been called his first Regionalist portraits. Although "Regionalism" in art came to mean the Midwest in the 1930s, "The Meal" features Tom's New England neighbors, George and Sabrina West at Martha's Vineyard. George, a Yankee farmer-fisherman, and his wife were deaf mutes. Benton painted their son, also mute, in the oil "Josie West." All three, parents and son, are unadorned—quintessentially folk. Can we assume that Josie's portrait appealed to him as much as did "Missouri Musicians" to Leverett?

Looking back to the 1930s, we marvel at that period's wide attention to folk culture. Then, Holger Cahill brought folk art to Manhattan's Museum of Modern Art. Before the decade closed, phonograph company executives had learned to repackage blues and mountain music as "folksong" for urban audiences. While one federal unit, the Index of American Design, called fresh attention to craft object, another unit, the Archive of American Folk-Song, dispatched collectors to "the field."

As we hear political culture of the '30s through field recordings, we see it through cameras held by FSA photographers, for Dorothea Lange and her peers left us thousands of folklife documents. Similarly, *Porgy and Bess* and *The Cradle Will Rock* elicited tags such as "folk opera" and "vernacular music," respectively. Aaron Copland used folksong in his ballet *Billy the Kid,* as did Virgil Thompson for his film score of *The Plow That Broke the Plains.* In fiction, William Faulkner turned Yoknapatawpha's folk, black and white, into universal models. Some of the decade's mediators held to no firm ethnographic guide; others, like Ben Botkin, undertook to spread widely Horace Kallen's seminal concept of cultural pluralism.

Pundits, today, disagree as to the value of using folklore in building the belletristic palace. While some composers, authors, and artists conceive the folk item only as common stone, others appreciate folk material intrinsically. It is not the stone's sole destiny to firm the palace wall. To value folklore is to see the stone's color, to feel its weight, to know its power. Such knowledge does not diminish the achievement of "stonemasons" like Faulkner or Benton. Rather, our attention to their sources deepens appreciation of tasks in unrolling varied cultural scrolls.

Granting Benton's dazzling achievement in folk interpretation, we can return to his verbal key, "folk pattern." He stood on very firm ground in depicting a particular fiddler or roustabout, but, I feel, he ventured onto faulty ground in naming guiding and bonding national values "folk." In such endeavor, he touched unsettled semantic issues built into this word, for it stretches from some to all Americans. No single artist has ever limned all our discrete communities: ethnic, regional, religious, occupational, linguistic, ideological. No artist has isolated one hue to replace the banded rainbow.

Folklorists who guard disciplinary towers will not welcome Benton, even retrospectively, to their domain. I have stressed his documentary contribution—reportorial and imaginative—not to award him post-humous credentials, but, rather, to assist in today's appraisal of national continuity and change. Perhaps, Benton is now most important to those who are engaged in analysis and presentation of American complexity. From whom do collectors and interpreters of folklore derive strength; to whom do they offer their talent? Does Benton's art reinforce contemporary formulations of cultural singularity or of diversity? How? We go to many sources for answers to these questions. By way of example, I cite but one source.

In 1954, Benton illustrated Lynn Riggs's *Green Grow the Lilacs* for the Limited Editions Club. Revised as the musical *Oklahoma!*, it carried, far and wide, a benign view of folk culture. For the play's handsome printing, drama critic Brooks Atkinson wrote an introduction which touched large issues: "But the folk about whom disarming little plays used to be written have been gathered into the multitudes of Americans who participate in a common culture."

I do not believe that Atkinson's views were shared by Benton, nor that the latter's art helped weld a "common culture." Tom painted his way from Martha's Vineyard to the Red River to Hollywood. In this hegira, he did not limn all Americans, but he did catch the likenesses of many. Melting pot images of "gathered multitudes" did not shore his populism, nor did he impose mainstream vision on those caught in backwaters.

Through five decades, Benton offered a superb set of folk representations. Technically disciplined and emotionally engaged, he called wide attention to hidden brothers and sisters. He had no need to place them in Eden or Hades; pragmatically, he placed them in their "natural" settings. Hill fiddler, steel puddler, cotton picker, track layer, lead miner, wheat cradler, and hymn singer fit into Tom's cosmos. Despite years of railing against politicians, in agora and academy, Benton sought to connect folklore and political culture. He struggled long and hard to situate his populism between Wall Street and Union Square. Like fellow creators, at times, he strayed from base.

We find ourselves during the 1980s looking back at 1930s art with a kaleidoscope in hand. Each turn brings an exciting configuration: revisionistic, ambivalent, mournful, gleeful. Wanda Corn, in a major reappraisal of Grant Wood's work, sees his art, "founded on grassroots imagery and local history," as "in eclipse." Some critics, less sympathetic than Professor Corn, assert that Wood, Curry, and Benton, together remain in eclipse: spiritually vacant, cliche-ridden, anachronistic, reactionary. From my perspective, such laden language blocks the constant task of demystifying cultural experience.

As long as corporate and technocratic society continues to relegate many Americans to the margins, we must renew our search for promises within traditional artifact and enactment. In this spirit, I close my commentary on Benton's depictions by noting his use of old sorghum mills as emblematic of current views of folk community. The sketch "Sorghum Mills," dated to 1932, is included in *Benton's Drawings*. His Missouri Capitol mural, "Politics and Agriculture" (1936), holds a similar mill vignette, also selected for the lithograph "Missouri Farmyard." Finally, in 1968, the artist completed a magnificent oil and tempera "Sorghum Mill."

I have not counted all such Benton mills, but his 1968 painting marks well his keen attention to folklife. With its gaunt farmers, creaky mill, white mule, massive cane pile, energizing fire—all set off by autumnal hills—the painting illustrates a platonic folk practice. Thus, it makes a quiet ideological statement about traditional culture. Some viewers do project beyond these descriptive pictures to see social life constituted at "pullings," where the final skimmings are boiled into precious candy, and, as well, community mores are congealed. Each folk custom carries a complex associational web.

Documentary films and *Foxfire* articles now portray picturesque molasses-making. I have helped walk a mule around a cane press, not as a young farm laborer, but as an adult folklorist at the Smithsonian Festival of American Folklife. Of hundreds of country customs (quilting/carving/cooking/singing) none serves better than sorghum making to demonstrate for legislators and bureaucrats the need to preserve American folk culture. In the Age of Jackson, Senator Thomas Hart Benton trumpeted that western frontiersmen were the equal of their tidewater cousins—perhaps their betters. His namesake, Tom, in print and painting, insures that frontiersmen in forgotten vales, with tired mules and antiquated tools, still belong within our polity.

Americans have cultivated sorgo cane for centuries. Walt Whitman noted that Civil War soldiers relished rationed sorghum molasses. A few farmers, from Florida to Kansas, continue to produce 'lasses at the home place, but most buy factory-refined sugar and bottled syrup at the supermarket. When a participant offers old ways and treasured values at a folk festival, indeed, he produces a delicacy, but, mainly, he offers a message built into the term "folk." Sorghum makers—men, women, and children—articulate a pride in the past, as well as a belief in the continuing utility of handicraft. They connect their culture to democratic concern.

Men and mules in tandem have a long pedigree in national discourse. Zora Neale Hurston titled her superb Florida collection of Afro-American tales and beliefs, *Mules and Men.* Jimmie Rodgers immortalized a black work lyric in "Mule Skinner Blues," later altered by Bill Monroe into a bluegrass-music favorite. We *hear* Hurston's tale tellers and Rodgers' skinners when we *see* Benton's sorghum makers and patient mules.

Tom Benton's depictions touch our people's deepest experience. His art, also, directs thought to questions of how our polity reached its contemporary dimension. Benton's folk do sweeten days as they reaffirm Jeffersonian ideals. At work and play, they root present in past. They urge constant attention to American promises.

REFERENCES

Allbright, Thomas. 1983. "Street Artist of the Depression." *San Francisco Chronicle, Review,* November 27: 14.

Atkinson, Brooks. 1954. "Introduction." In Lynn Riggs, *Green Grow the Lilacs.* Norman: University of Oklahoma Press for the Limited Editions Club, New York.

Baigell, Matthew. 1971. *A Thomas Hart Benton Miscellany.* Lawrence: University Press of Kansas.

———. 1974. *Thomas Hart Benton.* New York: Abrams.

Benton, Thomas Hart. 1937a. *An Artist in America.* New York: McBride.

———. 1937b. "Artist Thomas Hart Benton Hunts Communists and Fascists in Michigan." *Life* 3 (July 26): 22–25.

———. 1942. Letter to Alan Lomax, Library of Congress, Archive of American Folk-song, January 21.

———. 1968. *Benton's Drawings.* Columbia: University of Missouri Press.

———. 1969. *An American in Art.* Lawrence: University Press of Kansas.

Corn, Wanda. 1983. *Grant Wood: The Regionalist Vision.* New Haven: Yale University Press.

Craven, Thomas. 1937. "Thomas Hart Benton." *Scribner's* 102 (October): 33–40.

Fath, Creekmore. 1969. *The Lithographs of Thomas Hart Benton.* Austin: University of Texas Press.

Green, Archie. 1979. "Charles Louis Seeger (1886–1979)." *Journal of American Folklore* 92:391–99.

Lawless, Ray. 1961. "Thomas Hart Benton's Jealous Lover and Its Musical Background." *Register of the Museum of Art,* University of Kansas, 2 (June): 32–39.

Leverett, Wilbur. 1976. Letter to editor. *JEMF Quarterly,* no. 44: 174.

Marling, Karal Ann. 1981. "Thomas Hart Benton's *Boomtown*. Regionalism Redefined." In *Prospects* 6:73–137.

Reuss, Richard. 1979. "Folk Music and Social Conscience: The Musical Odyssey of Charles Seeger." *Western Folklore* 38:221–38.

Rosenfeld, Paul. 1933. "Ex-Reading Room." *New Republic* 74 (April): 245–46.

Seeger, Charles. 1975–76. Letters to Archie Green.

Stokstad, Marilyn. 1980. "El Greco in the Ozarks." In Elizabeth Broun et al., *Benton's Benton.* Lawrence: Spencer Museum of Art, University of Kansas (32–48).

Weintraub, Linda. 1984. *Thomas Hart Benton: Chronicler of America's Folk Heritage.* Annandale-on-Hudson: Bard College, Bloom Art Institute.

The Archive's Shores

n the mind's eye we see an island as bounded by a regular and continuous shoreline, although a careful look after reveals discrete beaches — sandy or rocky, open or mysterious, tranquil or tempestuous. Within American libraries, museums, and universities, archives often appear to be peaceful islands, at a distance from the mainland, figurative retreats for document and disc, manuscript and photograph. As a young sailor during World War II, I prepared for Pacific island hopping at Jamestown, Virginia. Journeying to Washington, D.C., while on leave, for a first visit to the Library of Congress, I saw its Archive of American Folk Song as a cool room within an immense marble building. It took me three decades to connect this room with outside domains of political tension and philosophic discourse.

Working at the Library during 1966, I edited an album of railroad songs from archival field recordings and learned that tie tampers and brave engineers used their chants and ballads variously: to pace work, to commemorate death, to challenge injustice, and to establish consensus. From 1968 to 1976, I was at the archive frequently, at times to study but mainly to prepare myself for visits to Senate and House chambers. There, in office and lobby, I conducted a long folklife "seminar," and, as the American Folklife Preservation Act wound its way to presidential signature in 1976, I had ample time to puzzle over the archive's complexity.

In time, we shall have a full history of the American Folklife Center, its germinal course and everyday achievements. Here, I want to consider the visions of three widely different individuals whose energies are now integral to the center: Robert Winslow Gordon (1888–1961), John Avery Lomax (1867–1948), and Horace Meyer Kallen (1882–1974).

Gordon and Lomax served, respectively, as first and second heads of the archive; whether or not Kallen ever visited it, I do not know.

My choice of a pair of insiders and of an unfamiliar outsider is deliberate, for an island's shores are altered both by wild storm and placid eddy. By invoking images of insularity, I wish to explore the ideas which have shaped the first public-sector unit in the United States devoted to folksong, folklore, and folklife.

We generally trace the origins of the American ballad quest to literary studies by Harvard's Francis James Child and see behind him a line of rhetoricians and antiquarians. Inspiring the trio of Gordon, Lomax, and Kallen was another Harvard professor, Barrett Wendell. Himself uninvolved in folksong study, Wendell was a gentleman, eccentric, patriot, and tory, engaged in ambivalent floundering between orthodoxy and heterodoxy. For him, American literature at its best derived from Mother England, and remote regions beyond the Berkshires produced only inferior writing. Yet this Brahmin, in asking his students to consider literature in relation to their experience, touched in them deep feelings of particularity and pluralism.

Looking back at his own odyssey, John Lomax saw his beginning at the Archive of American Folk Song in the initial encouragement to collect given him by Professors Barrett Wendell and George Lyman Kittredge at Harvard. Lomax dedicated his autobiography, *Adventures of a Ballad Hunter* (1947), to Wendell; previously, this teacher had written a warm introduction for his student's first book, *Cowboy Songs and Other Frontier Ballads* (1910). Over the years, Lomax enjoyed telling, and perhaps embroidering, his calling's opening tale.

As a Texas farm boy in Bosque County, Lomax had heard nightherding cowboys singing. Leaving home for college, he carried secretly a roll of trail songs in his trunk. At the University of Texas, when a distinguished philologist dismissed these as "tawdry, cheap and unworthy," Lomax, in shame, burned the packet. Years later, in advanced work at Harvard, when Wendell encouraged his respect for cowboy song, the Texan felt a phoenix rising from the ashes.

Cowboy Songs carried a prefatory message from "Teddy" Roosevelt which closed, "It is . . . of real importance to preserve permanently this unwritten ballad literature of the back country and the frontier." In the book's introduction, Wendell complemented the sentiment, "I commend [cowboy ballads] to all who care for the native poetry of America." The linked phrases "back country," "unwritten literature,"

the FARMER comes to town

"*The Farmer Comes to Town*," by Charles Pollack, *1936, for U.S. Resettlement Administration song-series leaflet (American Folklife Center, Washington, D.C.).*

and "native poetry" seem commonplace today but were provocative in 1910. At that time, many leaders in academic and governmental circles judged the collecting of folksong as a peripheral activity.

Accordingly, pioneers like Gordon and Lomax engaged in a double mission—asserting that American literature was more than a branch of English letters and asserting as well the vitality of folk literature within American life. In this sense, folklorists, no matter how closely they held to mainstream ideological positions, advocated the merit of expression by neglected people.

In Washington in 1933, John Lomax picked up the tasks of the archive's creator, Robert Gordon. Despite differences in personality, both men were in substantial agreement on matters of then-current ballad theory. An obvious contrast between the pair lay in the ability of Lomax to tell his story dramatically in print and from platform, while Gordon remained largely mute, unable to publish his collectanea in a major book or to pen an autobiographical account.

Gordon's tenure at the Library was brief, running from 1928 to the trough of the Depression, 1932. Unfortunately, the Librarian of Congress, Herbert Putnam, and the chief of the Music Division, Carl Engel, failed to understand their archivist. At first, all three shared a grand vision of a national folksong repository, but Gordon was too much a bobcat to be tamed in a stone cage. He saw himself as a creative scientist; his supervisors needed a bureau-builder. When the private funds that created the position were exhausted, Putnam ended Gordon's appointment. The blow haunted Gordon until his death, and for decades he worked quietly as a technical editor in the Washington area. Only recently has Debora Kodish told the story in an article for the *Quarterly Journal of the Library of Congress* and reported Gordon's unselfish public contribution.

Gordon, born a Maine Yankee, seemed to take to mechanical devices as readily as Lomax had to cowboy song. At Harvard, between 1906 and 1917, Gordon tinkered with cameras, cylinder recorders, and early radio sets, preparing himself for eventual field work while teaching at the University of California, Berkeley. With an *Oakland Tribune* reporter, he sought chanties from the few windjammer crews still sailing through the Golden Gate. Gordon developed rapport with shellbacks and stevedores, no matter whether all their poetry conformed to canons of ballad scholarship. Waterfront workers remembered him as "the guy with the derby hat and the phonograph."

Many hands hammered out the archive's governing concept, the intrinsic worth of folksong within American letters. Enlightened readers shared the ballad's glamour by reading Bishop Thomas Percy and Sir Walter Scott. At home, authors such as Irving, Cooper, Hawthorne, and Twain decolonized literature by attention to local legend. George Caleb Bingham and William Sidney Mount—steeped in Jacksonian democracy—depicted on canvas homespun fiddlers on flatboats and at barn dances. Joel Chandler Harris popularized Uncle Remus's animal tales; the Fisk Jubilee Singers carried spirituals north; Scott Joplin emblazoned ragtime coast to coast; W. C. Handy placed blues sheet music in many parlors. By the time Gordon arrived at the Library, a wide audience had been prepared to receive the songs of camp meeting and campfire, of hill and range.

Gordon sought machines both to discover and to extend such expression and was eager in his acceptance of technology. For a century collectors have used sound-recording equipment and cameras in the field and have issued their findings in many forms. But the problem inherent within the cylinder or disc machine, the perforated film track, or the magnetic tape and cassette is that all these instruments document tradition and at the same time distort and interfere with it. Hence, by definition, sound apparatus stands like Janus facing antiquity and modernity. Because technology preserves vernacular music in its subtle nuances and also corrodes tradition, robbing the folk of treasures, scholars have been made uneasy by "talking machines" and "canned music." Gordon escaped such anxiety because of faith in science. Not only was he ahead of many peers in his sheer facility with recording equipment—taking to it as an extension of his senses—but he reached out, during the Library years, to acquire commercial discs of folk music from Victor and sister firms.

Barrett Wendell's influence on John Lomax is treated in both their writings; however, I have not found similar references suggesting a dialogue between Gordon and his professors on recording or photographic devices. I am curious to learn whether any early ballad scholars prepared students to collect old lore with new gear, already on the market, or discouraged the use of these tools because they distorted folk material. When did it become proper to teach "the ballad" with a mechanical phonograph or a motion-picture projector in the classroom? When did school teachers turn to the Library's Archive of Folk Song for field recordings as instructional aids?

I think that Gordon sensed no ambivalence about the "progress" implied by recorder or camera. In his cosmos, folksong represented truth, roots, authenticity. Hence, a device which lengthened an old folksong's life glowed in reflected light. But what if the same device shortened life? Using contemporary judgment, we suggest that Gordon anticipated neither that a phonograph might level traditional walls, nor that it might help enclaved groups in their counterhegemonic wall-raising. Those folklorists only aware of the homogenizing thrust in mechanical apparatus have not observed that the wide extension of inexpensive recording and playback equipment has given local citizens a bit of control in holding at bay society's robots.

The matter of understanding all facets of the recording process surfaces presently within the Folklife Center as it reissues Omaha Indian (and other tribal) music "caught" about (and after) 1896. Clearly, these "curiosities" function as revitalizing factors in present-day Omaha life. Records, thus, advance ongoing campaigns for cultural equity. We feel it necessary, with this enlarged sense of the sound recording's contribution, to follow a single disc as it moves away from field or studio and reenters the resilient community in which listeners alter group identity. Ultimately, we must label early cylinders deposited in the Library not as archaic toys but as survival tools.

The Archive of American Folk Song retained its original name from 1928 through 1955, when it dropped the qualifier *American*. This shift marked response to the fact that, before World War II, the collection had already been broadened to include international material. No one in the Library made a conscious decision to shape an inclusive unit; rather, collectors deposited disc and manuscript from remote lands. Even before these items were accessioned, however, the word *American* had become troublesome to the third head of the archive, Alan Lomax, and to the wartime Librarian of Congress, Archibald MacLeish.

From the inception of the American Folklore Society, in 1888, its members agreed that lore in the United States came in a babel: Passamoquoddy, Papagayo, Cajun-French, Pennsylvania-Dutch, to name a few tongues. Neither Gordon nor Lomax remained immune to linguistic reality, but, like most of their peers, they focused on English-language song. I do not mean to paint the archive's pioneers into too narrow a corner. Great in enthusiasm, they saw their public mission as related to Major John Wesley Powell's ground-breaking work —speech, myth, music, custom, artifact—in the Smithsonian Institution's Bureau of American Ethnology. In Gordon's reach to commercial records, he knew that foreign-series discs paralleled then-current "race" and "hillbilly" categories. In early field work for the Library, Lomax recorded the sacred Mexican play "Los Pastores" at San Antonio.

Despite this wide start in collecting, a limiting formula stunted the archive—a nativistic view of Anglo-Saxonism. Some nineteenth-century collectors had used the term primarily in philological reference, but others knew it as a shibboleth for purity of race and imperialistic policy. Some ballad scholars held an embedded belief that Anglo-Saxon lore (curiously, also tagged *Elizabethan*) was not only quintessentially American but also an antidote to Catholic, Celtic, alien, radical, or assorted dark-skinned terrors. Many New England jingoists became active in movements to restrict immigration; some opposed the rise of institutions formed by newcomers; others retreated into a state of bitter melancholy, persuaded that their America was doomed.

Within folkloric circles, the term *Anglo-Saxon* was used broadly to touch society and culture. To illustrate, John Lomax opened his "Collector's Note" for *Cowboy Songs:*

> Out in the wild, far-away places of the big and still unpeopled west—in the cañons along the Rocky Mountains, among the mining camps of Nevada and Montana, and on the remote cattle ranches of Texas, New Mexico, and Arizona—yet survives the Anglo-Saxon ballad spirit that was active in secluded districts in England and Scotland even after the coming of Tennyson and Browning.

Today, we look back at the talismanic phrase "Anglo-Saxon ballad spirit" as part of the conventional baggage of folklorists trained in the past. Lomax may have used it formulaically without implying that other people lacked poetic impulse. We know that he had encountered black cowboys and Mexican vaqueros who were spirited singers with laden songbags. Liking their music, he struggled to accommodate his explanatory phrases to the world about him.

Anglo-Saxonism, when Lomax began to collect, held spatial and temporal significance as it tied to lateral labels. Theodore Roosevelt liked *Cowboy Songs* because the book illustrated the replication on our frontier of "conditions of ballad growth which obtained in mediaeval England." However, Lomax knew in his bones that black and Tejano buckaroos were neither Anglo-Saxon bards nor medieval exemplars. Throughout his life the tension implicit in such knowledge proved difficult to contain. While active at the Library, Lomax "discovered" a magnificent black folksinger, Huddie Ledbetter, in a Louisiana prison. The collector published a huge book on "Leadbelly," managed his early concert appearances, and, finally, quarreled with him. Regardless, Lomax could never compress this black singer into a xenophobic mold.

Alan Lomax accompanied his father John on collecting trips in the South and assisted him at the archive. To mark Alan's enthusiasm, I quote a line from a letter dealing with a visit (1935) to the Georgia coast, Florida, and the Bahamas: "This has been the most exciting field trip I have made and, really, its story can only be told in a long, rambling novel." We need this novel, long overdue, as well as a reflective autobiography. It is our loss also that B. A. Botkin left no critical account of his years at the archive (1942–45). Alan Lomax and Ben Botkin, together with their friend Charles Seeger, carried a heady mix of liberal and radical, populist and Marxist values to the archive during the New Deal period.

In the years from 1950 to 1970, the archive turned inward, reflecting both internal Library policies and an external climate of civic conformity. Further, the activists who came together in the Kennedy years to lobby for the National Endowment for the Arts and the National Endowment for the Humanities were not tuned to folk culture. These partisans of high art and formal learning hardly seemed aware of panoramic folk tradition. Essentially, the builders of the endowments established their agencies initially to distance attention from rurality, artisanship, ethnicity, and regionalism.

The impetus to change in Washington comes from all points of the compass: a chance happening, a planned position paper, a legislative program, a newspaper report. In 1969, drawing upon experience at the Festival of American Folklife, Sen. Ralph Yarborough of Texas introduced a bill to create a folklife unit within the Smithsonian Institution. Time and circumstance altered his plan, for in 1976 the American Folklife Center saw light within the Library of Congress. In 1978 the Archive of Folk Song affiliated with the center, and in 1981 it acquired the name Archive of Folk Culture. (It must be noted here that the archive's staff, in the New Deal years, had already gone well beyond folksong collecting.)

To return to the archive's founding in 1928, I reiterate that it stemmed from the long drive to free our literature from European belletristic antecedents. Barrett Wendell never grasped the genius in Melville's *Moby-Dick,* leaving that to others. Yet this teacher inspired Bob Gordon to sweet chanties heard on the Pequod. Despite Wendell's pronounce-ment that American literature was "inexperienced" and "innocent," Gordon helped his fellow citizens see their elusive art in full flower.

We sense folksong's appeal and message by attention to a 1978 archive LP: *Folk-Songs of America: The Robert Winslow Gordon Collection, 1922–1932*. This field album, intrinsically educational, becomes a fitting companion to John Dos Passos's trilogy *U.S.A.* or Vernon Louis Par-rington's *Main Currents in American Thought*—contributions in fiction and criticism that, interestingly, came from the pens of two of Wen-dell's students. I position Gordon's cylinders and discs as illumination for both Parrington and Dos Passos to underscore my view that archi-val beaches can be washed by Jeffersonian waters.

Had the archive's story ended in 1976, this essay could not have in-cluded a commentary on cultural pluralism. Because archive is now joined to center, we may note the voicing of cultural pluralism's mean-ing in congressional offices while the folklife bill drifted from legisla-tive hopper to White House desk. In his initial bill, Yarborough de-clared "that the diversity inherent in American folklife has contributed greatly to the cultural richness of the nation and has fostered a sense of individuality and identity among the American people." Upon hearing this declamation by a Texas populist, I knew that we raised our red, white, and blue flag with manila lanyards of black, brown, and yellow.

Senators and Representatives have enjoyed the Library of Congress from its inception as their special reference center. Because of prox-imity and constant use, they have identified more closely with the Library than with parallel learned institutions in Washington. Hence, during the early 1970s, a majority of these lawmakers saw no problem in extending the archive's role in documenting folksong (preservation) to novel modes of dissemination (presentation) for folklife. In effect, "passive" archival practices took on an "active" dimension of display for a rainbow of American expression.

Cultural pluralism's bibliography is extensive; its theoreticians are few. Here, I feature only one, Horace Kallen, largely unknown to folk-lorists. Professor Kallen taught philosophy all his life; versed in es-thetics, he wrote extensively about the arts. However, his contribution to folklore was not that of field collection, archival categorization, or popular interpretation. Rather, he articulated a concept which helped resolve the turmoil of many American scholars caught between adherence to the state's dominant ideology and affection for a particular group's expressivity.

Kallen was born in Silesia, Germany, and his Jewish parents brought him as a child to Boston's West End. There, he "grew up among Bostonians neither properties nor proper." His earliest orthodox doctrines, which came from the Hebrew Bible, were countered by New England teachers who worshipped another set of founding fathers. At Harvard, he was close to many superb teachers, among them William James, George Santayana, and Barrett Wendell. Recalling college days, Kallen reported that he lived not in Cambridge but in an "otherworld," his parents' immigrant home. Additionally, he lived as a social settlement resident in the North End where he met socialists and anarchists, testing his creed against theirs.

Associated with the New School for Social Research in Manhattan from its founding in 1919, Kallen for a period edited *Advance,* the organ of the Amalgamated Clothing Workers. He was also very active in peace, civil liberties, and consumer cooperative movements. Kallen did not subscribe to a separation of scholarship from society, saying dryly that he "never attained that fullness of pedagogical withdrawal which custom and prejudice ordained for the practice of philosophy." We are in his debt for his rejection of campus ethos.

My focus on Kallen's cultural pluralism pulls one thread out of rich cloth but a thread crucial to all folklorists. During his youth he was conscious of fracture between his Jewish and American self. Many immigrant children feel this pain, but not all are able to externalize it creatively. In Wendell's class, Kallen tentatively linked his fate with those Hebrew prophets this Puritan teacher enshrined. Wendell not only brought back from ashes Lomax's packet of cowboy songs but also rekindled Kallen's interest in ancestral past, helping him reconcile seemingly antithetical ideals.

While Kallen was teaching at the University of Wisconsin, the United States was seized by fears of hyphenated Americans and shrill demands for immigrant-restriction laws. Wisconsin sociologist Edward Ross presented "scientific" arguments for harm inflicted on the body politic by newly arrived foreigners. Drawing on a personal sense of Jewish marginality and public debates by Zionists, Kallen immersed himself in minority issues. He buttressed empathy for beleaguered people by borrowing aspects of the elder Bob La Follette's progressivism. William James's striking image of a pluralistic universe, antithetical to monistic dicta, helped the young philosopher find language then new in the political arena.

At the end of 1914 Kallen prepared an academic paper, "Democracy and the Melting Pot," in response to nativist agitation. This address reached a lay audience in the *Nation* (February 18 and 25, 1915), where the word *versus* displaced *and* in the paper's title. In 1916, he called upon Americans to champion the "perfection and conservation of differences"—language close to that used in the 1970s to advance folklife legislation.

While teaching in the New School and associating with foreign-born needle-trades workers, Kallen drew together several articles on diversity, equality, and comity in *Culture and Democracy in the United States* (1924). Dedicated to Barrett Wendell, the book attacked *Kultur,* countering it with cultural pluralism (a locution then new in print). In essence, Kallen assailed melting-pot assimilationists and Anglo-Saxon supremacists, while he equated pluralism and democracy.

As early as 1915, Kallen had pointed to Switzerland as a model democracy, a commonwealth of cultures. Patrician critics of his 1924 book spoke derisively of crazy quilts and Balkanization. Returning in 1956 to his cause's wide implications, he suggested that our experience precluded a republic of ethnic or linguistic sub-nations. Reflection on totalitarianism had turned liberals away from dogma of race or geist tied to the state. Accordingly, Kallen stressed the vitality of cultural components within the polity over strange constitutional forms. With Whitmanesque prose, he centered cultural pluralism in expressive rather than political behavior. Contemporary folklorists are wise to turn his formulas into inquiries by asking: What kind of diversity can a sovereignty accept? How does such diversity integrate with our heritage of individual freedom and sectional consciousness? Must we see national sustaining culture always as seamless and absolute?

Rulers of large society have usually treated arts and letters as props for national cohesion, while artists and writers have often seen their work as opposing monolithic rule. In our Vietnam era of "cultural revolution," black nationalists, white-ethnic revivalists, and counterculture hedonists became especially strident. Conservatives charged militants, chauvinists, and flower children with subversive divisiveness. Liberals called up varied catchwords to type the changed nation: *mosaic, tapestry, symphony.* Figuratively, folklore collectors became tile setters, weavers, or conductors. Those folklorists who eschewed political envelopment employed their knowledge of traditional language and literature, customary behavior, and the mythic paraphernalia of identity to describe the American cornucopia.

In a 1955 memorial essay to his friend and classmate Alain Locke, Kallen asserted that he had first verbalized the concept of cultural pluralism about 1906, while an assistant to Professor Santayana, Kallen noted, "It has taken these two generations for the term to come into more general use and to figure in philosophic discourse in this country." At his ninetieth birthday (New School, 1972), he expressed oracular satisfaction that his early "upsetting" ideas had been vindicated. Folklorists have assisted in this vindication, not directly as polemicists, but by gathering tribal and ethnic lore and displaying its magnificence.

Metaphorically, folklorists have not upended the melting pot as much as they have sought to treasure its discarded slag. Folkloric work with "non-Anglo-Saxons" has touched Native Americans, Afro-Americans, and immigrants from all the globe. Some collectors of folklore have paralleled the pioneer documentation of Jacob Riis and Lewis Hine in ghetto and factory, at times absorbing progressive belief in civic reform. More recently, some have been caught up by the Civil Rights movement, which itself contributed to the widening of congressional horizons. Some proclaimed, in the 1970s, that traditional artistry and folk wisdom were integral to American experience; hence, the government's major arts/humanities foundations altered their course.

I shall not gloss Kallen's coinage further but instead shall allude to great differences in this century among black leaders (such as Marcus Garvey, James Weldon Johnson, and W. E. B. Du Bois) caught, like immigrants, between rival goals of assimilation and separatism and lashed by demagogue and eugenicist. The issues long voiced in the struggle against racism still echo in our land. Afro-American lore, serving both as lance and shield, also became an instrument used in the division between integrationist and nationalist. Was Brer Rabbit to be left behind on plantation field or to be recharged as a combative warrior on new battlefields?

We need to probe deeply the interaction between white and black intellectuals who accepted, rejected, or modified theories of cultural pluralism. We can begin with Alain Locke, who identified himself as "a philosophical mid-wife to a generation of younger Negro poets, writers, artists." By urging them to see African art and to hear Afro-

American speech and music, he made formal, for many, their link to the discipline of folklore. Literally, he sent them to archive and gallery to immerse themselves in proverb and headdress, ringshout and figurine. Balancing training in ethics and esthetics with reading in anthropology, Locke suggested that the term *value relativism* defined his worldview.

This usage draws us back to Franz Boas, Ruth Benedict, Margaret Mead, Edward Sapir, and their students who generally favored the term *cultural relativism* in their studies. Professor Benedict was influenced by the young critic Randolph Bourne, who, with great flair, championed the organic and creative impulse within immigrant communities. After Benedict's widely read *Patterns of Culture* (1935) appeared, a number of folklorists adopted her exemplifying prose. The path of anthropological language into federal agencies has been better charted than that of philosophical pluralists.

We have yet to describe Kallen's presence in Washington. For example, Sen. Paul Douglas of Illinois had long admired his friend Jane Addams for her work with immigrants at Chicago's Hull House. In lauding her, he referred to Kallen's seminal "Democracy versus the Melting Pot." The Douglas reference is unusual; I believe that most Congressmen who subscribed to cultural pluralism learned about it in attenuated form. Some absorbed it out of the politics of ethnicity; others, from religious renewal; still others, from studies about the artistic landscape. Writers as widely scattered as Louis Adamic, Will Herberg, Milton Gordon, Geno Baroni, Michael Novak, Ben Botkin, and Constance Rourke all drew upon or altered Kallen's texts. These individuals, in their separate writings, contributed to legislative dialogue on the widest horizons of American experience.

Until 1967, the Library of Congress's archive remained the federal government's major unit for the transformation of folkloric codes into public actions. After 1967, the Smithsonian's Festival of American Folklife gave high relief on the National Mall to the twined rubric of cultural pluralism, value relativism, and cultural relativism. Festival participants hardly made explicit use of these labels; rather, musicians and dancers performed while craftsmen worked. Auditors and viewers heard a gospel hymn lined out or saw a wood carver fashion an ox yoke. The private ceremonies of groups set apart from America's common culture became public enactments in a colorful "outdoor museum." Perhaps a few visitors on the Mall connected their pleasure to

Kallen, Locke, or Benedict. Significantly, a handful of Senators and Representatives made the connection.

The Smithsonian's annual event cemented the word *folklife* to a congressional policy of cultural diversity. Previously, Prof. Don Yoder at the University of Pennsylvania had bridged the teaching of folklore in the United States to European folklife studies (regional ethnology, cultural geography, material culture). A report by Yoder on his extension of the keyword *folklife* to American usage, as well as a report by Ralph Rinzler, the festival director, on the Smithsonian experience would help identify the core ideas now built into the term.

By focusing this essay upon three students of Barrett Wendell, I have tried to reveal one archive's formative concepts. Gordon, Lomax, and Kallen wrought their designs out of mundane and, at times, painful experience. Like other Crusoes, they gathered sticks and stones from the tidal pools about them to construct the platforms upon which they exhorted and prayed. Only from today's juncture can we distinguish sharply their guiding constructs: American literature's coming of age, folksong's worth, power in recording device and process, diversity as a federal agency norm.

Professor Wendell's Washington apprentices served Americans well by eclipsing their New England teacher's narrow views about literature. Gordon and Lomax, trained in arcane debates about the ballad's origin, helped enfranchise vernacular culture. They enlarged the Library of Congress holdings to include discs with magic power of recall. Sir Patrick Spens and Mary Hamilton, Stackolee and Pearl Bryan, John Henry and Mother Jones now live in a marble mansion.

The achievement of Gordon and Lomax, great enough, led after half a century to the archive's affiliation with the Folklife Center, itself born out of legislative attention to ethnic identity, race tension, cultural accessibility, historic preservation, and resource conservation. In these pages I have touched, but not spelled out, matters of ethnicity and the access to art and letters by rank-and-file citizens. However, I have neglected entirely matters of preservation and ecology. Perhaps a personal note, here, will hint at the center's labyrinthine mandate.

In urging Congressmen, before 1976, to vote for the folklife bill, I learned how differently each member defined the word *folk*. Concretely, it meant string-band tune, good-luck amulet, blessing of the fishing fleet, yarn swapping, corn dance, covered bridge. Abstractly, it meant language retention, Negritude, pleasure in hand skill, savoring dry wit in colloquial humor, respect for Indian belief, I felt complimented when folklorists were likened to Rachel Carson and John Muir, and when I was asked whether we had a Sierra Club or Audubon Society. Finding it necessary to explain folklife to legislators tuned to Cambodia and Watergate, I could not go beyond their common-sense notions that some culture was endangered and that federal dollars for arts and letters, in a democratic society, had to be spent equitably. On Capitol Hill, I suggested that a mountain ballad resembled a redwood tree, snail darter, colonial farmstead, or Amish buggy.

Clearly, as Senators and Representatives considered the folklife bill, they reshaped the concept of cultural pluralism pragmatically by welding it to preservational strategy for human artifact and natural environment. Without knowing in detail the history of their own folksong archive, they tempered the ballad passion of Gordon and Lomax with queries embodied in Kallen's blueprints: How is power shared within a society divided by race, class, language, and creed? Where does expressive culture intersect with political and economic force? Does diversity enhance or negate our social compact?

These provocative questions switch past to present. The folklorists who now choose to work at the Library of Congress and, by extension, at sister agencies cannot escape the burden of reformulating statements of national purpose. We try to complement the netting of a blues lament or the framing of a patterned quilt with attention to studies in normative theory and reports of ideological conflict. Public-sector folklorists should read the historians who have detailed the ambiguities within cultural pluralism. Beyond such insight, it is useful to consider the work of political economists and sociologists on the right who find pluralistic creeds wanting and, as well, of critics on the left who scorn pluralism's utility either as analytic tool or social template.

Armed with the findings of fellow scholars, folklorists can help unravel American complexity. We are sensitive to that array of elements which defines polity and principle: region, religion, language, ethnicity, race, occupation, class, gender, age. We know songs and stories in English, our common language; we know the jokelore of mestizo and creole; we know rituals of migrants, castaways, and refugees. Many contemporary followers of Gordon and Lomax continue to choose documentary projects; others, touched by Kallen's teaching, choose advocacy for creative group or expressive cluster. Archivists, who daily intertwine preservational and presentational modes, of necessity mix roles.

Within this setting of juxtaposition in tasks, I return to my opening figure of repository as island. Clearly, the present Archive of Folk Culture, now integral to the Folklife Center's function at the Library of Congress, cannot be isolated from centuries of American experience or thought. Neither filiopietistic adulation nor revisionist carping focuses our vision clearly on granite cliff or coral strand. To see our archive as a uniformly contoured circle suggests dim sight. To sense it as a tranquil abode suggests only partial comprehension. The archive's land-mass is irregular; its beaches, indented; its shores, varied.

NOTES ON FURTHER READING

This list of selected references is grouped by the four main individuals and three central ideas of my essay. Items are arranged chronologically within sections.

Wendell

Self, Robert T. *Barrett Wendell.* Boston: Twayne, 1975. (Includes full bibliographic citations.)

Lomax

Lomax, John Avery. *Cowboy Songs and Other Frontier Ballads.* New York: Sturgis and Walton, 1910.

———. *Adventures of a Ballad Hunter.* New York: Macmillan, 1947.

McNutt, James Charles. *Beyond Regionalism: Texas Folklorists and the Emergence of a Post-Regional Consciousness.* Austin: University of Texas Press, 1982. (This thesis includes a Lomax bibliography.)

Gordon

Kodish, Debora. "A National Project with Many Workers." *Quarterly Journal of the Library of Congress* 35 (October 1978): 218–33.

———. *"Good Friends and Bad Enemies": Robert Winslow Gordon and the Study of American Folklore.* Forthcoming from the University of Illinois Press.

Kallen

Kallen, Horace Meyer. *Culture and Democracy in the United States.* New York: Boni and Liveright, 1924.

———. *Cultural Pluralism and the American Idea.* Philadelphia: University of Pennsylvania Press, 1956.

Ballad Studies

Wilgus, D. K. *Anglo-American Folksong Scholarship since 1898*. New Brunswick: Rutgers University Press, 1959.

Leach, MacEdward, and Tristram P. Coffin, eds. *The Critics and the Ballad.* Carbondale: Southern Illinois University Press, 1961.

Porter, James, ed. *The Ballad Image: Essays Presented to Bertrand Harris Bronson.* Los Angeles: UCLA Center for the Study of Comparative Folklore and Mythology, 1983.

Recording Tools

Brady, Erika, et al. *The Federal Cylinder Project, Vol. 1: Introduction and Inventory.* Washington: American Folklife Center, Library of Congress, 1984.

Gronow, Pekka, Richard Spottswood, et al. *Ethnic Recordings in America: A Neglected Heritage.* Washington: American Folklife Center, Library of Congress, 1982.

Cultural Pluralism

Matthews, F. H. "The Revolt against Americanism: Cultural Pluralism and Cultural Relativism as an Ideology of Liberation." *Canadian Review of American Studies* 1 (Spring 1970): 4–31.

Greenbaum, William, "America in Search of a New Ideal: An Essay on the Rise of Pluralism." *Harvard Educational Review* 44 (August 1974): 411–40.

Higham, John. "Ethnic Pluralism in Modern American Thought." Chap. 10 in *Send These to Me.* New York: Atheneum, 1975.

Gans, Herbert J. "Symbolic Ethnicity: The Future of Ethnic Groups and Cultures in America." In *On The Making of Americans: Essays in Honor of David Riesman,* ed. Herbert J. Gans. Philadelphia: University of Pennsylvania Press, 1979.

Mann, Arthur. *The One and the Many: Reflections on the American Identity.* Chicago: University of Chicago Press, 1979.

Wacker, R. Fred. "Assimilation and Cultural Pluralism in American Social Thought." *Phylon* 40 (December 1979): 325–33.

Gleason, Philip. "Americans All: World War II and the Shaping of American Identity." *Review of Politics* 43 (October 1981): 483–518.

Stitching Patchwork
in Public

n the United States, we live with a sense of contrast between special and common interest. Although boundary lines remain unclear in dividing zones—margin from center, section from nation, private from public—we invest the public zone with awesome power. The word *public* holds strong associations: commonweal, general welfare, service to others, selflessness. Historically, this key word refers to those people who constituted the Hellenic city state. Over time, this then narrow body politic came to include Greek and barbarian, man and woman, master and helot. Further, within the modern state, the many children of helots, putting stigma behind, assign to each other the quality of constituting the whole and wholesome public.

We understand the term *public domain* to cover the people's land, unencumbered. Similarly, songs and stories in the public domain belong to all people, not to private copyright holders. Today, the locution *public house* seems quaint when applied to an inn or saloon. By contrast, the modern terms *public service* and *public sector* are extended from supplying utilities and guarding health to new functions: conserving endangered forms of expression, advocating minority rights, placing cultural equity on the political agenda, seeking links between natural conservation, historic preservation, and ethnographic documentation.

Who accepts such present-day duties as central to professional life? The answering phrase *public sector folklorist* emerged but recently. For a decade these innovative agents have stitched their skills and ideals into figurative patchwork. During 1975 teachers and students in a graduate seminar at the University of Texas used "folklore and the public sector" as a course title.[1] By 1981 the compressed *public-sector folklore/folklife*

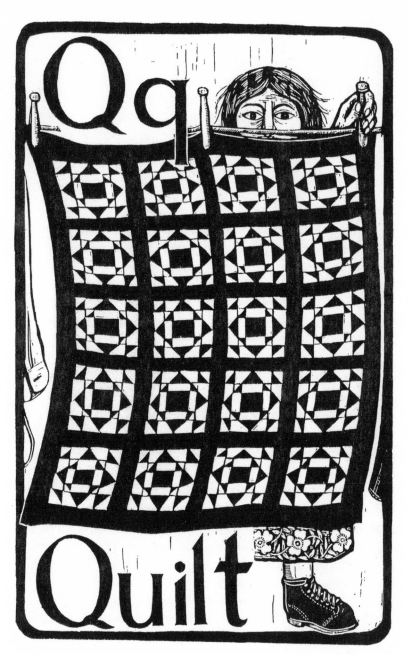

"Quilt," by Mary Azarian, woodcut for notecard, Plainfield, Vt., 199—.

had become a compass pointing to employees within governmental agencies, as well as to their demarcated skills.

New names do seem stiff; one does not casually roll into ordinary speech "public-sector folklore/folklife" to identify governmental activity. Fortunately, others share our responsibilities if not full titles. Arts agency coordinators, cultural resource managers, park rangers, museum curators, library storytellers, and festival fieldworkers hold similar jurisdiction in the public area. Together, we and they thread folk expression into public-policy discourse.

These new workers in folk programs cannot estrange themselves from ideological dispute nor escape the tension built into governmental action. Much of the political debate engendered by President Reagan centers on whether or not his administration enlarges or diminishes American differences. Is the president's public singular or plural? Does he speak for all or a few of our citizens? In stark terms White House staffers present issues: sunbelt against rust belt, rich against poor, white against black, moral majority against secular humanist.

Folklorists hardly address these polarities directly, for our disciplinary experience has not been shaped at the convention rostrum nor during the torchlight parade. Rather, in complementing past teaching, we mainly have collected and commented upon discrete items of lore. Even when sensing the connection of quilt or ballad to social issue, we have felt more comfortable with the quilter or balladeer than with the legislator or bureaucrat.

The contrast touched here bases itself in intimacy and articulation. Folklorists are drawn initially to quilt pattern or purpose, to ballad tune or text. Like countless other creative forms, folk constructs carry a high affective charge. Familiarity with admired shapes or symbols becomes circular. The quilt's beauty or song's quality appears too obvious to need explication beyond a limited circle of disciples. We seem especially at a loss to join personal esthetic pleasure to public issue. Long training on campus helps one accept this sheltered site as "natural" turf while distancing self from Capitol Hill, statehouse, and city hall. Like a prince transformed into a toad, a folklorist may become diminished in the bureau chamber. Who helps cultural explorers in their own transformations?

I have long maintained linkage in teaching lore and engaging in its preservation and presentation. As well, I have asserted that folklorists should accept service to those from whom they gain kudos. This sense of parallelism joined to the welfare of others has shaped my views of tasks in public cultural projects. Field collectors have had the freedom to return to the laboratory with trophies caught by camera and tape recorder. Members of folk society often have been left stranded to face bullhorn and TV dish, bulldozer and tank. It seems but a matter of justice for teachers and officials to articulate their responsibilities to folk communities.

Public folk service, at its best, can be felt as an exciting calling—in spirit, aligned to the work of forest lookout and ghetto nurse. In this vein, one can *do* folk displays as one *does* literary criticism for a metropolitan newspaper or oral history for a neighborhood center. Essentially, fresh tasks and bold visions alter internal guides as we focus upon the complex traditions with a multicultural society.

The word *public* dominates the new workplace. Surely, it signifies more than a physical site removed from campus grove. In deciphering this very old word, we ask: How do we aid the large public by concentrating on groups set apart by region, ethnicity, occupation, language, religion, and similar institutional forces? Is it our main purpose to support a host of clashing identities or to assist individuals' and groups' subordinate differences in the quest for national unity?

Young professionals in the years ahead will address these concerns as they prepare objective reports on their museum exhibits, craft demonstrations, film showings, and festival happenings. Wise servants will match highs and lows in their accounts and close glowing papers with open-ended questions. Inevitably, public folklorists will develop special strategies as well as distinct rhetorics. We can assume, before long, a gathering of self-contained reports into a sequential history of public sector folklife—origins, pioneers, monuments, emblems. A historian might well begin with the metaphor of patchwork coverings, bewildering in size and shape and not always congruously patterned or colored.

I can best assist colleagues in opening that history by calling up two experiences which stood behind congressional lobbying for the American Folklife Preservation Act. My formal report to members of the American Folklore Society, "A View from the Lobby" (1976), had outlined the enactment of initial legislation.[2] Dual anecdotes at this juncture illuminate this "view," as they add footnotes to my sense of the public I then served.

At year's end, 1962, the American Folklore Society met at Austin, Texas. Our Sunday morning closing session, sparsely attended, included a paper on the National Folk Festival by Sarah Gertrude Knott, the event's founder. An indefatigable and strong-willed crusader for public programs, she had come to vernacular culture by participating in the Carolina Playmakers. This group of student actors and writers at Chapel Hill had stimulated interest in regional folk drama in the early twenties. As well, she had worked with Bascom Lamar Lunsford after 1928 in his path-breaking folk festival at Asheville.

Many academic folklorists questioned Miss Knott's credentials. Undaunted by raised eyebrows and pedantic criticism, she plunged into festival politics and publicity. In Washington she had learned of early plans for an arts and humanities foundation. Intuition told her that folklore belonged within the yet-unborn endowments. Pleas to enlist academic support, both for lobbying and fund-raising efforts, fell on deaf ears. Rejecting naysayers, she marched directly to the Folklore Society's annual gatherings. In 1962 some members of the Austin audience were put off by her style; others dismissed her as an outsider.

MacEdward Leach, presiding at the AFS meeting and ever the gentleman, appointed a committee to respond to Miss Knott's challenge, for he was conscious that editors, publicists, and legislators had encircled the discipline and had defined our Main Street roles. The specter that haunted the AFS sounded like the Kingston Trio and resembled a *Life* magazine art extravaganza. Professor Leach selected me as committee chairman—my first formal assignment to carry the word beyond ivy towers, to ward off the popularizer's spell.

Following the annual meeting, I visited Mac in his University of Pennsylvania office. Eager to start, I asked him for an agenda, an action plan. Kindly, he informed me that he could provide no funds, no space, no paraphernalia, no troops; only good cheer. Needless to say, I returned to my prairie library post, and the "action" committee died of inactivity. However, the vivid lesson of Sarah Gertrude Knott, embattled in Washington and isolated from the academy, remained in mind.

On March 20, 1969, in the Ninety-first Congress, Sen. Ralph Yarborough, chairman of the Committee on Labor and Public Welfare, introduced the first folklife bill. Next, Jim Hightower, a feisty Texas populist, and I formed a citizens' lobby tied together by a proverbial shoestring. Ralph Rinzler, then heading the Smithsonian Institution's

Festival of American Folklife, worked as closely with us as his federal position permitted. Learning from past experience, I made a special attempt to enlist university people in the Citizens' Committee for an American Folklife Foundation.

Senator Yarborough scheduled hearings on his bill for May 18, 1970, and called a number of persons to testify, including Richard Dorson from Indiana University.[3] Sadly, Professor Dorson used the opportunity to criticize the bill, asserting that its proponents debased the coin of scholarship. Further, he charged that activists would lead the discipline into totalitarian darkness. I was dismayed but undaunted by these fears.

It seemed to me then (as it does now) that folklorists in the United States were committed to a democratic polity and worked within Jeffersonian traditions. In fact, lacking an overt political stance, we seemed better prepared than many university colleagues to explore matters of cultural pluralism. Field experience among isolated and marginal groups had helped us raise nettlesome questions about their relationship to the national state.

Memories from 1962 and 1970 surface to suggest that one does not come to public work out of philosophic abstraction alone. Before a Yarborough aide dropped the first folk bill into a Senate hopper, several of the bill's partisans had been drawn to folk expression: cowboy lament, street jive, Mormon myth, Blue Ridge pottery, bluegrass music, frontier tall tale. (Patchwork quilt, duck decoy, shrimp gumbo, jump-rope rhyme, or rain dance could well have played similar emblematic roles.)

Both Sarah Gertrude Knott and Richard Dorson enjoyed aspects of folk culture. One connected affection for song and dance with the political process; the other could not tie local legend and personal narrative to public issue. Standing between Knott and Dorson, I tried to bond festival tone and seminar spirit in order to see political codes structured into cultural enactments. As a youngster I had never in my wildest dreams anticipated lobbying. Yet in the sixties circumstance permitted me to nudge folklorists toward the public arena.

The full story of the American Folklife Preservation Act belongs in thesis and monograph. I have employed impressionistic anecdotes to touch upon one folklorist's vision of public service, as well as to note one individual's move from campus to congressional corridor. A committee's failure and negative testimony by a colleague placed temporary barriers upon a difficult road. With time's perspective we see that our path to legislative victory and the articulation of large purpose was neither easier nor rockier than that of other citizens in pursuit of public interest.

Notions of public interest date back to popular debate in Athens and its sister states. During Washington years I never questioned that folklorists had important contributions to make to large society; nor did I feel disloyal to the academy as I sought fresh venues for graduates. Instead, I urged students to ground their abstractions at the Potomac's edge and, by extension, at the Golden Gate National Recreation Area or Huey Long's State Capitol-building-mausoleum on the Mississippi's banks.

In seeking folklife space in governmental bureaus, I judged a colleague's correspondence to Congress to be as meritorious as a learned journal article. Someone had to open legislators' eyes. Dell Hymes's letter to Sen. Mark Hatfield stands out.[4] The linguist had called for the retention of tribal language in Oregon and the necessity for scholars to participate in this cause. Professor Hymes knew that the native people with whom he lived and studied formed but a small American band. Regardless, he knew that the strongest wall could crash when even the tiniest stone fragmented.

I shall not pause to name the many individuals who lobbied for and built early folk programs in federal, state, and local agencies. Rather, I look back to a few central paradigms that helped collector, curator, archivist, teacher step across the public threshold. Formulaic speech and mnemonics store energy and comment upon transformations. Accordingly, in triadic model I suggest that folklorists have been, and will continue to be, partisans of particularity, preservation, pluralism.

One: The identification of cultural particularity. Massive tomes picture the American grain, its pitch pockets and knots. Portraits of New Jerusalem abound from Plymouth Rock to Missouri's Hannibal, to Haight-Ashbury, to Cape Canaveral. Essentially, assertion of the nation's independence in 1776 from the mother country necessitated a decolonization of arts and letters. Not only did James Fenimore Cooper transfer Scott's heath to our forest and prairie, but Irving, Hawthorne, Melville, Twain, and their peers took the King's English out of royal hands.

Religious dissenters, fleeing Britain to the Continent before undertaking the wide Atlantic crossing, complained that Dutch syntax had corrupted their children's speech. In short, before any pilgrim met a Massachusetts Bay native, colonial language had begun to distance itself from received English. John Witherspoon, Princeton's president, coined *Americanism* in 1781 to provide an emerging language's label. A century later, laymen and scholars joined together to form both the American Folklore Society and the American Dialect Society whose members gathered regional speech, homespun locutions, backcountry yarns, native poetry, and local song.

Each discovery of an indigenous song or story marked particularity. In time, scholars questioned whether or not our letters were inferior to those of England or any other European power. Early in the twentieth century, Harvard professor Barrett Wendell had asserted that American literature was derivative and unformed. One of his students, Van Wyck Brooks, deflected such criticism by suggesting a need for a "usable past" and by asking aspiring writers to search for particular or native roots.

Among the critics and documentarians who sought strength in useful traditions, Constance Rourke's name shines. In books and reviews or from open platforms, she declared American lore to be abundant, various, subtle, and sinewy. Rourke drew spirit from great-grandfather George Mayfield, a frontier child raised by Creek Indians. In her own days, she taught at Vassar, accompanied lumberjacks to the first National Folk Festival at St. Louis, served as editor of the *Index of American Design,* and perfected a confident writing style designed to make our cultural roots accessible to a wide public.[5]

During the thirties ballad scholars merged notions of usable past and particular present by attention to Huddie Ledbetter's prison chants and Aunt Molly Jackson's coal-mine laments. For a century song-catchers from the Atlantic to the Pacific had declaimed that they heard Americans singing in wondrous tones. Lucy McKim, George Pullen Jackson, James Weldon Johnson, Langston Hughes, and others directed attention to spirituals, black and white, and, ultimately, to the many folk religions thriving in the United States. Path breakers from Henry Rowe Schoolcraft and John Wesley Powell to Elsie Clews Parsons, Zora Neale Hurston, Mary Elizabeth Barnicle, Holger Cahill, Ben Botkin, and Alan Lomax championed American vernacularity in dramatic ways.

One could not establish the worth of rank-and-file culture within national letters and avoid black shantymen on the Gulf, brown vaqueros in the Southwest, or red hunters on the Great Plains. In a nutshell, folklorists helped discrete groups intrude their wares into literary anthology, national museum, and public festival. To be a folklorist meant to resonate to the myriad contours of American experience.

Two: The linkage of cultural documentation to preservation and conservation movements. The word *preservation* appears in the earliest statements of the American Folklore Society, referring to the folk's retention of its special lore, as well as to scholarly attention to this lore by outsiders. We can best see folklorists as *preservationists* by understanding the charge within the word *tradition,* constant in discourse. Pioneer folklorists believed that songs and stories *preserved* themselves upon entering the stream of tradition. In collecting, folklorists helped a "natural" process with formal *preservational* tools: archive, anthology, disc, film.

Conservationists today join documentarians in attempts to recapture portions of the American past. The verb *capture* is deliberate; one must battle to deflect a highway around a shrine or to appreciate a nasal song style subordinate to ubiquitous network tones. The shibboleth, "you can't stop progress," seems more American than apple pie. When engineers drain swamp, nesting birds give way to autos nested on asphalt. Is there a brackish essence that leads to the parking lot? Why do we believe that water nymphs design concrete culverts? Tropistic force may help direct a flower or leaf to follow the sun, but tropism neither drains swamp nor develops a continent. We make pragmatic decisions about technology within human ethical frames and then are amazed that this technology helps situate our culture.

Conveniently, *conservation* and *preservation* overlap as terms linking organic life to the constructs of human hands.[6] Because we had no Rhine castles or hallowed cathedrals, preservationists turned to symbols of nationhood—Independence Hall, Mount Vernon, Gettysburg. The Antiquities Act of 1906 extended this umbrella of patriotism to pre-Columbian and living Indian site and eventually to slave cabin or work tenement. Such progression from natal hall to Ohio's Serpent Mound, to Lowell's textile factories parallels growth in cultural sensitivity to the achievement of muleskinner or cropduster.

Within our discipline we know that George Lyman Kittredge explored New England rural beliefs, John Lomax gathered Afro-American worksongs, and Américo Paredes extended our knowledge of Tejano border *corridos.* We do well to ask: What animated John Muir's fascination with the high Sierras? What drew Ann Pamela Cunningham to preserve Mount Vernon? What led Rachel Carson to salty tidal pools? When did guardianship of a wilderness area also protect the inhabitants for whom mesa or canyon spirit were sacred? Who first articulate this connection of site to belief system? Answers to such queries come from the Sierra Club and the Audubon Society as well as the National Trust for Historic Preservation and the American Folklife Center.

Three: The assertion of cultural pluralism. At inception in 1812, the American Antiquarian Society faced a dilemma, still troublesome. Its founders shared the English language and citizenship in the United States, but what forms did antiquarians seek—Scottish ballads alive in Virginia, arrowheads in Ohio's forests, mission relics in California? Fortunately, some collectors of Indian artifacts learned tribal languages as others joined tribal elders in resisting efforts to annihilate or assimilate native people.

The antiquary's step across the line from collector to partisan, not always articulated consciously, is crucial in picturing the lineage for public folk projects. This step, made in a day or stretched out to decades, must be framed by our historical understanding: English colonists carried dogmas of savagery to American shores; soldiers, settlers, and legislators attacked Indians on their homelands; courts have been slow in reasserting even partial sovereignty for native people. Somehow, in this dreary progression, a few collectors paused long enough to assess stereotypes and to form some association with native language and legend.

Deliberately or not, the antiquarian who had the capacity to appreciate Indian expression began to play a counterhegemonic role in public life. The shapers of national goals saw Huron and Apache as enemies of progress. Early ethnologists veered between formulas of a singular destiny for the United States and tentative commitment to emerging statements of pluralism. We need to focus spotlights on pioneer pluralists—Moravian sect missionaries, expedition artists, myth seeker—who put aside images of native barbarism.

Facing all the implications in present-day ethnography, we help ourselves by attention to the contributions of philosophy teacher Horace Kallen.[7] Out of his experience as a Jewish immigrant child in Boston and from his teacher William James's description of a pluralistic universe, Kallen came to value diversity, openness, and experimentation within the polity. Reacting against the anti-immigration policies of zenophobes, he developed a conceptual key, *cultural pluralism*. Unable to draw a precise blueprint to refashion the state, he did help public debaters see traditionary groups, native and foreign-born, as sacred.

Kallen, as a Harvard graduate student, reached to the concept of cultural pluralism about 1906. Entering the arena of public debate, in 1914 he published a paper, "Democracy and the Melting Pot." In an attack on Ku Klux Klan *kultur*, he placed his locution *cultural pluralism* in print in 1924. During the thirties anthropologists Ruth Benedict and Margaret Mead championed a similar formulation, *diversity*. B. A. (Ben) Botkin, in his long commitment to intercultural education and liberal social action, drew upon Kallen's ideas to help push folklorists into public directions. Significantly, in the fifties Ben made common cause with Sarah Gertrude Knott upon the festival platform.

Cultural pluralism conveys varied meanings to scholars. Some focus upon black music as the most visible aspect of minority culture. Others champion the crafts of our newest refugees from Cambodia or Laos. Still others return to Indian beliefs found on the reservation and in the urban ghetto. Directly stated, folklorists do plug pluralistic messages into political circuits. In the act of commenting upon many cultures, we reveal the capacity to slow down assimilative as well as technological progress. Imaginatively, we reach under the melting pot to retard its flame. This skill in decoding expressive life helps fellow citizens make sense of tags in public discourse — coat-of-many-colors, mosaic, patchwork quilt.

I have pulled a conceptual set (particularity, preservation, pluralism) out of the past and linked it to patchwork. Obviously, Americans have long struggled to stitch together one quilt of many pieces as they have also puzzled over the old motto, *E Pluribus Unum*. Ten thousand events in our chronicle reveal how difficult it has been to forge unity, whether by imposition or consent. Generally, folklorists in the United States have worked within mainstream norms, accepting them as part of the natural order. We have been comfortable with dominant ideology — empiricism, pragmatism, parliamentary democracy, progressive reforms, the free market.[8] Only a handful of folklorists, using radical theses, have challenged majoritarian consensus.

In this past decade of advance by folklorists, some have worked to clarify their public roles. They have looked at the connection of daily tasks — netting a song or displaying a basket — to large statements of American identity. In rhetorical modes: Do folklorists best thread separate patches to the national cover, or do they best aid discrete groups to stitch their own small coverings? No facile answer presents itself; a single flashback to an episode in President John Quincy Adams's career offers perspective on the cultural dynamics built into such political questions.

In the War of 1812, as in the Revolutionary War, tribal people allied themselves with rebellious backwoodsmen as well as with the Crown's redcoats. At Ghent in 1814, Adams helped negotiate a treaty shaping American sovereignty. The English, unprepared to abandon their frontier allies and desiring to hem in the upstart nation, had suggested a neutral corridor at the Appalachian rim. Adams bristled at this proposed barrier, for he believed that Indians would benefit by Washington's territorial expansion to the West. Adams equated savagery and wilderness, seeing both as antithetical to national progress.

We need ponder this enlightened statesman's rhetoric about Indians as "wandering hunters," for it underlies much of America's challenge to subject and subordinate people. Reporting from Ghent to Secretary of State James Monroe on September 5, 1814, Adams wrote:

> Their [Indians'] only right upon land was a right to use it as hunting grounds; and when those lands where they hunted became necessary or convenient for the purposes of settlement, the system adopted by the United States was by amicable arrangement with them to compensate them for renouncing the rights of hunting upon them and for removing to remoter regions better suited to their purposes and mode of life. . . . To condemn vast regions of territory to perpetual barrenness and solitude, that a few hundred savages might find wild beasts to hunt upon it, was a species of game law that a nation descended from Britons would never endure. It was as incompatible with the moral as with the physical nature of things. . . . The proposal of dooming a large extent of lands, naturally fertile, to be forever desert by compact, would be a violation of the laws of nature and of nations, as recognized by the most distinguished writers on public law. It would be an outrage upon Providence.[9]

This flashback to Ghent should not suggest that Adams's views are lost in history. On September 3, 1985, Bill Moyers, in a CBS television program, asked, "Whose America Is This?" Reporting on illegal aliens in Florida, Texas, and California, Moyers gave doomsayers—some from the Federal Immigration Service—a chance to verbalize fear that "in ten years we will not have an American nation as we know it today." [10] The Spanish language aroused his interviewees' anxiety as did the sight of "wetback" workers on demanding construction jobs. Clearly, in the year 2000, we will not have a singular state made up of citizens only in the image of John Quincy Adams. Perhaps the main task of today's folklorists, by document and display, is to ease the transition from Adams to Moyers and beyond to the children of cotton pickers and hod carriers.

Teachers of folklore, planners of festivals, and advocates of folk-life funding have experienced frustration in explaining the word *folk* to political figures doling funds to cultural agencies. Americans hold no simple definition of the signifying *folk,* for it covers, alike, guitarist in Stetson, pioneer-day celebrant in sunbonnet, and ironworker in hard hat. Our very key remains problematic because a thousand years of babel have worn it to shapelessness. Germanic marauders first carried *folk* to Britain; Beowulf's narrators voiced *folk* as did King Alfred's scribes; it was hoary when it came down to Chaucer and Caxton.

In early usages *folk* denominated a single tribe, race, or nation, as well as an inner subgroup of retainers, followers, or serfs. The connotative span runs from horizon to horizon—from a tribe unified in custom and vital in spirit, to an inferior set of beings enclaved in the state. Obviously, our naming label *folk* lumbers under a semantic overload as it accommodates notions both of power and marginality, strength and weakness, all or some. Afrikaners in Pretoria declaim *Die Volk* in its oldest emotive sense (singular, wholesome, mystical), while American journalists often reduce *folk* to the zany conduct of motley folk heroes—bank embezzlers, aging rock stars, sports titans, centerfold queens.

No folklorists in the United States and few public officials of consequence have fallen back recently on *folk* to justify belief in an all-powerful people, bonded by one soul. Instead, folklorists have operated with notions of diversity and contributed to dialogue on regionalism and community empowerment. Oriented to expressive culture's dazzling range, they have shored up the claims to attention by *all* the totem carvers, *all* the patchwork stitchers.

Americans are well acquainted with the now-magic wand *public re-*

lations. Constantly, messages (seen and heard) extol product, person, place: buy this, enjoy that, fear them, join us! Few governmental folklorists seek personal publicity, but each festival brochure or exhibit catalog we edit makes known our documentary and presentational skills. In this sense, we are defined by that which we picture and report. A public folklorist brings a stonemason to the National Mall, a sail maker to the Hyde Street Pier, a bead worker to the Academy of Science, a quilter to the State Fair at Columbus. Even when the presenter mutes formal message, the craftsworker's hands trumpet legitimacy: Not every product is plastic; not every skill, robotized; not every craft object, uniform. As folklorists enter public service, their academic colleagues, too, seek new publics.[11] Newspaper columnists and TV editors have relished the comments by university-based teachers about consumer response to Procter & Gamble's logo, a crescent moon against a field of stars. Folklorists have not been surprised that the firm, facing business loss, has withdrawn its trademark and denied that this design stood for the "Church of Satan." Similarly, bizarre tales of poodles in microwave ovens and alligators in city sewers have generated considerable publicity for explicator and analyst.

I confess ambivalence over such attention to our discipline; folk studies deserve wide attention, yet I am troubled by press and screen preoccupation with trivia, nostalgia, and latrinalia. Clearly, scholars must be free to examine all human experience, as their peers in government treat the expressive life within bounded communities and this life's ideological dimension.

The alligator-in-the-sewer story and the Church-of-Satan belief become useful when interpreted as political metaphor. Demons do inhabit my cosmos; they subjugate native people, destroy time-tested lore, abuse political consent, and poison physical and moral environments. They inhabit Washington and Moscow, Santiago and Kabul. They flaunt titles: President Marcos, General Jaruzelski. Hence, I am wary of all the giants and goblins who oppress the vulnerable.

Elsewhere in this book, individual folklorists describe public projects. As an audience member at museum display and park performance, I have enjoyed such events. In varied sites neighbors now show folklife in its infinite variety, unencumbered by sensationalism. Their offerings defuse notions of exotica, as they open eyes and ears to everyday life's sustaining symbols. In a narrow sense, the specific setting for these public folk displays is a tax-funded agency. In a large sense, such events are framed by journalistic reports that comment upon power relationships throughout the world.

In the classic trilogy, *U.S.A.,* John Dos Passos brought experimental techniques (biographical portrait, camera eye, newsreel) to expand his narrative. Folklorists, too, need a constantly running newsreel as supplement to catalog, program book, or annual report. In this vein, I select a few vignettes from the press in the period during which this essay has jelled. These selections describe neither item nor process of folklore. Instead, they report on the shaping of our identities.

Gentrification's Price—San Francisco Moves: Yuppies In, the Poor Out (*Los Angeles Times,* April 3, 1985)

In recent years, there has seemed to be a new consciousness and fear spoken and unspoken—that America is losing its white, English-speaking identity. The nativist movement, or set of backlashes, also explains "the new patriotism." (*New Yorker,* October 29, 1984, p. 132)

Ozark Lead Mine Strike Turns Bitter Amid Violence. Striker Gary Priest, 41, who has followed his father, grandfather and great-grandfather into the St. Joe mines [said] "I'm going to be the last generation of Priest to work here. It used to be like a family. It isn't any more." (*Los Angeles Times,* October 18, 1984)

Indiana family faces loss of a farm where its roots go back 200 years. Someday the Clarks of Hamilton County could vanish much like their predecessors on the land, the Delaware Indians, victims of the changing times and government policy. (*San Francisco Examiner,* March 3, 1985)

Libyan leader Moammar Khadafy offered yesterday to arm a black army in the United States to create a separate state and destroy white America. (*San Francisco Chronicle,* February 25, 1985)

American Indian Movement leader Russell Means said yesterday at Bogota, Columbia he will try to recruit U.S. Indians to battle with Nicaraguan Indians against Nicaragua's government. (*San Francisco Chronicle,* May 24, 1985)

Schools Are Becoming the Battleground in the Fight against Secular Humanism. One teacher in Georgia says she hesitated before assigning *The Scarlet Letter* because of its references to witchcraft and adultery. (*Wall Street Journal,* August 6, 1985)

Raisa [Gorbachev]: No frumpy babushkas for this svelte socialist. She's not a peasant, clearly she's a paid-up Russian folklore princess. (*San Francisco Chronicle,* November 19, 1985)

[Dispatch from National Party meeting at Silkaatsneck, South Africa]: Several thousand whites gathered here for prayers, songs and a historic pageant. [Carel Boshoff, guiding light of the Afrikaner Volkswag (People's Sentinel), warned,] What we are undergoing is the darkest hour of our nation's existence. (*Washington Post,* October 10, 1985)

In the journalistic pastiche above, I have selected items highlighting this essay's conceptual elements. Readers can provide other newsreel bits. Of concern here is not the pungency of any given selection, but the role of daily reportage in marking intergroup sensibilities. One hears, as chaff, an eccentric tale about franchised food; one learns, as news, a report of death in Belfast or Beirut. In the classroom a professor may explain an urban legend as a strategy to take the edge off catastrophe, to cope with threats beyond personal control, to exorcize hidden anxiety. Such functional and psychological analysis of narrative serves scholars well.

Public folklorists, in presenting quilters or balladeers and their sisters and brothers, depart from classroom techniques, for the move from academy to bureau alters rhetorical modes. On campus, to develop a thesis, the teacher reads a text, retells a tale, shows a slide, plays a tape, or runs a film. In the park or museum, traditional narrators offer their *own* stories, craftsworkers demonstrate their *own* competence. Wise interpreters respect the integrity of those they introduce and are circumspect in framing analysis. Inviting a guest to a display event or public performance in order to enhance professional standing is not the folklorist's ultimate purpose. Beyond the invitation, some sense of the community in which traditional expression lives must guide the outsider's vision.

By connecting artistic act to nurturing setting, by striving constantly to explicate meaning within enactment, folklorists lay bare the ideological underpinnings of their choices. Folklorists volunteer to collect within the city slum, upon the eroded land, or at the Appalachian mine mouth; hence, they accept a special relationship to subjects. No matter how much one balks at terms *folk society* or *traditionality,* the sight of fellow citizens at the margins of privilege cannot be blotted from view. Such comprehension does not imply that all the people with whom we work are unlettered or downtrodden. However, to know this fact does not excuse one from seeing alienation and exploitation.

Lest I seem to picture tradition carriers as living only in the shadows of dismal tracts, I can report a warm visit to a Florida public library display.[12] There, a net mender, neither poor nor unhappy, plied his craft in the lobby. Browsers and borrowers paused at this unusual sight. Net mending is not strange in a harbor town; but why the library setting? What message did the folklife specialist intend in bringing the craftsman to the lobby? I suggest several possibilities: to preserve the net maker's access to tools and twine; to honor his craft; to comment upon continuities from sailing and fishing to the library's educational purpose; and, in this paper's imagery, to see the net as yet another bright patch on the body politic.

If one folklorist can comment on microheated poodles and subterranean alligators, another can comment on the scarred landscape of ideological conflict. We do well to mute esoteric analysis in introducing a festival or library guest, but such understatement need not diminish acceptance of the public's stake in our showing and telling. A thousand routines within folklife, throughout the land, make graphic the citizenry's interest in traditional culture. Returning to the example of the net maker's public role, obviously, he reveals traditional techniques to new audiences. Simultaneously, folklorists in libraries, upon festival grounds, and at interagency conferences metaphorically plait nets and stitch quilts. We strengthen public sector folklore by sharing the stage with our guests and, importantly, by seeing ourselves as actors in an analogic drama.

In stepping back from the stage, we return to statements of professional intent as well as to multiple definitions for the word *folk*. I am aware of such multiplicity after working with the rainbow of American folk groups. Some cling to the past; others engage gleefully in their own transformations. In helping those who value autonomy, I reject singular notions of nationhood. I do not see America flowing only in the Hudson or the Columbia. Nor do I cleave to a monolithic formulation of a homogeneous folk from Point Barrow to the Rio Grande, Diamond Head to Kitty Hawk.

Thoughts on the word *mainstream* bring my stitching to a close. While lobbying for folklife preservation, I heard many cynics say that the public didn't want to retain fossils: custom, belief, song, story, patchwork. In a ludicrous simile, one representative's aide told me that preserving folklife was akin to recalling dinosaurs to life. He admonished me to leave lore in museums and to bring backwards people into the mainstream.

The tag *mainstream* has served journalists as a synonym for place and person—hypothetical residence for Middle American, Main Streeters all. Folklorists know that the man-in-the-street, as well as the common man, long beloved in political rhetoric, is neither common nor only of one gender, color, humor, or locale. This knowledge flows from the city state's long march—philosopher king to helot and the latter's sisters, cousins, aunts.

Perhaps the anecdote is apocryphal that tells of the brave mountain girl whose dialect had been corrected and who told her teacher, "I don't want to be mainstreamed." This defiant youngster brings intensity to my underlying queries: Does the president open or close national doors? Where do cultural administrators find models other than those stamped out in White House media events? Do folklorists serve large society best by bringing people into America's dominant current or by encouraging them to swim against the current and even to bob in the shallows?

Fortunately, we are not required to make final political choices for the many individuals whose artistry we document and display. However, in our attraction to expressive life of all groups within the nation, we gain a sense of the modern state's cruel puzzles. The technological wizards, who deploy weapons into space, cannot always help aged residents displaced by instant condos. The masters of satellite communication, who beam programs over the globe, cannot always hear the fiddler at the village square. Surely, the tested rubric *public* still includes the displaced and the quiet.

Some folklorists are unhappy with notions of neglect, marginality, enclavement, ambiguity, powerlessness. Recently, a few teachers in the humanities have discovered corporate culture and have sought positions in managerial realms. When populism runs strong in the United States, monopolies are pictured as juggernauts. When populism runs thin, private enterprise throws off negative cloaks and casts doubt on governmental duties. It is well to note in the eighties that public servants continue to warn of hurricanes and earthquakes, guard against disease, control toxic waste, educate for citizenship, and highlight expressive diversity.

Coming to the academy after seasoning in a bicultural family and after learning a waterfront trade, I could help articulate a legislative agenda for folklife. While tramping congressional halls, I began to shake out disciplinary guides—particularity, preservation, pluralism. Reflecting on folklore's keywords and relishing pictures from America's corners, I enjoyed connections in teaching and preaching. Above all, I avoided anxiety over being stranded at the mainstream's edge. My apprenticeship in public sector activity revealed that our tasks are endless and our threads, limited; the patchwork we stitch, vivid and vital.[13]

NOTES

1. Archie Green, "The Naming Tag 'Public-Sector Folklore,' a Recollection," *Public Programs Newsletter* 3 (Sept. 1985): 16–17.

2. "P.L. 94-201—a View from the Lobby," reprinted in appendix to this book [orig. publication].

3. U.S. Senate, Committee on Labor and Public Welfare, *American Folklife Foundation Act* Hearings, 18 May 1970.

4. Dell Hymes's letter to Senator Hatfield, reprinted in appendix to this book [orig. publication].

5. Joan Rubin, *Constance Rourke and American Culture* (Chapel Hill: University of North Carolina Press, 1980); Samuel Bellman, *Constance M. Rourke* (Boston: Twayne, 1981).

6. See Ormond Loomis, *Cultural Conservation* (Washington, D.C.: Library of Congress, 1983).

7. Horace Kallen, *Culture and Democracy in the United States* (New York: Boni and Liveright, 1924); *Cultural Pluralism and the American Ideal* (Philadelphia: University of Pennsylvania Press, 1956).

8. Archie Green, "Interpreting Folklore Ideologically," in *Handbook of American Folklore,* edited by Richard M. Dorson (Bloomington: Indiana University Press, 1983), pp. 351–58.

9. Worthington C. Ford, ed., *Writings of John Quincy Adams* (New York: Macmillan, 1915), 5:115. See also Charles F. Adams, ed., *Memoirs of John Quincy Adams* (Philadelphia: Lippincott, 1874), 3:28.

10. Moyers's quote from CBS press release. See Terence O'Flaherty's TV column in *San Francisco Chronicle,* Sept. 3, 1985, p. 50.

11. See, for example, three articles in the *New York Times:* "The Once-Simple

Folk Tale Analyzed in Academe," March 5, 1984, p. 15; "Folklore Thriving in Cities," Feb. 25, 1985, p. 30; "Folklore Mirrors Life's Key Themes," Aug. 14, 1985, p. C1.

12. I attended "folk days" in the St. Petersburg Public Library, March 30–31, 1984. Having observed similar events elsewhere, I note the lack of published reports on such close-to-home presentations.

13. Thanks to Burt Feintuch for helping to turn an "after-dinner keynote talk" into an essay.

Remembering Jack Fitch, Pile Butt and Artist, on Labor Day 1994

U nion activists use Labor Day to sum up past glories or to call for holding the line against job erosion and civic loss. We celebrate great leaders, masters of rhetoric or political maneuver. Seldom do we pause to remember obscure figures—ash haulers, wood hewers, freight handlers, cafe hashers, skirt hemmers, faith healers.

Who will write the obituaries for San Francisco's remaining blue-collar workers? After a steel erector falls to his death or a fisherman drowns in the Bay, we may learn something of their lives in a newspaper accident story. Perhaps the evening news adds a picture of twisted girders or wreckage on the tide.

What if these workers die alone in cheap hotels, charity wards or street doorways? When they outlive their buddies or leave no heirs, who recalls their adventures or sorrows? Who gathers to mourn them?

Jack Fitch. Born Sept. 17, 1899. Died Feb. 27, 1994. Another handful of years and he would have spanned three centuries.

Circumstances brought us together in the mid-1950s on a memorable job in San Francisco and, subsequently, permitted me to interview him for a book on labor lore.

We met at Market Street's huge Furniture Mart. Cahill Brothers had contracted to add a new floor to the building—tear out concrete roof, extend walls, raise penthouse, keep elevators running night and day.

Jack handled with ease the heavy timbers (temporary penthouse) nested around the elevator shaft's top while we jackhammered out the old structure. We kept quiet eyes on humming motors and whirring cables, all whispering danger.

Jack Fitch, "Untitled"
(Courtesy Ames Gallery, Berkeley)

Retiring on Social Security and a carpenter's union pension in 1966, Fitch turned back to an early love, oil painting.

He lived at 567 Minna St., filling the top floor of a rented flat with easels and paintings. Using oils, canvas and masonite, he created a personal gallery. When he ran out of wall space to hang works, he painted new ones atop the old.

In 1983, Fitch reluctantly told me something of his story, noting that it had been uneventful. Born on a Minnesota farm, he seemed destined for a hardscrabble life. In his teen years, he lost his mother. When his father remarried, the stepmother "shoved me out into the world."

Fitch, a young "straw cat," followed the wheat harvest in North Dakota, meeting "red-card" Wobbly organizers for the Industrial Workers of the World.

Riding boxcars to the Pacific, Fitch felled timber in the Northwest, helped raise San Francisco's O'Shaughnessy Dam in the Hetch Hetchy Valley, cut mountain-lake ice for reefer rail-cars and toiled on the Colorado River's Hoover Dam. During these years of migratory labor, Fitch joined the ɪ w w, traveling with a red card hidden in his shoe.

In 1928, on a Western Pacific Railroad bridge gang on the Feather River, Fitch broke into pile driving, joining a craft union, the Brotherhood of Maintenance Way Employees.

Like many construction hands, he gravitated to San Francisco for jobs on the Golden Gate and Bay bridges. On September 8, 1933, he joined Pile Drivers Local 34, holding a card until his death. "Pile butt" is the nickname for a member of a pile-driving crew. When a piling is driven downward, tip first, the butt end is pounded by a huge hammer.

Despite reminders to me that he had lived just like countless other pile butts, Fitch had keen ears for job lore. He alerted me to new terms.

"Sand monkeys" walked ahead of ox or horse teams, spreading sand on icy roads to keep wagons (with sleigh runners) from sliding downhill, thus killing the dray animals.

To prevent the sand from freezing, the boys kept it in hot buckets. Jack sketched verbal pictures of steaming sand and scurrying boys on wintry days.

"Chickadees" were boys who followed the lead wagon and shoveled droppings out of the snowy road. Why "chickadees"?

Fitch paused, "Just like a bird pecking for seeds in cow dung."

Fitch never married and lost touch with his farm relatives. In San Francisco, during New Deal years, he enrolled in WPA art classes in the Montgomery Block. He also took a few lessons with Spencer MacKay at the California School of Fine Arts. Beyond these classes, he remained self-taught.

He did not tell me why he turned away from academic painting or found it unsatisfactory. In time, he took up a style, often labeled "folk" — flat surfaces, skewed perspectives, bright colors, idealized figures, bucolic sites.

I never heard Fitch call himself a "folk artist." Nor did he use parallel terms: "traditional," "naive," "visionary," "primitive."

Fitch selected a few limited subjects from his past: lonely men in city cafes, "girls" sunning themselves in front of Nevada "cribs," a mother bathing her child, families on porches, mountain meadows, forest landscapes.

In my visits to his flat, I never saw a scene of a bridge, dock, wharf, pier, jetty, caisson or derrick. I asked if he'd paint (for me) a pile-driving rig, one that he knew from decades of familiarity.

He indicated that, long ago, he had painted from memory a Minnesota logging-camp bunkhouse—men chewing "snoose" (snuff), shooting the bull, searching for lice, drying clothes around pot-belly stoves—but that now he only treated pleasant matters.

"Would you sell me a painting?"

"No, I want to keep and enjoy them all."

Previously, I had never met a folk narrator who so flatly refused to part with a song or story.

Internalizing my thoughts, I probed the boundary between my concerns and his privacy. On our Furniture Mart job, Jack had not confided his artistry. Nor had I confessed to him a deep interest in workers' culture.

Over the years, I had worked with many waterfront and construction stiffs who used free time to follow sports, hunt and fish, or serve in community causes. Fitch painted. We shall never know how many paintings he finished and covered over, or how much of his "uneventful" life he played back in his mind while living in a private art gallery.

Dwelling South of the Slot, close to Skid Road for half a century, Fitch found some social life in Local 34, an unusual union bridging interests of waterfront red-hots and building trades hard-hats, who pulled together extremes in trade-union philosophy.

Fitch avoided sectarian union politics. He did remember enjoying a special cultural event in 1934.

Two fellow workers, Jack Kaufman and Joe Murphy, active in the Jack London Guild, had performed in "Singing Jailbirds," a Wobbly drama by Upton Sinclair based on the San Pedro maritime strike in 1923.

Fitch had no formal education after leaving home. Like other itinerant workers, he learned to judge blowhards on the job and piecards at the union hall.

Beyond work and art, he kept to himself, living austerely in a neighborhood of "urban blight." When he learned of my folklore interest, he suggested that I read James Stevens's "Paul Bunyan." I failed to convince Fitch that his deeds held as much value as any fantasy about a legendary lumberjack.

For many years, Fitch regularly attended the Pile Drivers' annual old-timers lunch—steak, wine, raffles, talk, companionship.

Introduced as the oldest member present, he would not make a speech. Rex Jones, another Local 34 veteran, usually accompanied Fitch. Missing Fitch at the 1994 gathering, I queried Jones. He replied, "He died a few weeks ago."

Such news, even for old-timers, never comes easily. Jones doubted that Fitch had left a will or had promised his bank funds to an art school or labor archive.

I asked, "Could we rescue a few of his paintings for the union hall?"

Jones said I'd have to see someone at City Hall to learn if they had been saved or carted to the dump.

Although I had long been content to write about workers as creators and carriers of tradition, I was at a loss to know how to rescue Jack's paintings. If they were saved, where would they be hung? Who would read their messages? Would Jack's art hold meaning for young pile butts who now hone his tools and carry on his craft?

On June 10, Pile Drivers Local 34 wrote to the San Francisco public guardian to request the Fitch paintings for exhibit in the union hall and for donation to area museums.

However, the paintings had been transferred to Butterfield & Butterfield for auction sale this month. A spokeswoman declined my request to photograph one of the paintings to accompany this article. The irony, for a former Wobbly, is that the proceeds will go to the state, along with his considerable savings.

(Perhaps someone who reads this piece will advise other old-timers to consider the wisdom of bequeathing job-related memorabilia, photos, journals, publications and other historical materials to their union, a museum or an educational institution.)

Today, these words represent a belated appreciation for Jack Fitch and all the other former sand monkeys, chickadees, wheat threshers, timber beasts, ice cutters, bridge builders, pile butts and everyday artists who slip away quietly within the shadow of the world they erected and maintained.

Rest in peace, Jack. You did not greet Labor Day, 1994. Your adze and maul have been put away along with your camel's hair brushes. Ask for directions to the heavenly art store. Stock up on oils, canvas and masonite. And paint a few pile rigs for Saint Peter.

Kelly Girl

The CEO in a company downtown needed some short-term help. He called the Kelly Agency and asked for a temp who would enjoy a modern office. The Kelly manager said she'd have a very good worker there at 10 A.M., the next morning.

That day the CEO was ready at 10. He was surprised to hear a scratching at the door. He opened it, and in jumped a dog—nice brown hair, soulful eyes, trim legs. Pausing to catch his breath, the boss asked, "Are you the Kelly girl?" The dog barked, "Bow-wow."

Not knowing what to do, the man asked, "Can you type?" The dog jumped into the chair at the desk, hit the keys with its paws, and barked, "Bow-wow." Next, the boss asked, "Can you make coffee?" The dog trotted over to the corner, heated up the Silex, handed the man a steaming cup, and barked, "Bow-wow."

Worried about what to do, the boss asked, "Do you use the computer?" The dog hunched up to the keyboard, flicked a switch button, waited for the screen to light up, and barked, "Bow-wow."

The CEO, amazed, had only one card left. He asked, "Are you bilingual? Pleased as punch, the dog purred, "Meow!"

Source: Charlie Chavez, proprietor of El Manito Barber Shop, 3112 Twenty-fourth Street, San Francisco, told me this story on June 16, 1993. I wrote out his text the next day.

BACKGROUND

"Kelly Girl" may have derived from a shaggy-dog story, but I have found no printed analogs. Told in San Francisco's barrio by a Mexican-American barber, it blends views of downtown office routines with

"The Typist," by Claire Mahl, for WPA *Federal Arts Project, 1938. In Mary Francey,*
American Women at Work *(Salt Lake City: University of Utah, Museum*
of Fine Arts, 1991). (Courtesy of Price Development Co., Salt Lake City)

ironic concern for present-day multicultural issues. Whether or not
other storytellers stressed different strands of ambiguity within this
tale, I do not know. Charlie had heard "Kelly Girl" from another cus-
tomer some weeks before he passed it along to me, but offered no special evaluation of the previous jokester's status or politics.

Torching the Fink Books

Andrew Furuseth, nearing his long journey's end as head of the Sailor' Union of the Pacific, joined his "boys" on the San Francisco waterfront, in 1934, at a ritual bonfire. Seafarers, longshoremen, and allies in other trade unions assembled, not far from the fink hall, to burn their hated fink books. This scene has long been remembered as emblematic of the Pacific Coast Maritime Strike—the Big Strike.

Technically, the Marine Service Bureau, a government agency, had issued identification booklets in which the ship's captain noted the details of a seaman's voyage and graded his performance. These employment records served to punish labor militants and to enforce union-free conditions at sea.

Rank-and-file sailors asked why they were expected to carry a blacklisting instrument in their own hip pockets. By staging a bonfire on the docks to express their feelings, seamen turned fink books, badges of oppression, into ashes; thus anticipating bright days of freedom on ship and shore.

Waterfront labor history reveals tales of heroism in which members fought and shed blood to replace the fink hall with the union-regulated hiring hall. The latter institution acquired the characteristics of a sacred temple; the former, the devil's domain.

The act of naming fink books paralleled this derogatory word's extension by trade unionists to scabs, strikebreakers, and related contemptible scum. Among other labor usages, we find fink hall (a government or company sponsored hiring hall); fink herder (an individual who supplies non-union crews—a shanghaier—a crimp); fink fac-

"Steady as She Goes," artist unknown. Sailors' Union of the Pacific pamphlet, San Francisco, 1937.

tory (a Maritime Academy training vessel or government-controlled school).

Over the years, scholars have asked how the term fink became widespread in labor circles. In my own studies, I have found more than a dozen fanciful explanations for origin, and literally hundreds of examples of usage in print and everyday speech.

To begin: "fink" the German-language name for finch (a family of singing birds) led to combinations such as "dreckfink" and "schmutzfink" which meant a bird pecking at or wallowing in dirt, mud, or excrement. A vulgar speaker might say that a fink resembled a shit-eating bird.

In time, "finkenschaft" emerged as a German noun to describe a group of students not in a "burschenschaft" (a fraternity sanctioned by the university). Elitists branded such non-in-the-clique-persons as undisciplined, slovenly, or barbaric. American collegians, who distinguished Greeks from Barbarians, accepted fink to range from campus nonconformist to habitual lawbreaker.

Harry Lundeberg, who succeeded Furuseth as secretary of the SUP, knew "skab" and "streikebryter" in his native Norwegian as labor words, and "finke" as a bird. In American vernacular English, he voiced stumblebum, hophead, dope-peddler, floater, Harvard stiff, and college boy, as synonyms for fink. Lundeberg considered campaigning against such lowlifes to be the highest duty of a unionist.

Naturalists have linked various birds with manure or carrion and still others, including the finch, with the squealing and singing of criminals, and with cheating or swindling by rogues. A stool pigeon decoys the unwary; to gull a person is to dupe him. As a young shipwright, I heard old timers warn me against seagulling or bypassing the union hall while seeking work. Only a fink would stoop to such behavior.

We sense the longevity of fink/finch in colloquial speech by reading Chaucer's *Canterbury Tales*. One of the pilgrims, the Somonour, holds an office in an ecclesiastical court by summoning sinners in cases of adultery and similar crimes. He is a despicable character, leprous and lecherous. He takes bribes; he fleeces those unfortunates who reside in his district.

Ultimately this court officer pulls a finch, a phrase which hides an obscenity, fornication. Translated, it means he plucks birds or seduces young girls. In short, Chaucer's Somonour is the all-time, all-purpose fink.

The many shadings for finch stand behind the use of fink as informer, snitch, gumshoe, shadower, secret agent, busybody, parasite, traitor. Fink itself carries hidden meanings; sailors knew fink house as a brothel or whorehouse, and fink is a prostitute. We enter a maze when we attempt to trace the exchange of such terms from the labor movement to the underworld, and back again.

Whale-ship crews used fenks (also pronounced finks) to describe the fibrous parts of whale blubber and other stinking offal. Seamen who worked the try pots (blubber boilers on deck) would skim off the refuse and discard it overboard. We do not know when a mariner first applied fenks/fink to a hooker, but the figure of speech, "You're lower than whale shit that sinks to the bottom of the sea" persists. Obviously, a miserable fink prostituted himself and consequently deserved no fate better than that in the shadows of the deep.

Because seamen regularly peppered their speech with fink, many listeners assumed it to be a waterfront coinage. However, to my knowledge, the earliest citations in the labor press represent other trades.

On November 17, 1910, the *Industrial Worker* ran a twelve-stanza poem by Lionel Moise, "The Workin' Stiff." He noted labels used to describe itinerants: cat, scissor-bill, bindle-stiff, tramp, Johnny Yegg, fly-by-night, scamp, fink. Moise's fink did not scab or strikebreak; rather, he harvested wheat, picked fruit, lined track, cut timber, stoked coal, dug ditches, and rode the rods seeking work.

The *International Socialist Review* (July 1912) reported a strike by Chicago newspaper workers in various craft unions. The *ISR* editors prepared a cover with a photo caption, "Five 'Cops' Guarding one 'Fink.'" This is the first clear use of fink in the context of a labor dispute. Hearst had enough clout to get city police to protect cowardly finks.

In the two examples above, an old negative term, fink, gains new meaning in both the context of migratory work and a bitter newspaper strike. Economic actions provided one setting for linguistic shifts; politics, another. Radicals, who favored speech rich in invective, especially targeted seafarers' unions. In long-forgotten sectarian wars, sailors ridiculed waterfront commissar George Mink by calling him Mink the Fink.

Words shift about and are recycled as social conditions change. New circumstances demand fresh locutions. At sea, vessels that fly under "flags of convenience" are no better than Barbary pirates ships in their disregard for humane standards. A half-century ago, crews called such rustbuckets, fink ships. It is time to apply this term to these hulls held together by bailing wire and phony registration papers.

Finks are now called replacement workers. Fink halls come disguised as career-enhancement centers. Sadly, only a few unions still control hiring practices. Some workers are told to rustle/hustle their jobs in the comfort of home by using computers as substitute dispatch tools.

Alas, finks thrive in cyberspace. Perhaps a twenty-first-century bonfire is needed to symbolically torch future fink books and engulf virtual fink halls in flame.

Peter Tamony
(1902–1985)

eter Tamony would have enjoyed for its absurdity the Kellogg's Corn Flakes 1993 television ad, "Taste them again for the first time." Can a first time ever be re-experienced? Tamony, working with words, knew that speech constantly appears in fresh guises. Taking pleasure in shifting old forms to new, speakers do proclaim firsts for recycled usages. However, I never heard Peter express belief in personal reincarnation, or the ability of a friend to make two initial entrances.

Curiously, I did meet Tamony twice for the first time: once, in 1941 at San Francisco's Dawn Club, then an innovative hot jazz venue; once in 1952, a few miles from the club, at his own Mission District flat/study/library. These two meetings, never logged in a diary, loom in mind's eye. I continue to see myself in Peter's presence, underground at the Monadnock Building and above ground at his residence. He looks over my shoulder as I write; he laughs as odd details surface; he commends me for conjuring a felicitous phrase.

At the Dawn Club, Peter collected tickets, greeting newcomers as if they had entered a charmed circle. He knew reporters, fans, critics, barflies, sharing Dixieland's excitement with all. A raw shipwright on the waterfront, I saw Peter's companions as quintessential San Franciscans, *hip* in that day's parlance. At the bottom of the club stairs, he seemed to guard much more than the entrance to a music hangout. Essentially, he welcomed citizens to a privileged forum.

By 1952, I had acquired books, phonograph records, and a few prints. Having ventured into "uptown" employment as a building-trade carpenter, I sank roots in a San Francisco neighborhood. While remodeling our Eureka Valley cottage, I attended union meetings, try-

Blues Singer, *by Miguel Covarrubias, in* Negro Drawings
(New York: Knopf, 1927).

ing to make sense of labor's post-war changes. Gradually, I fell in with a set of book collectors especially interested in labor history and lore.

After a stay in San Quentin, Jack Lawlor, a Noe Valley longshoreman and ex-felon, had been placed in Tamony's "care." Lawlor and I shared occupational yarns, rare book finds, and bibliographic details with ship's clerk Mitch Slobodek and ilwu librarian Anne Rand. Jack set out to introduce me to Peter, affirming that our interests ran in parallel channels. Literally, Jack helped me to ascend to Peter's aerie — more treasures than I had ever seen in a private collection; yarns spilling out of a leprechaun's bag.

Upon meeting Tamony in 1952, I tried to explain that I had met him a decade previously at the Dawn Club. He brushed aside my account in that it had not led to the camaraderie of word swapping. He implied that my initial exposure to Lu Watters, Turk Murphy, and other jazz greats had been entertaining, but not as vital as my "real" meeting with him — one in which we revealed to each other fascination with the American language. Somehow, he would help me treat speech as a cocoon to be opened.

Peter and I remained close until his death, July 24, 1985. I modeled my word studies (*dutchman, sabotage, Wobbly, fink, hillbilly music, cosmic cowboy, popsicle union, vernacular music*) on his papers on *jazz,* and assisted his sister Kathleen in transferring Peter's monumental collection to the University of Missouri, Columbia. Here, I salute a mentor and reflect on creative scholarship outside the Academy.

I look back at Peter Tamony as a keeper of a Celtic clan's lore, a bard in a magic three-storied castle — not in legendary Erin but rather in San Francisco's Mission District. Born on October 9, 1902, in his parents' upstairs flat, Peter attended the neighborhood's parochial boy's school at Father Peter Yorke's St. Peter's Church. In his childhood years, this portion of the city exemplified working-class life, with some youngsters beginning their march toward professional careers. Peter, reflecting on schooling, called himself "Father Yorke's favorite altar boy." From this challenging mentor — an agitator for Irish freedom, "modernist" in church dogma, and partisan of organized labor — Peter learned Latin rudiments, respect for book learning, and flamboyant rhetoric's power.

About 1905, the Tamony family purchased a flat at 2876 24th Street (near Bryant). Peter lived there until his final days in the St. Francis

Hospital. This act of physical continuity, of living in one house for eighty years, marked a persistent journey in self-education and an articulated sense of community. Peter's roots in Irish-American life were obvious to all who talked to him. He wore his ribbons jauntily as a native "born and bred" San Franciscan; his enthusiasm for THE CITY bordered on chauvinism. He stayed in his neighborhood long after it became a Latino barrio, and enjoyed crossing the street to La Galeria de la Raza, a meeting place for Chicano artists, writers, and activists.

Visiting scholars invariably asked Tamony how he became interested in words, and why he turned his flat into an archive. Literally, for more than half a century, he packed hundreds of cardboard cartons with a million citations of dated examples of language in action: file cards, newspaper clippings, notes from remembered conversations, quotations from formal literature. He supplemented these holdings with an assortment of books, pamphlets, broadsides, posters, cartoons, letters, and complementary ephemera. However, word citations formed the collection's core—a massive alphabetical-chronological treasury of raw data.

While classical etymologists trained themselves in the ancient roots of European languages, Tamony turned his etymological quest into an exploration of American experience: the Gold Rush, beat scene, sports, jazz, show-biz, stock market, labor disputes, politics, erotica. Deliberately, he sought arenas where new events shaped and re-shaped the meanings of old words. Consequently, his case-study articles on given terms drew upon the disciplines of history, literature, and popular culture.

Beyond this wide commitment to text-in-context, Tamony employed word-play, at times favoring a near-Joycean style. His fondness for alliteration burst conventional bounds. I cite but one example from his paper on *shill* at outdoor fairs: "The shouting of spielers. The shill/sheal/shell of the 'pea-and-shell game.' The shambling shuffle of the sauntering shillagalee" (*ACC,* #16, 13). To a reporter puzzled by his most convoluted prose, he explained modestly, "I like to wake people up to the possibilities of their language."

Tamony's personal linguistic awakening reflected both Irish-American culture and an early affection for sports. His father, an immigrant from County Donegal, became a laundry teamster and steam-laundry proprietor; he died in 1918. This death turned Peter away from considering college to work as a messenger boy and code clerk in the Crocker

"*Tamony in His Library*," *by Bob Dunn, date unknown. (Courtesy Peter Tamony Collection, Western Historical Manuscript Collection, University of Missouri)*

National Bank. William H. Crocker, one of the Central Pacific's "Big Four" railroad builders epitomized San Francisco's moguls—Republican in politics, patron of arts and letters, libraries and museums. Under Crocker's watchful eye, Peter seemed poised on the threshold of a financial career.

A few doors away from the bank, Tamony found the Mechanics Institute Library on Post Street and became an avid reader. At the bank, college-trained clerks—"bon ton" speakers commuting from Berkeley and Piedmont—made Peter aware of his plebeian origins and urban-Irish speech rooted "south-of-the-slot" (below Market Street). This consciousness of the mix of ethnicity, class, and language in moral judgments helped Peter achieve sophisticated word studies well before he encountered practitioners of sociolinguistics or psycholinguistics.

As a teenager, Tamony began to notice that sports writers "made errors" in their stories as they used contrasting terms in describing similar events. His Christian Brothers parochial-school teachers had impressed upon him correct (prescriptive) modes of grammar and lexical choice. Sports columnists turned Peter's eyes and ears to plural and vivid (descriptive) patterns in speech. In short, how could two writers use contrasting terms to describe the same field action, and both be "right"?

Contracting tuberculosis at the age of twenty, Tamony spent a year at Canyon Center, a Redwood City sanitarium. There, he intensified reading of classics such as the *Arabian Nights* and the *Golden Bough,* as well as H. L. Mencken's then-provocative *American Mercury.* Upon Peter's return from the sanitarium, he made heavy use of the Mechanics Library for general reading, and the Sutro Library for English dialect dictionaries.

In 1932, Peter read, literally, from cover to cover all seven volumes of Farm and Henley's pioneer work, *Slang and Its Analogues,* making notes on familiar usages close to his own Mission District, Irish-American speech. About 1935, a friendly staff member in the Public Library gave Tamony access to closed stacks where he could examine the full run of Tad's (Thomas Aloysius Dorgan) cartoons, "Indoor and Outdoor Sports," in the *San Francisco Call.*

William Randolph Hearst had syndicated Tad's features nationally; the cartoonist helped extend "lowlife" usages such as *ballyhoo, drugstore cowboy, hardboiled, dumbell, applesauce, skiddoo, fliver,* and *the real McCoy.* From the beginning, Peter had been receptive to street talk, graphic art, sports reporting, and contemporaneous sound recordings. With his self-directed apprenticeship out of the way, he made an initial scholarly contribution to *American Speech,* "The Origin of Phoney" (April, 1937).

The bout with tuberculosis in 1922 had also pulled Peter away from his starting job at the Crocker Bank to one a stone's throw from home in Peter J. Haggerty's real estate office. PJ, an immigrant ship's caulker turned Democratic politician, related tales touching the earthquake/ fire, civic graft, patronage, saloon mores, ethnic clash, occupational customs, and, above all, the art of politics.

With the election of Franklin Delano Roosevelt in 1932, Haggerty became superintendent of San Francisco's Mint, thus enlarging his sphere of influence as well as that of his young associate. In 1938, Tamony secured a prized notary-public license from California's New Deal Governor Culbert Olson. With Haggerty's 24th Street office as a base, Peter became a "tax man," learning IRS codes by filling out forms for neighbors. Most IRS hands congregated in Young Democratic Clubs, where Peter's buddies involved him in early campaigns for public housing, then seen as a social panacea.

In those heady post-Depression days filled with personal and political hope, Peter and other jazz neophytes reached out to new music, making friends across the color line. The move to folk and folk-like music in the setting of New Deal reform involved a complex of esthetic shifts within American society. In the 1920s, some white intellectuals had been drawn to jazz and used its verve to freshen their poetry, fiction, and drama. During the "Jazz Age," this music served as a raw substance to enrich formal art and literature. Only a few critics saw African-American forms as intrinsically rich metal rather than as earthbound ore destined to be refined. Tamony's discovery of hot jazz and blues stands as representative of a wide awakening in the 1930s, a breaking of cultural and social barriers.

In childhood, Peter had known the jigs and reels of Hibernian picnics and fraternal gatherings. As a teenager, he favored basketball over social dances where he would have heard then-current popular music. Upon reading *Esquire* in 1934, he encountered unknown jazz terms as they seeped into white consciousness. Bud Rowland, a San Francisco instrument repair man put Peter in touch with black musicians who could explicate jazz language.

At that time, the Musicians' Union segregated Negroes into an unofficial Mason-Dixon enclave in the Fillmore District. Sweet's Ballroom in Oakland, a swing band venue, did feature black performers but divided audiences — white on Sunday, colored on Monday. Despite such practices, Tamony talked with Vernon Alley, Wilbert Barranco, Bob Barfield, Jerome Richardson, Saunders King, and other San Francisco black artists, knowing that they used an active language as it moved from gin mill and night club to lecture hall and cinema studio.

In 1935, Tamony began to collect jazz and blues records in great numbers, consciously selecting material from the race series rich in examples of black speech. He patronized Melander's Record Exchange at 172 Eddy Street where one could buy used 78-rpm discs for a nickel each. In those years, Peter brought obscure race records to radio shows which featured hot jazz, for example, Ted Lenz's "Jive at 11:05" on KSAN. During 1939, Tamony served as organizing secretary for the Record Collectors (Swing-Hot) of Northern California, arranging an important get-together (April 23) for members at the Golden Gate International Exposition.

Tamony, with characteristic humor, recalled the meeting. Previously, he had been invited to Treasure Island to talk on dialect. No one showed up to hear him except two lads who blundered in looking for their pet snakes on loan from the Josephine Randall Museum. While waiting for the non-existent crowd to arrive, Peter "cased the joint," finding a splendid auditorium with a piano and a radio-record player console which might be used for club gatherings. Fletcher Henderson, then appearing with Benny Goodman at the Fair, promised but failed to attend one of Peter's sessions. Nevertheless, 500 fans including local musicians did come; they agreed to organize San Francisco's Hot Music Society.

This dynamic Society owed initial success to the fact that its founding members included most of the Bay Area jazz disc jockeys. The new group made its public debut with Freddie Blue and His Six Dixielanders on Monday night, December 18, 1939, at the Dawn Club in downtown San Francisco. For subsequent sessions, Tamony secured Police Chief Charles Dullea's permission to serve spirits until 2 A.M. Local 6, American Federation of Musicians, made a special dispensation for "bonafide members" of the Hot Music Society to jam with featured musicians on Monday night. Technically, Peter recognized members as he collected their tickets.

In time, the Dawn Club's performers moved in varied directions: to the Fairmount Hotel to play for Nob Hill's glitterati; to the Green Room in the basement of the International Longshoremen's and Warehousemen's Union hall on Golden Gate Avenue adjacent to the Tenderloin. Peter helped bring Bunk Joyhnson, a New Orleans veteran trumpeter, to the union hall. Bunk and his peers gave San Francisco jazz a good times, hijinks audience, literally as bop and cool jazz moved in from the East Coast.

During 1952, when S. I. Hayakawa arrived at San Francisco State College to teach a summer course on popular music, Tamony sat in. He had been out of the classroom since 1918, but knew the professor's *Language in Action* (1941) as it had popularized semantics. Similarly,

Dr. Hayakawa had read Tamony's articles in *American Speech* and enjoyed the latter's presence on the Haight Street campus. The two word enthusiasts "hit it off," remaining friends through "Sam's" tenure in the United States Senate.

Present at a Hayakawa lecture in 1952 with Turk Murphy and Vernon Alley offering musical examples, I recall the message. Hayakawa championed hot jazz, opposing it to sweet; he identified black musicians as creative innovators, putting down white Tin-Pan-Alley popularizers for compromising the vitality in African-American expression. I liked part of the presentation, but felt troubled by Hayakawa's ignorance of old time and country music. He seemed oblivious to Uncle Dave Macon, the Carter Family, Harry McClintock, Jimmie Rodgers, Roy Acuff, or Hank Williams. Hearing my criticism of the semanticist's "tin ear," Peter encouraged me to study hillbilly music, to seek correlations between the intellectual discovery of white and black folk culture.

Among Tamony's friends in journalism, Ralph J. Gleason played a significant role. At Columbia University in 1939, the latter had started a mimeographed journal, *Jazz Information,* to which Peter subscribed. After the War, Gleason moved to California; he and the wordsmith met at a Kid Ory session in the Green Room, 1947. When Ralph became a critic for the *San Francisco Chronicle,* and as he helped launch *Rolling Stone,* he made extensive use of Peter's files. Tamony did not share Gleason's joy in rock-n-roll music or the rock generation's excesses, but the etymologist could not resist feeding words to the critic.

During 1958, Gleason initiated a prestigious quarterly journal, *Jazz.* Only five issues appeared; Peter contributed an innovative article to each on the terms *jazz, bop, jive,* and *swing,* as well as one on the locutions within Bessie Smith's "Gimme a Pigfoot" (Okeh 8949). For this article, "Bessie: Vocumentary," Tamony coined a keyword suggesting that a musical disc holding speech in its grooves became a vocal documentary, or, *vocumentary.* This neologism did not spread widely, but its underlying concept still guides scholars pursuing multiple uses inherent in sound recordings.

In July 1963, Tamony contributed an article to *Western Folklore,* detailing the many meanings of *hootenanny,* then especially significant to folksong revivalists. Wayland Hand at UCLA, recognizing a kindred soul, invited Peter to submit a series of articles on words for *Western Folklore.* In turn, this encouraged Peter, in July 1964, to privately publish and circulate a hectographed series, *Americanisms: Content and Continuum*. Totally free from editorial tampering, Tamony packed these articles with supercharged prose, acerbic wit, and a lifetime of thought on linguistic development.

Although Tamony served as a consultant to the *Oxford English Dictionary,* and puzzled through the meaning of hundreds of words, he never wrote out a full theoretical statement of his views. Perhaps he freed himself of this burden by virtue of independent studies, away from academic codes of advancement or tenure. We talked about this matter as I made my own jump from the construction trades to the University of Illinois. As best I understood it, Peter felt that his many findings on individual terms spoke for themselves. Such "theory" as he needed integrated itself in his descriptive studies.

Living by empirical and pluralistic creeds, Tamony eschewed grand design and singular formula. Yet, in his *Americanisms* papers, he did articulate commonsense thoughts on word formation and movement. A few examples follow:

A. Words are seldom "corruptions." That condition is in skulls, and on the pages of dictionaries, glossaries, etc. (*ACC,* #17, 12)

B. Editors and their etymologists of two-word and two-line origins, who feel one word "comes from" another, would not have to note so many origins "unknown" if successive extensions of meaning were recorded as they developed. (*ACC,* #16, 12)

C. To reach currency, a word must be grounded in varied social processes. . . . Neologisms do not pop out of the mouths of individuals, as many think, but are evoked in a speaker-hearer complex to reflect a succession of things or a cavalcade of events that seek to be metamorphosized. (*ACC,* #11, 5)

Perhaps etymology and dialectology attract free souls, distant from ivy halls, in that all humans hold the potential to explore their speech. Who is not expert on personal messages? Who can not demystify signs and symbols familiar since infancy? Who guards lexical chambers against amateur intruders?

Whether students remain on campus or venture to the agora, the conjunction of sound and sense seems to stimulate alternate explanations based on phonetic or semiotic arts. In an on-the-job setting, I heard a fellow worker offer a nativity scene for *gandydancer* as coming from Hindu track workers who worshipped Mahatma Gandhi. The "woodbutcher" (carpenter) assured me that he had been present at a Montana railroad construction site when "ragheads" (turban wearers) chanted "Gandhi, Gandhi" as they wielded rail tongs and tamping bars.

Tamony cautioned me against accepting such fanciful "origins." He urged me to read widely, listen clearly, and seek the constant interplay of phonemic and morphemic building blocks. One of his illustrations notes *broad,* describing a woman of loose morals; this label/libel dates to 1914 in use by American criminal crews: "*Broad* has sound and sense reinforcement from *bawd,* and is back-stopped by *broad gauge,* a railroad usage encapsulating the struggle between proponents of *broad-gauge* and *narrow-gauge* tracking, and the misconception that a part of the human anatomy enlarges with use" (*ACC, #12,* 1).

Peter never hectored me with trendy phrases or blinding concepts. Rather, he drilled with demonstrated examples of word extension from scene to scene. He made me conscious of *extension* as the key tag for a continuous and dynamic process—speakers transfer word meanings as wagon teamsters used to transfer trunks. Some words achieve fame upon delivery; others slip in under the door mat; still others never survive the trip from the depot.

To this day, I recall Peter's treatise on *hip,* not in a journal article, but as a one-on-one talk fest in his quarters—walls of books, tons of files. Without resorting to formal citation from either books or files, he talked to me as if we strolled in an ancient olive grove. He had no other chore than to reveal how words crawled and flew, skipped and jumped.

Many centuries ago, *hip,* an anatomical name, had shifted to denominate action and state of being when a wrestler pinned an opponent to the mat. "He's down, beat, on the hip, hipped." In time, drug addicts similarly used *on the hip* to signify a high while stretched out to indulge opium in a hop-house (den). Thus, *hip,* with great elasticity, came to invoke both consciousness of defeat in athletic circles and elation in the narcotics realm.

Sports fans and drug addicts together gifted *hip* to jazz cats who needed a term to encompass distance from the strictures of straights and squares. *Hipsters* found themselves both up/down, high/low, in relationship to conventional society. After Peter first explained *hip* to me, Haight Street hippies pushed the music fan's "in the know" or "with it" to cover contradictory states of beatitude, superiority, dissent, and scruffiness.

When Tamony discoursed on *hip,* he ranged freely from Will Shakespeare's Shylock to Tim Leary's dopey hype. Peter also alerted me to the conjecture of peers who centered analysis in vowel changes from *hip* to *hep* or *hep* to *hip.* Knowing that it might be hip to say hep in some circles, he also charmed me with a series of alternate etymologies, none of which dated back to wrestling speech.

Ella Fitzgerald warbled "get your hip boots on"; hence, a few fans based *hip* in the proper act of lacing boots to the hips. Some traced *hip* to the drill-sergeant's chant "hep, hep, hep"—meaning get in step, stay alert, be right. Others derived *hep* from the name of a famous criminal, detective, or saloon keeper (Joe Hep) and scoured city directories to make the point. Still others favored the phonetic *help/hep* tie, "God hips those who hep themselves."

I have no conscious memory of Peter invoking "folk etymology" to explain a locution after the fact of its extension from scene to scene. He did not waste time in "put-downs" to those who coined "fanciful origins." Although his studies were most imaginative, he saw himself grounding each word's story in social events and chronological appearances. Thus, I had but to open eyes and ears to advance beyond my initial hearing of *hip* as a jazz/swing honorific.

In his lifetime, Tamony rarely traveled far from home. He did tell me of a long train trip to Lexington, Kentucky, to accompany a narcotics prisoner to jail, and a trip to Seattle, Washington, to testify (victoriously) in a copyright trial on *hootenanny.* To make up for clinging to San Francisco experience, he read penetratingly in linguistic journals, corresponded widely, and attended University of California public lectures.

From time to time, Tamony entertained visitors with personal tours in San Francisco, and with feasts in fabled restaurants. On our forays, he associated particular persons and watering holes—Ben Botkin, Wayland Hand, Fred Cassidy, Dwight Bolinger, and other scholars had dined with him at Breen's, Taditch's, Earthquake Magoon's, or the Palace Hotel. He savored the memory of a "get-together" at the Old Poodle Dog, December 27, 1975, when the American Dialect Society toasted his work. Peter reciprocated with a case of Wente Brothers California wine. He democratically shared this same generosity with rank-and-file waterfront workers. Jack Lawlor and others left Peter's flat with gifts—often rare books in the visitor's field of interest.

One instance of Tamony's breadth in encouraging students need be cited for its lasting effects. In the 1950s, several American record collectors corresponded with John Edwards, a hillbilly disc collector in Sidney, Australia. I urged John to come to study folklore at UC with Bertrand Bronson or at UCLA with Wayland Hand and D. K. Wilgus. Peter shared my interest in such a journey, generously offering to help make it possible. We planned to raise funds by contributing to a "Friends of John Edwards" committee.

Edwards never made the trip; upon his untimely death at year's end, 1960, Eugene Earle, Ed Kahn, and I formed the John Edwards Memorial Foundation. In 1965, Tamony gave the JEMF, housed at UCLA, his huge stock of more than 2,000 race records. In time, we transferred JEMF holdings to the University of North Carolina, Chapel Hill. Presently, Peter's vocumentary discs serve students delving into African-American expressive culture.

I offer a note on Tamony's choice in records. While searching for jazz and blues items as dialect sources—locutions pressed into grooves—he found similar discs: hillbilly, cowboy, corrido, calypso, foreign language in general. However, he disciplined himself to concentrate on race records. His flat had limited space; his purse was finite; time to transcribe, precious. In retrospect, the New Deal's intellectual climate encouraged the discovery of black vernacular music. A jazz band could play on campus in Berkeley, in a radical union hall, or in an elegant hotel. Decades elapsed before country, old-time, western swing, or bluegrass musicians achieved comparable impact in the Bay Area.

Peter retired in 1958, simply by shifting back from Haggerty's office to the Tamony upstairs flat. He and his sister Kathleen had never married; Kate, upon her own retirement from office work, undertook to help Peter with his massive filing tasks. They divided long days into reading, clipping, collating, filing, and corresponding. In 1980, Tamony suffered a stroke which required hospitalization and physical therapy. This illness set him back emotionally; he had assumed that leaving bad habits behind in his youth would save senior years for continued study.

In the years 1960–1982, while away from San Francisco, I kept in touch with Tamony by visits and letters. Returning home, I resumed weekly visits to the upstairs flat. Conscious of Peter's and my age, I attempted to obtain a modest grant from the San Francisco Foundation to hire a student to help arrange the Tamony files for archival deposit. We anticipated an initial computer-based survey of holdings and an anthology of his varied articles. To my consternation, the foundation program executive rejected our request.

By 1984, Tamony could no longer lift the carton trays holding his word files. He overcame isolation to a degree by corresponding with Gerald Cohen at the University of Missouri, Rolla. Professor Cohen reprinted some of Peter's articles in *Comments on Etymology,* gathering other file material for future publication. Shortly before Peter's death, I indicated that I had willed my books, records, and files to the University of North Carolina. Would he like me to pack and ship his holdings to Chapel Hill?

For a moment Tamony felt encouraged, sensing continuity in his concerns. On reflection, he indicated that he could not deal with North Carolina's distance from THE CITY, his beloved San Francisco. A few weeks later, my wife Louanne and I joined Kathleen and a band of remaining friends for Peter's last rites at St. Peter's Church and burial at Holy Cross Cemetery.

Tamony left no will. For decades, he and Kathleen had shared their collection-filled flat. Conscious of time's demands, she asked me to make overtures to our Public Library and Stanford University. Years before, Peter had tried, unsuccessfully, to interest the University of California in his holdings. With local doors closed, I turned to Rolla, Missouri. Although Gerald Cohen had never met Peter, he understood the scope of his achievement, as well as the responsibility of associates to safeguard the word files.

At year's end, 1985, Professor Cohen visited Kathleen, suggesting that she might donate the entire cache to the University of Missouri. Sensing Cohen's respect for her brother, she agreed—no haggling over value, no limiting conditions. University librarian Tom Shaughnessy and director of the Western Historical Manuscript Collection Nancy Langford flew to San Francisco and arranged with Kathleen for the physical shipment of seventeen tons of material to Columbia.

San Francisco's great loss ended most happily. Nancy Langford, linguist Donald Lance, historian David Roediger, and archivist Randy Roberts formed a loyal crew to preserve and expand Tamony's gathering. In 1986, various University units joined in presenting the first annual "Peter Tamony Memorial Lecture on American Language." Despite Columbia's distance from San Francisco, Peter would have been happy at this yearly talk fest in sight of his cartons and tools, among them the hectograph machine upon which he "hand-printed" *Americanisms: Content and Continuum*. Yes, Columbia does continue Peter's life work.

We also find continuity in monographs touching Tamony's life, reprinting selected articles, or following his leads. I cite four items as researchers' entry points:

A. *Peter Tamony: Word Man of San Francisco's Mission*. Marjorie McClain, Folsom, Calif., Wellman Publishing, 1986. (Biographical sketch illustrated with photographs and graphics.)

B. *Studies in Slang, Part I*. Gerald Cohen, Frankfurt, Verlag Peter Lang, 1985. (Articles by Tamony and others.)

C. *Studies in Slang, Part II*. Gerald Cohen, Frankfurt, Verlag Peter Lang, 1989. (Articles by Tamony and others.)

D. *A Tad Lexicon*. Leonard Zwilling, Rolla, Mo., 1993, Etymology and Linguistics Principles, Volume 3, ed. Gerald Cohen. (Tad's career and word list; in Tamony's moccasins.)

Kathleen Tamony died on December 28, 1987, also at the St. Francis Hospital. During visits with her in the preceding two years, Louanne and I gave her news from Missouri. Randy Roberts shared her brother's passion. Peter would have reveled in such a willing apprentice. Jerry Cohen and Don Lance seemed indefatigable in reporting and lauding Peter's findings. Nancy Lankford "dug" Kathleen's spirited decision. The Lexicography Discussion Group of the Modern Language Association and the American Dialect Society had planned to honor Kathleen at their year's end, 1987, meeting in San Francisco; her death prohibited this event.

However, we know that as long as students remain curious about *hip, jive, rap, malarkey, hunky-dory, scarf, gonzo, scissorbill, sandlot, fuzz, camp, hot dog, funky, dyke, trip, Frisco,* or their related colloquial terms, Peter's work will be applauded. Although concerned whether his studies would continue in San Francisco, he never doubted that his curiosity about vernacular speech would infect others.

This memorial to a companion and mentor opened with an account of two initial meetings: jazz club; residence. I close with a final vignette set in the upstairs flat on 24th Street. At the end, Tamony remained calm, accepting Charon's call, not dwelling on his life of study or his immense collection, not fretting about the disposition of his files. Instead, he queried me about my then-current project, *Work's Many Voices,* a multi-LP reissue set of American songs drawn from 45-rpm discs. In turn, I asked when he first had encountered the expression *single* to designate a recorded song. Lost in time, he replied, "Too long ago to remember."

I could only offer a glass of water, and tug to smooth his sheets, unable to bring this musical term into his own chronology—listening to and writing about jazz, buying records, helping fans across the continent. Going to a bookshelf, I removed Robert Gold's *Jazz Talk,* and read the entry for *single* (from a singer or pianist working a club gig alone to a single 78-rpm disc): "The best single of the month is Barney Bigard's 'Lost in Two Flats'" (1940). That had been my CCC year on the Klamath River, and Peter's Hot Music Society efforts in San Francisco. He smiled, nodded at Gold's book, and said, "Why don't you take it along?" Frozen, I failed to thank him, knowing that it would be the last book he would ever give to any friend.

Peter Tamony and I, defying convention, met twice for the first time. In the decades of his mentorship, I conjured varied tropes to picture him, among them—word wizard, lore keeper, Celtic bard. In mind's eye, I continue to see him as a carter pushing a wheel barrow of words to a cliff's edge, and pausing to question whether to tilt the load into the abyss or to pull back to safe ground. As surreal as this image seems, it serves to evaluate his life work.

Never breaking completely out of his stance as a self-educated scholar and old-fashioned storyteller, Tamony helped me in the difficult transition from waterfront trade to seminar room and lecture hall. *Jazz Talk,* his closing hand-to-hand present, represented his countless gifts to citizens seeking language to explicate the human condition. We all live in a cocoon of speech heard and felt. Peter Tamony exampled others to puzzle their way out of each immediate, enveloping cocoon.

n looking back at four decades of writings touching vernacular culture, I have imagined myself a geologist traversing a roadcut, examining exposed strata, contorted intrusions, and metamorphosed formations. Pausing to examine particular expressions in music, speech, or art, I have likened them to gems or fossils embedded in rock. The age and circumstances of composition of a ballad, blues, tale, talisman, cabin, or canoe often remains mysterious, yet challenging. To questions of origin, I have added matters of form, use, and meaning in studies of literary and social texts.

I am not a geologist. As a folklorist, I seek metaphors to describe our terrain. We borrow variously: "melting pot," "mulligan stew," "patchwork quilt," "coat of many colors," "trails converging," "pluralistic universe." Six decades ago in California's Siskiyou Range, Lawrence Roberts, a Karok Indian, taught outdoor skills to ragtailed "three-C boys": how to work productively and safely in an environment of woodland sounds and water currents. Our spike camp rested between the fir-and-cedar-flanked Klamath River and the rainbow-tinted Marble Mountains. Roberts explained that spirits animated all nature; our task was to decode the role of salmon or serpentine. For example, this latter jade-green rock, abundant underfoot, could be carved into sacred amulets.

Roberts, too, was not a geologist. Rather, as a Forest Service/ Civilian Conservation Corps foreman, he led Depression-buffeted youngsters in their work. His understated messages have served me well over the years. He would appreciate my likening of a ballad to a rock-embedded gem. In his mind's eye, songs or stories became pebbles in the pouch of a ceremonial dancer. Fossils, in his cosmos, still

Man with Drill, *by Charles Turzak, 1931.*
(Courtesy Joan Turzak van Hees Studio and Gallery, Orlando, Fla.)

lived. This distant memory is out of sequence in my backward glimpse, yet it helps situate one starting point on a journey.

My gathering of a dozen articles—academic and popular—raises many questions, among them: What gave such intellectual activity coherence? Why did *folklore* emerge as a term to encompass my diverse interests? When did *vernacular studies* emerge to resolve some of the dilemmas faced by all cultural explorers?

As a youth, I had no conscious ambition to become either a writer or a folklorist; indeed, I had no knowledge of the latter as a possibility. While an adult, I seldom used such categories in self-description. Instead, I favored at appropriate times the titles *shipwright, librarian, teacher,* and *lobbyist.*

Shipwrights work a lifetime reading abstract blueprints and never commit their daily toil to paper. When I shifted from blue-collar to white-collar employment, writing came with the new territory. Bob Cantwell, in his introductory essay for this gathering, describes the elements that marked my path through the roadcut. Here, I retrace a few steps that seem, in retrospect, to have been defining. Perhaps the highlighting of anecdotes of growth will lend color to the selections.

Some writing forays transpired well before I made any career choice. While a Roosevelt High senior in Boyle Heights—an immigrant enclave on the east side of Los Angeles—I served as editor of our yearbook. My task consisted mainly of coordinating required picture shoots with the printer's business representative and selecting the book's theme. Without reflection, I fell readily into a clichéd subject: graduation as the start of a sea voyage, and our school principal as a seasoned pilot. Out of what ancient well of platitudes did I find words to frame my first editorial?

After I entered UCLA, an assignment in freshman English awakened me to the pleasure in writing. Bradford Booth, fresh from the Ivy League, had just arrived as an instructor. For our term papers, he gave students freedom to select topical subjects. I chose the then-newsworthy CIO (Committee for Industrial Organization), identified with recent sitdown strikes. Professor Booth encouraged me to pursue labor studies and to prepare to contribute in this arena.

Later transferring to Berkeley, I heard some of the polemical thunder then dividing San Francisco waterfront trade unions. At the University of California–Berkeley I had the good fortune to enroll in classes taught by Ira Cross and Paul Taylor, proponents of Wisconsin-based labor economics. I knew that they had studied under John Commons; they exposed me to the generational relationship between teachers and students. Although I held these professors in awe, I did not enter their beckoning field.

As children, my sisters Judy and Mitzie and I listened to our father tell of his escape from czarist Russia, where he had participated in the abortive 1905 revolution. For a few days, a coalition of young idealists governed Chernigov, a provincial center in the Ukraine. When the Cossacks recaptured the town, the rebels faced prison in Siberia or death. Many fled west, helped by sympathizers who ran an underground railway like that of American abolitionists. Father's adventures imparted a keen sense of geography: Russia, Finland, England, Canada, the United States.

In adulthood, I returned to his central narrative with abundant curiosity. What were father's politics in 1905? How did he respond to the failure of revolutionary dreams? He was neither a disciplined Bolshevik nor an orthodox Marxist. Rather, as a member of the Jewish minority, he gravitated to a mild socialism that stressed the cultural values of each constituent group in the polity. Later in America this creed found realization in Workmen's Circle activity. During my teen years, I saw him move enthusiastically to embrace Franklin D. Roosevelt's liberalism; he remained an unreconstructed New Dealer for life.

My parents devoted considerable resources to cultural matters. Agnostics in religion and puritans in behavior, they sought grace by attention to art, music, drama, and literature. They never believed that expressive forms were reserved for an elite. It seemed natural to be taken to museums, concerts, and lectures. Long before hearing the term *cultural pluralism,* I had seen neighborhood children in kimonos, sombreros, or peasant dress as they celebrated Japanese moon dances, Mexican Cinco de Mayo festivities, and Slavic holidays.

Mother sang while doing housework—Ukrainian, Russian, and Jewish folksongs, as well as favorites from opera and the musical stage— although many years elapsed before I recognized the boundaries of her repertoire. She, too, had migrated from Chernigov to Winnipeg and finally to Los Angeles. Along the way, she added a few popular hits— "Alexander's Ragtime Band," "Charlie Chaplin"—to her songbag. I never thought to ask her why she stopped learning new pieces after she left Canada.

In the mid-1920s we purchased a battery-set radio. Of the music we heard on it, cowboy ballads made the deepest impression on me. Harry "Haywire Mac" McClintock emerged as the first defined star in my firmament. In junior high (1930–32), while helping the school librarian, I discovered *Cowboy Songs* by John Lomax. This book made a tremendous impression in that a few of the ballads it included were already familiar to me via the radio. Also, it provided a model of strange activity— searching for folksong.

Father's early trade, harnessmaking, fell victim to the automobile's rise. Like other immigrants, he tried his hand at various jobs: a millman making wooden boxes, a greenhouse gardener growing flowers, an expressman (teamster) at the railway station moving travelers' trunks and bags home. Eventually, he settled in a small secondhand furniture store combining repairs and sales. When his children left home, he gave up entrepreneurship to close out his work days as a warehouseman. As a lifelong champion of workers, he felt it ironic that his final dues supported Teamster president Jimmie Hoffa.

Even before I encountered cowboy songs in the library, I had read my way into a Wobbly (IWW, or Industrial Workers of the World) universe. My elder sister Judy subscribed to Mencken's *American Mercury;* about 1928, it carried articles by Louis Adamic on Seattle Wobblies, San Quentin class-war prisoners, and San Pedro fish-cannery women. A few years later, Adamic wrote *Dynamite,* a book on violence in workers' causes. He represented my first reading in labor history, as well as an exposure to anarcho-syndicalist ideas.

In my early teen years, I began riding the trolley car downtown to the main public library. Books in hand, I regularly stopped over in nearby Pershing Square to listen to the soapboxers and swamis, cultists and combatants, who bathed in the sunshine of endless debate. As Depression years gave way to the New Deal era, the square's partisans of reform and revolution vied for attention. I accepted this rhetorical mulligan as a free-lunch gift, selecting choice morsels and rejecting others beyond my taste or ken.

At Berkeley, I found my parents' values merging with those of gifted teachers and community activists. To be a worker engaged in trade-union activity appealed to me as the most desirable choice I could make. Accordingly, I enrolled in a New Deal relief agency, the Civilian Conservation Corps, for a year on the Klamath River. There I learned the rudiments of roadbuilding and firefighting, as well as a smattering of occupational and regional lore. Without reflection, I absorbed a conservation ethic that decades later blossomed under the rubric *ecology.*

Ready for new tasks, I located in San Francisco and made a start at Western Pipe and Steel, then building Maritime Commission vessels. The job required me to join a waterfront local of the Carpenter's Brotherhood, a cause I eagerly accepted. Bits and pieces of the shipwright experience appear in various writings of mine. I can sum up years of working-at-the-trade by reporting that they embraced naval duty in the Pacific and China, as well as marriage and children.

The rewards of a skilled trade are many, including the means to buy books and records. My choices ranged from Paul Bunyan yarns to William Faulkner novels, mountain music to exotic calypso and flamenco tunes. Although I did not consider myself a serious disc collector, this hobby gradually led to my shift from tradesman to folklorist. In the 1950s, I corresponded with George Korson, John Greenway, Joe Glazer, and Bill Friedland, querying them about recorded labor and occupational songs. With their encouragement, I undertook a discography of coal-mining music.

This initial task of "junking" (searching) for obscure records and then plumbing their stories cut across conventional academic fields. It also promised to add details to labor history and ballad scholarship, usually unrelated disciplines. The link between collection/acquisition and sanctioned scholarship is strange; somehow, I felt that song histories intensified the value of sound recordings.

Autobiographical accounts smooth out detours in a road and fill in the potholes. Distressed at abandoning my trade and leaving companions behind, I looked ambivalently at a second calling in the realm of learning. In 1960 at the University of Illinois, I completed library-science courses and took a faculty position at the Institute of Labor and Industrial Relations. Winds from the outside reached the prairie campus; I volunteered as faculty adviser to the Campus Folksong Club and was excited by unanticipated responsibility. Our club cut across town and gown divisions; we included fiddlers, guitar and banjo pickers, and professors—the latter group largely from math, science, and engineering. Judy McCulloh, Doyle Moore, and Harlan Daniel were three among many CFC stalwarts who could describe a tune family, design a poster, or unearth long-buried song histories.

In 1966 I enrolled at the University of Pennsylvania for a folklore degree. Under the prodding of MacEdward Leach, the coal discography grew into a thesis and, eventually, a book, *Only a Miner*. It appeared as the movement for Appalachian identity gathered force and fortuitously led to new friends—Loyal Jones, David Whisnant, Rodger Cunningham—who in their special ways deepened my thoughts on the relationship of nation to section.

The "folksong revival" offered divergent fare: Joan Baez, New Lost City Ramblers, Merle Travis, Dorsey Dixon, Glenn Ohrlin, Sarah

Ogan Gunning. We chose our favorite artists, argued their merits, and used component elements of song/singer/style to debate the issues of the day. *Tradition* became a keyword, an open sesame, a point of honor. During these years, I joined Gene Earle, Ed Kahn, Bob Pinson, Norm Cohen, and others in chartering the John Edwards Memorial Foundation, an archival center dedicated to vernacular music. Undertaking more than institution building, we embraced the conflict engendered by pitting "hillbilly" styles against the dominant forces of Nashville's Music City U.S.A.

In 1967 Ralph Rinzler had initiated the Festival of American Folklife at the Smithsonian Institution. A few years later, I added to his presentations several groups of trade-union craftsmen, starting with ironworkers in high steel. On the National Mall, the "hardhats" coolly demonstrated their skill in steel-frame erection alongside Native American basket weavers and Appalachian quilters. The tradesmen also precipitated controversy over who should be selected to represent "the folk" at public events. Some partisans felt that contemporary unionists could not be included under the rubric *folk*. Others knew these ironworkers to be more "authentic" than the then-ubiquitous singers of folksong. Like numerous related disputes of the day, this one was not resolved.

Meanwhile, Jim Hightower, an aide to Senator Ralph Yarborough (Texas), drafted legislation to give political structure to the Smithsonian's folklife venture. Throwing the bill into the hopper, Jim challenged the National Endowments for the Arts and Humanities. Cultural policy could no longer be the sole province of prestigious entertainment palaces or learning centers. A byproduct of this Congressional endeavor was increased vocational choices for folklorists. Heretofore, we had worked mainly in the academy; the bill offered the possibility of public-sector employment.

When Jim left Capitol Hill, I ventured into lobbying with an innocent's conviction. Other citizens joined the crusade; here, I'll name only three as representative: Wayland Hand, Judy McCulloh, and Joe Wilson. Congress passed the American Folklife Preservation Act in 1976, establishing the American Folklife Center at the Library of Congress. This modest agency lent visibility to preservation/presentation efforts by asserting the significance of folk expression in a society dominated by elite and popular institutions.

With lobbying behind me, I completed a few years of teaching at the University of Texas. Austin stands in my memory for collegiality—staff and students worked together, resisting atomization. From Roger Abrahams to Roger Renwick, Nick Spitzer to Deborah Kodish, they operated with a spirit of solidarity. Cosmic-cowboy music filled the air; good companions gathered at the Split Rail and Soap Creek Saloon. On campus, I taught two then-new seminars in public folklore and saw my students fan out to pioneer in arts/humanities positions.

When I retired in 1982, Louanne and I returned home to San Francisco, resuming a quiet role with family and friends. I have continued to write, mainly on the same topics that have concerned me for past decades. My current project, a book on tin-man trade signs, takes up tinkers'/tinsmiths' material culture. My interest in these and other artistic forms—whether seen as fossils or harbingers of change—has remained strong as my exploratory powers have diminished.

Two recent activities mark the retirement years. I have been concerned that students continue to study occupational folklore. The pleasure in sharing data and strategies with colleagues, such as Bob McCarl and the late Dick Reuss, had proved especially rewarding. Thus I established, with much help, a graduate scholarship in this field at the University of North Carolina. The effort called latent traits of diplomacy into play; Dan Patterson and Terry Zug guided me through the administrative maze governing such programs.

Currently, I assist Chris Strachwitz in his Arhoolie Foundation. In some respects, it is similar to the John Edwards Memorial Foundation in its attention to vernacular music. It differs in that Chris, the proprietor of Down Home Music (El Cerrito, California), brings business practice to bear on discographic research and educational efforts. He reminds me that "roots" music is too precious to be trusted entirely to one section of society.

The autobiographical account above suggests an unreal, straight-ahead progression, without unanticipated detours to slow the traveler. In selecting the dozen pieces that appear in this gathering, I have placed them chronologically, offering a variety of themes and sources.

"*Dutchman:* An On-the-Job Etymology" is my first published study of an esoteric term I heard in shipyard employment at the "Pipe." With the passage of time, it reminds me of my good fortune in teachers James Allan and Benjamin Carwardine, who took me in hand in 1941. This paper also reflects lessons in language by mentor Peter Tamony, a native

San Franciscan. By contrast, the shipwrights hailed from Scotland; Jim Allan had worked as a merchant seaman and pile driver. Benny Carwardine, a Clydesider, had apprenticed in "Red Glasgow," where he acquired trade secrets with the tenets of left-libertarian unionism. In America he gave his prodigious intellect to the cause of industrial unionism, fighting both craft privilege and Stalinist dogma. I viewed him as a sage, imagining that in previous incarnations he had helped launch the *Golden Hind* and the *Flying Cloud*.

"Hillbilly Music: Source and Symbol," a major article in 1965, ranges freely through fields of music, language, and literature. Inspired by Tamony's work on the etymology of jazz, it has proved useful to country-music historians. It pleases me to report that this paper has attracted scholars—among them Wayne Daniel, Bill Malone, and Gene Wiggins—who have both modified and expanded my research with their findings.

"Laborlore" appeared in the 1971 program book of the Smithsonian Institution's Festival of American Folklife. To enlarge the scope of trade-union lore, a then little-known field, I focused on material other than music. John Neuhaus, a San Francisco "double header" (member of both the International Association of Machinists and the Industrial Workers of the World), had gifted me with a folktale, "The Striker's Wife." I had met John about 1952 and had memorialized him in the *Journal of American Folklore* (1960). In 1996, I returned to his contribution in *Calf's Head and Union Tale*.

Following my research for *Only a Miner,* I wrote "A Folklorist's Creed and a Folksinger's Gift," an offering to an Appalachian exemplar, Sarah Ogan Gunning. Her strength always amazed me; how did she internalize radical and traditional modes of conduct? Sister to Aunt Molly Jackson and Jim Garland, she appears in books by Jim and about Molly. Sarah recorded two LP albums and starred in *Dreadful Memories,* an Appalshop video. Ideally, my essay, the discs, and the film should be treated together to appreciate a life now distant in time and place.

In listing mileposts, I mentioned my stay in Texas at the close of my teaching years. "Austin's Cosmic Cowboys: Words in Collision" served many purposes: it caught the spirit of exciting music cutting across community lines; it appeared in a tribute to a colleague, Américo Paredes; it reflected long interest in graphic art—lithograph, etching, cartoon, advertisement. Very early in my research, I reported pictorial findings that commented on the sound-recording industry. How did "talking machine" executives determine proper images to promote hillbilly (Appalachian), race (Negro), and foreign-language discs? My Graphics Series ran from 1967 to 1985 in the *JEMF Quarterly;* editor Norm Cohen helped make the sixty-eight features possible.

Occasionally, a *JEMF* article reached a second audience beyond that of record collectors. I had been interested in Thomas Hart Benton since the mid-1930s, when heroic, affirmative art, folk culture, and New Deal politics seemed to converge. "Tom Benton's Folk Depictions" appeared in a handsome Bard College exhibition catalog as a step in the "rehabilitation" of an artist left behind by proponents of abstraction and introspection in painting.

Delivered orally at a conference in Washington, D.C., "The Archive's Shores" represents a long commitment to public folklife. When the Folksong Archive at the Library of Congress celebrated its fiftieth birthday, I commented on the intellectual roots that had sustained the unit. Subsequently I expanded my remarks into a formal paper for the *Folklife Annual,* published by the American Folklife Center (which had incorporated the Archive in 1976).

As the Center grew, it sought alliance with historic preservationists and natural conservationists in sister agencies. Over the years, I have addressed this matter frequently. At an early gathering of public folklorists at Bowling Green State University in Kentucky, I spoke on "Stitching Patchwork in Public." Themes for that conference still resonate: particularity, preservation, pluralism.

In recent years, I have tried to reach an audience other than that of academic journals by writing for the popular press. In this vein, the *Examiner,* a San Francisco daily, ran a Labor Day op-ed piece, "Remembering Jack Fitch." Jack worked as a pile driver all his life; he buoyed himself by "Sunday painting" on canvas and masonite. He may never be "discovered" by dealers and collectors of folk art—not that it will make any difference to the handful of pile-butt buddies who recall him. He left no work scene to be shown in his union hall. Yet I am impelled to see Jack in full dimension: talented, idiosyncratic, isolated, skeptical of all creeds emanating from boss, labor leader, or pundit.

For most of my life I have listened to and told stories; I don't know when I became aware of scholarly efforts in folktale analysis. *Calf's Head and Union Tale* brought together sixty-six occupational yarns, many in multiple variants. "Kelly Girl," told in the Mission barrio, is one of

Zapata Calavera, *artist unknown, ca. 1915, Jean Charlot Collection,*
Library of Congress. In Ron Tyler, Posada's Mexico
(Washington, D.C.: Library of Congress, 1979).

these tales that still eludes me. Deceptively simple, it comments on
"women's work," job authority, and bilingualism.

"Torching the Fink Books" is a short piece written for the monthly
newspaper of one of America's oldest unions, the Sailors' Union of the
Pacific. Previously, I had written a long essay on *fink,* the pejorative
term, in *Wobblies, Pile Butts, and Other Heroes;* "Torching" condenses that
essay's findings and adds new material to a never-ending study.

I close by circling back to Peter Tamony in a personal tribute (previously unpublished). Peter had figured in my study of *dutchman,* the first
selection in this reader. He lived many lives: Irish leprechaun, superb
raconteur, local chauvinist, generous friend. His command of Ameri-

can speech was unexcelled. That the University of Missouri acquired his massive word collection is a miracle in which I gladly participated.

Seemingly, certain subjects have predominated in most of my writing: vernacular music, graphic art, word study, public cultural policy, laborlore. At times, I have focused on one; sometimes, the discrete elements become hopelessly entangled. I have assumed that pleasure in scholarship — reading or writing — stems from separating the strands.

Of my chosen fields, laborlore remains enigmatic. It challenges me; I return to it constantly. In searching for this subject's source and meaning, I revisit certain autobiographical details. In effect, I am again in the roadcut.

A Los Angeles picnic/meeting for Eugene Victor Debs at Selig Zoo in July 1925 marks a beginning. It would be less than candid, though, to imply that socialist speeches or songs then consciously influenced me. My recollection of the event is one of avoiding adults by playing Tarzan in the zoo's bamboo thickets. The meaning of this childhood act eludes me. What does the incident say about my exposure to the radical movement's rhetoric?

However, memory begins to "kick in" with Nicola Sacco and Bartolomeo Vanzetti, anarchist martyrs executed in Boston on August 23, 1927. My parents took me to rallies for the prisoners before their death. At memorial meetings, their lithographed portraits were draped in black bunting; the assembled mourners sang funeral dirges. Perhaps the contrasting images of Debs (not retained) and of Sacco-Vanzetti (retained) involve no more than the beginning of a child's recollective power.

Whether one deals with autobiography in proper time sequence, or writing as a mechanism cutting across chronology, the very act of composition smooths out features of the journey. To revert to my geologic image: in memory, upended strata magically become horizontal; dusty rock fragments transform into conglomerate; creatures long extinct "live" in an antiquary's cabinet.

Previously I have alluded to leaving my trade as generating ambivalent feelings — betrayal on one hand, promise on the other. This sense of unease occurred again when I chose to give up teaching at the University of Illinois. My sons, David and Derek, had joined the navy and were posted to Vietnam; daughter Debra took a job on a quarter-horse farm. Free of parental responsibility, I pulled up stakes and headed for Washington, D.C.

The decision to lobby in House and Senate chambers on behalf of the folk—enclaved groups, citizens at the margins of power, people left behind by "progress"—was not premeditated; looking back, it seems fated. I could no longer call myself a shipwright, but lobbying seemed a natural extension of work at my trade and its concomitant trade-union affiliation.

My attention to politics is rooted in childhood; it had always been more philosophical than practical, for I conceived political issues in utopian rather than in backroom terms. I internalized conflicting creeds—visionary, pragmatic—and admired Wobblies who favored direct (job) action over voting. However, when offered the chance to influence public cultural policy by walking congressional corridors, I marched ahead, accepting the opportunity to enact our legislation.

Neil Rosenberg, in *Transforming Tradition,* has related my efforts on Capitol Hill to preliminary work with the Illinois Campus Folksong Club. He might also have referred to earlier work on the San Francisco waterfront. I viewed my lobbying role as that of a teacher with the entire Congress as a classroom. Not only was the substance of folklore interesting, but it had the potential to help Senators and Representatives walk the high road. I believed then, and still do, that if tax funds are allocated for cultural activity, our social charter requires an equitable, democratic distribution of those resources.

Do we ask too much by calling for equity and democracy in cultural life? The peasant fiddler is as worthy as the symphony violinist; the village cobbler more precious than a pair of boots. Poets and pamphleteers have penned odes to the people. It seems naive to reiterate that peasants and villagers create/utilize art. Facing a time of instant and incessant mechanical talk, coupled with policies of ethnic cleansing, the truism that folk expression is valuable needs to be trumpeted.

A question remains that has troubled a few of my colleagues: how to explain my infatuation with laborlore? I have used this coinage narrowly to cover union material and broadly to include the expressive culture of all workers. Laborlore can be as particular as the job custom of picking up one's tools five minutes before quitting time, or as complex as matters of class and caste identity.

Many partisans view union songs as the most appropriate expressions in our repertoire, trumping tales, customs, rituals, and material artifacts. Rather than clinging to well-known chestnuts, I have tried deliberately to expand our field of attention. I cite two recent articles on material culture in *Labor's Heritage,* "Labor Landmarks: Past and Present" and "Tin Men on Parade," that plow new ground. The preservation and conservation movements have long treasured Mt. Vernon and Yellowstone; museum curators guard cigar-store Indians. It is time we promote alliances between conservationists and unionists.

I have labeled the shipwrights who caulk the ferryboat *Eureka* for the National Park Service "blue collar preservationists." This same phrase is applicable to unionists, coast to coast, who clean up Mother Jones's Cemetery, erect a monument to Cesar Chavez, or persuade a port authority to save an obsolete, dysfunctional copra crane in a now-restored-to-nature harbor creek. Laborlore commitment consists of more than celebratory writing; it includes interaction with civic leaders and technicians in agencies that range from parks to public works.

In this afterword, I have reported some of the steps along my path: Debs, Sacco-Vanzetti, Wobblies, Wisconsin-based labor economics, the shipwright's trade, joining a union. My shipyard teachers have all departed. Fortunately, others have continued to instruct me in the relationship of craft skill to democratic unionism, among them piledrivers Mike Munoz and Bill Myers. Names alone do not convey the intensity, indeed passion, generated by this combination of friendly counsel, reading, and experience.

Around 1915, a now-forgotten University of Chicago professor, Robert Hoxie, formulated a structural typology that has served me very well in laborlore studies. He characterized American unions as *business, uplift, revolutionary,* and *predatory.* These categories rise and fall; new names become fashionable. Today, revolutionary and predatory unions have all but vanished; uplift (reform) unions operate within the Democratic Party fold; business unions willingly transform themselves into corporate clones. It is painful to watch a crippled union drift like a rudderless ship in distant waters.

This typology may seem something of a digression in a collection on vernacular culture, but I have invoked Hoxie deliberately. Some students assert that only militant workers in class-conscious unions produce and convey lore, and that by definition it is contestational. I reject this formula, for I believe that *all* workers, organized or not, ideologically pure or not, create lore. A handful of scholars collect or study occupational tradition; similarly, a few museum curators honor the artifacts that mark workers' aspirations. Few unions accept formal responsibility for preserving/presenting cultural material. No unions employ folklorists as professional staff members.

Inattention to a human resource—time tested, wise, expressive—whether by government, media, or trade union, troubles me. Labor leaders give many reasons for their callous neglect of lore, their ambivalence about heritage. Not surprisingly, unions reflect the norms of the society that surrounds them. Pejorative talk about folk culture flows from art-council administrators, university deans, and union officials. I have touched on this matter previously and shall return to it in a future essay.

It is not my intent in this concluding statement to exaggerate my adventures or glaze over the difficulties in my travels. I have already alluded to troubled transitions from shipwright to librarian and professor to lobbyist. In this vein, I recall two roads not taken while I was still an undergraduate.

Colleagues have asked why I did not prepare myself for a career in folklore by taking anthropology classes from Alfred Kroeber and his peers at the University of California. In retrospect, I must say that in 1939, the world of work beckoned more seductively than that of a career recording native languages in preparation for campus teaching. As a young New Dealer, I was dimly aware of John Collier's efforts to reform tribal government, but they did not inflame me as did waterfront labor. Ironically, when I enrolled in the CCC, a few of Kroeber's students were in Klamath country studying Yurok and Karok lore. I was oblivious to their presence, and they to mine.

Similarly, ballad scholar Bertrand Bronson taught at Berkeley, but I did not avail myself of his encyclopedic wisdom, either. I had no knowledge of the corpus of traditional folksong that preceded the few cowboy ballads I had encountered. Decades elapsed before I read and heard my way back from John Henry and Gregorio Cortéz to Mattie Groves and Gypsy Davey. It is futile to think that I could have anticipated future paths in folklore while still a sophomore. Nevertheless, self-recrimination has been an unwelcome companion on the road.

A positive memory complements these confessions. I did not take up serious writing until the late 1950s. As a guest at the University of Louisville in 1977, I contributed a paper titled "Reflexive Regionalism" to *Adena,* the campus literary magazine. Editor Leon Driskell asked why I wrote in the passive voice. He was surprised, if not shocked, to hear me reply, "What's that?" Without formal training in composition, unknowingly I had fallen into a stylistic trap. Driskell illustrated with a handful of deadly, inactive usages. I saw the light! Since that day in his office, I have tried to write as I speak.

Finally, I return to a keyword in my book's title, *vernacular;* I employ it broadly in my chosen fields. *Folk* has been and remains a contentious disciplinary term. Through the ages, it has acquired contradictory meanings. I am not sanguine enough to believe that we shall resolve our semantic disputes by substituting the rubric *vernacular* or *folk.* Nevertheless, I live in hope.

The former term has a long history dating back to ancient Rome, when it designated a slave born in his master's house; hence nativity. *Vernacular* came to signify regional or social dialect, substandard speech, and "homemade" architecture or landscapes. Critics extended the term to Mark Blitzstein's 1937 proletarian musical, *The Cradle Will Rock.* Although committed to steel-mill labor's cause, the composer did not include indigenous music actually performed by steel workers in their varied ethnic and regional associations.

Like other signifying words, *vernacular* has been used loosely. However, its utility is fourfold: long service as a descriptive term in linguistic and artistic studies; economy in bridging differences where folk and popular forms interact; association with the practices of vast numbers of people; neutrality regarding causes and revivals.

The need for clear language to describe imprecise cultural categories is apparent in my choices for this book's pictures. I have favored black-and-white over color; prints over photos or paintings. My selections reveal a personal taste and indirectly comment on art standards. Do any of these illustrations qualify as vernacular art? Is such art positioned in a bin between avant garde and folk expression? Is it defined by medium used, audience achieved, or judgment rendered?

Jose Guadalupe Posada (1852–1913) made zinc etchings for newspapers, broadsheets, chapbooks, and *corridos* (ballads). He was neither a folk nor a fine artist, but bridged these realms. He reached into Mexican folk tradition for Day of the Dead beliefs and gifted his contemporaries with compelling *calavera* figures (skeletons) that startle us today. I view Posada as the platonic vernacular artist against whom we measure this term's utility. When attempting comparisons—Thomas Nast,

Norman Rockwell, Rube Goldberg, Andy Warhol—we see the difficulties in categorizing expressive culture.

Such matters will continue to confound scholars. Here, I turn to some of the mentors and students who have guided me through the roadcut. I am acutely aware that I have not named all, or in any special order. I keep in touch with a few childhood playmates and add companions by accepting new projects. I follow convention by crediting my sources in articles, but this practice does not measure the gifts of those outside the academy.

Two friends from Boyle Heights, Michio Kunitani and Norman Granz, with whom I shared political and cultural adventures, are not cited in these pieces, but they represent many individuals along the way who shaped ideas found in this book. Michio helped me in the transition from campus "sandbox" groups to the national American Veterans Committee, which in turn challenged old-line organizations. Norman and I attended wPA theater dramas, musicals, and public lectures before I "graduated" to his innovative Jazz at the Philharmonic series.

Lead Belly, Billie Holiday, Miguel Covarrubias, The Hot Mikado, "Intoxicated Rat," "Smoke on the Water," John Dos Passos, Yoknapatawpha County, and "The Commonwealth of Toil" all tumbled into my consciousness within the space of a few breathless years. The effects of these separate pleasures are intertwined; their voices continue to echo. I have long been mystified by the lasting power of initial sights and sounds.

Cultural nomads do not live in a bubble, sealed off from other experience. Bob Cantwell, in his foreword, has unraveled the plural, and at times hidden, strands in my writing. Brian Finnigan has offered a different explanation of my work geared to British cultural studies (*Folklore Historians*, 1988). Sandra Bressler has documented my lobbying efforts in a University of Pennsylvania thesis, "Culture and Politics" (1995). These three have helped me look back at ideas and actions. Also, I have looked ahead via the current work of friends. Among them, Maria Hetherton uses Chicano and Cajun music as teaching tools in an Oakland, California, school. Patrick Huber has completed a thesis on textile-song recordings at the University of North Carolina. Paula Johnson resolves problems in the exhibition of maritime labor at the Smithsonian Institution. Stephen Wade pursues individual song studies in a forthcoming book based on his CD, *A Treasury of Library of Congress Field Recordings*. I see my *Torching the Fink Books* reflected in their respective endeavors.

A happy rite remains. The twelve selections gathered here acknowledge, by internal reference or footnote, my debt to friends and fellow workers at the time of their initial publication. I look back at mentors who have slipped away. How did Lawrence Roberts fare after those CCC days? Where are the shipwrights and pile butts who taught me trade secrets? What happened to the activists who consciously or inadvertently shaped my visionary politics? Can we ever unravel and name all the threads in our growth?

At the University of North Carolina Press, I am grateful to editor Elaine Maisner, assistant managing editor Pam Upton, and designer Rich Hendel, and to outside readers Julia Ardery and Burt Feintuch for their close scrutiny of this book in manuscript form. From the vantage point of eight decades, I should list in one grand summation all who served me over the years. I refrain, except to name one, Louanne Green. She has read and criticized my writing endlessly and has struggled to keep me focused. To her, and to all the others, thanks for your help while I sought gems in the contorted strata.

BIBLIOGRAPHY OF ARCHIE GREEN'S WRITINGS, 1959–2000

1959

"A Discographic Appraisal of *American Balladry from British Broadsides.*"
Caravan, no. 15 (February 1959): 7–13. (Folksong fan journal, New York.)

"The John Neuhaus Collection of 'Wobbly' Songlore." *Western Folklore* 18
(July 1959): 256.

"Will the Weaver's Hillbilly Kinfolk." *Caravan,* no. 18 (August 1959): 14–23.

1960

"Streets of Hamtramck." *Western Folklore* 19 (January 1960): 58–60.

"The Death of Mother Jones." *Labor History* 1 (Winter 1960): 68–80.
University of Illinois ILIR Reprint 82.

"John Neuhaus: Wobbly Folklorist." *Journal of American Folklore* 73 (July 1960):
189–217. University of Illinois ILIR Reprint 88; also reprinted in *Folklore of
the Great West,* edited by John Greenway, 312–27 (Palo Alto, Calif.:
American West, 1969).

Review of *Songs of Work and Freedom,* by Joe Glazer and Edith Fowke. *Labor
History* 1 (Fall 1960): 334–36.

"*Dutchman:* An On-the-Job Etymology." *American Speech* 35 (December 1960):
270–74.

1961

"A Discography of American Coal Miners' Songs." *Labor History* 2 (Winter
1961): 101–15. University of Illinois ILIR Reprint 93.

"Born on Picketline, Textile Workers' Songs Are Woven into History." *Textile
Labor* 22 (April 1961): 3–5.

"A Discography (LP) of American Labor Union Songs." *New York Folklore
Quarterly* 17 (Autumn 1961): 186–93. University of Illinois ILIR Reprint
109.

"Mary Magdalene Garland Stewart Jackson Stamos: 1880–1960." *Kentucky
Folklore Record* 7 (October 1961): 129–30.

"Ben Robertson Meets Aunt Molly." *Kentucky Folklore Record* 7 (October 1961):
133–39.

Adobe Bricklayer, *by Kenneth M. Adams, 1934. In Clinton Adams,*
Printmaking in New Mexico, 1880–1990 *(Albuquerque: University of New Mexico
Press, 1991). (Collection, University Art Museum, University of New Mexico;
gift of Lawrence O. Hogrefe)*

"An Aunt Molly Jackson Discography." *Kentucky Folklore Record* 7 (October
1961): 159–69.
"The Carter Family's 'Coal Miner's Blues.'" *Southern Folklore Quarterly* 25
(December 1961): 226–37. University of Illinois ILIR Reprint 114.

1962
Review of *American Murder Ballads,* by Olive Burt. *Journal of American Folklore*
75 (January 1962): 73–74.
"Folksong Record Reissues: Alternative Approaches." *Autoharp,* no. 10
(May 4, 1962). (Student publication, University of Illinois Campus
Folksong Club.)
[With Dick Adams]. LP brochure notes for *Philo Glee and Mandolin Society.*
Stringband music by Doyle Moore/Jim Hockenhull/Paul Adkins, a
student-faculty trio. Campus Folksong Club CFC 101, May 1962.

1963

"A Carter Family Bibliography." *Sunny Side Sentinel,* no. 2 (January 1963): 3–12. (Fan club journal, Drake, Ky.)

[With Fritz Plous et al.]. LP brochure notes for *Green Fields of Illinois,* by various local performers. Campus Folksong Club CFC 201, May 1963.

LP liner notes for *'Mid the Green Fields of Virginia,* by the Carter Family. RCA Victor LPM 2772, October 1963.

1964

LP liner notes for *Blue Sky Boys,* by Bill and Earl Bolick. RCA Camden CAL 797, January 1964.

"Campus Report: University of Illinois." *Hootenanny* 1 (March 1964): 5–9. ("Folksong revival" magazine.)

"A Carter Family Handbill." *Sunny Side Sentinel,* no. 4 (May 1964): 5–9.

[With Judy McCulloh.] LP brochure notes for *The Hell-Bound Train,* by Glenn Ohrlin. Campus Folksong Club CFC 301, June 1964.

Foreword to *Minstrels of the Mine Patch,* by George Korson, i–xiv. Hatboro, Pa.: Folklore Associates, 1964.

"Dorsey Dixon: A Place in the Sun for a Real Textile Troubadour." *Textile Labor* 25 (November 1964): 4–5.

LP liner and brochure notes for *Babies in the Mill,* by Dorsey, Howard, and Nancy Dixon. Testament T 3301, December 1964. Liner notes reprinted as "Dorsey Dixon: Minstrel of the Mills," *Sing Out!* 16 (July 1966): 11–12.

1965

"American Labor Lore: Its Meanings and Uses." *Industrial Relations* 4 (February 1965): 51–68. University of Illinois ILIR Reprint 150.

LP brochure notes for *The Carolina Tar Heels,* by Dock and Drake Walsh and Garley Foster. Folk-Legacy FSA 24, March 1965.

"Hillbilly Music: Source and Symbol." *Journal of American Folklore* 78 (July 1965): 204–28. John Edwards Memorial Foundation Reprint 4.

LP brochure notes for *Sarah Ogan Gunning.* Folk-Legacy FSA 26, December 1965.

1966

LP brochure notes for *Tipple, Loom and Rail,* by Mike Seeger. Folkways FH 5237, March 1966.

LP liner notes for *The Railroad in Folksong,* by various performers. RCA Victor LPV 532, August 1966.

Record reviews of *Songs and Ballads of the Bituminous Miners* and *Songs and Ballads of the Anthracite Miners. Ethnomusicology* 10 (September 1966): 361–63.

"Several Scenes in Search of a Tag." In program book for Philadelphia Folk Festival, September 9–11, 1966.

1967

LP liner notes for *Mountain Sacred Songs,* by various performers. County 508, February 1967.

"Commercial Music Graphics." *JEMF Newsletter,* no. 6 (June 1967): 48–53. Graphics 1, "Okeh's First Atlanta Session." (Series continued through 1985. Items 1–30 originally untitled; titles supplied retroactively in Winter 1974.)

"Fiddlin' John Carson and Henry Whitter." *JEMF Newsletter,* no. 7 (September 1967): 15–17. Graphics 2.

"Columbia's Fiddle, Guitar, and Banjo Records." *JEMF Newsletter,* no. 8 (December 1967): 43–45. Graphics 3.

1968

Review of 15 LPs. *Western Folklore* 27 (January 1968): 68–76. University of Illinois ILIR Reprint 188 (titled "Recorded Labor Songs: An Overview").

"Victor's *Olde Time Fiddlin' Tunes." JEMF Newsletter,* no. 9 (March 1968): 8–13. Graphics 4.

"The Workers in the Dawn: Labor Lore." In *Our Living Tradition,* edited by Tristram Potter Coffin, 251–62. New York: Basic Books, 1968. University of Illinois ILIR Reprint 200.

"MacEdward Leach, 1892–1967." *Journal of American Folklore* 81 (April 1968): 108–10. (One of several untitled memorial reminiscences by various contributors.)

"The Beginnings of the John Edwards Memorial Foundation." *Ralph Stanley Fan Club Journal* 3 (May 1968): 19–21. Reprinted in *The Published Works of the Late John Edwards,* edited by John Atkins and Mike Craig, 1–5. Kingswinford, Eng.: Society for the Preservation and Promotion of Traditional Country Music, 1973.

LP brochure notes for *Railroad Songs and Ballads,* by various performers. Library of Congress AFS L 61, May 1968.

"Uncle Am Stuart on Vocalion." *JEMF Newsletter,* no. 10 (June 1968): 39–42. Graphics 5.

"Mac and Bob at Strawplains School." *JEMF Newsletter,* no. 11 (September 1968): 93–96. Graphics 6.

Review of *Screening the Blues,* by Paul Oliver. *Autoharp,* no. 32 (October 25, 1968).

"Columbia's Jigs, Reels, and Banjo Tunes." *JEMF Newsletter,* no. 12 (December 1968): 126–30. Graphics 7.

1969

"Andrew Jenkins' Christian Love Songs." *JEMF Quarterly,* no. 13 (Spring 1969): 23–26. Graphics 8.

"Jimmie Rodgers' 'In the Jailhouse Now.'" *JEMF Quarterly,* no. 14 (Summer 1969): 58–60. Graphics 9.

"Recorded American Coal Mining Songs." Ph.D. diss., University of Pennsylvania, 1969.

"Gennett and Champion Releases." *JEMF Quarterly,* no. 15 (Autumn 1969): 101–4. Graphics 10.

"Paramount's Southern Series." *JEMF Quarterly,* no. 16 (Winter 1969): 141–45. Graphics 11.

"A Joe Hill Song Checklist." In *Joe Hill,* by Gibbs Smith, 231–60. Salt Lake City: University of Utah Press, 1969. Book reprinted as *Labor Martyr Joe Hill* (New York: Grosset and Dunlap, 1972); reprinted in paperback as *Joe Hill* (Layton, Utah: Peregrine Smith Books, 1984).

1970

"D. K. Wilgus' Album Notes." *Journal of American Folklore* 83 (January 1970): 110–11.

"Buell Kazee Folk Song Recital." *JEMF Quarterly,* no. 17 (Spring 1970): 23–27. Graphics 12.

"Eck Robertson on Victor in 1923." *JEMF Quarterly,* no. 18 (Summer 1970): 70–73. Graphics 13.

Review of *Big Bill Haywood and the Radical Union Movement,* by Joseph Conlin. *Forest History* 14 (July 1970): 36–37.

Reviews of *The Nashville Sound,* by Paul Hemphill, and *Sing a Sad Song,* by Roger Williams. *Washington Post,* July 3, 1970, C3.

"Two Vocalion Record Sleeves." *JEMF Quarterly,* no. 19 (Autumn 1970): 114–18. Graphics 14.

"Two Cole Hillbilly Folios." *JEMF Quarterly,* no. 20 (Winter 1970): 167–71. Graphics 15.

1971

"Edison Envelope Stuffer." *JEMF Quarterly*, no. 21 (Spring 1971): 23–26.
Graphics 16.

"J. E. Mainer's Liza and Sambo." *JEMF Quarterly*, no. 22 (Summer 1971):
72–75. Graphics 17.

"George Korson and Industrial Folklore." *Keystone Folklore Quarterly* 16
(Summer 1971): 53–63. (Adapted from *Only a Miner*.)

"A Discography/Biography Journey: The Roberts-Martin-Roberts
'Aggregation.'" *Western Folklore* 30 (July 1971): 194–201. John Edwards
Memorial Foundation Reprint 20.

"Laborlore." In program book for Festival of American Folklife,
Smithsonian Institution, July 1–5, 1971.

"Four 78-rpm Album Covers." *JEMF Quarterly*, no. 23 (Autumn 1971): 116–21.
Graphics 18.

"Hear These Beautiful Sacred Selections." In *1970 Yearbook of the International
Folk Music Council*, edited by Alexander Ringer, 28–50. Urbana: University
of Illinois Press, 1971. John Edwards Memorial Foundation Reprint 26.

"Kentucky Thoroughbreds on Paramount." *JEMF Quarterly*, no. 24 (Winter
1971): 171–75. Graphics 19.

1972

Only a Miner: Studies in Recorded Coal-Mining Songs. Urbana: University of Illinois
Press, 1972.

"Vocalion Catalog of 1930." *JEMF Quarterly*, no. 25 (Spring 1972): 25–30.
Graphics 20.

Review of *Great Day Coming*, by R. Serge Denisoff. *Labor History* 13 (Summer
1972): 451–54.

"Victor's 'P' Album Series." *JEMF Quarterly*, no. 26 (Summer 1972): 77–89.
Graphics 21.

"Victor in Rural Schools." *JEMF Quarterly*, no. 27 (Autumn 1972): 141–47.
Graphics 22.

LP brochure notes for "Trouble at the Coal Creek Mines," on *Doc Hopkins*.
Birch 1945, October 1972.

"Cowboys by Thomas Eakins and Others." *JEMF Quarterly*, no. 28 (Winter
1972): 196–202. Graphics 23.

LP brochure notes for "Our First LP," on *The Carter Family on Border Radio*.
John Edwards Memorial Foundation JEMF 101, December 1972.

1973

"Coal Creek Troubles." In *Coal Creek Rebellion* (pamphlet). Huntington,
W.Va.: Appalachian Movement Press, 1973. (Adapted from *Only a Miner.*)

"Folksong on Campus." *JEMF Quarterly,* no. 29 (Spring 1973): 18–23.
Graphics 24.

"Labor Day 1971." In *Folklore from the Working Folk of America,* edited by
Tristram P. Coffin and Hennig Cohen, 409. Garden City, N.Y.: Anchor
Press, 1973.

"Sacred Recordings." *JEMF Quarterly,* no. 30 (Summer 1973): 62–66.
Graphics 25.

"Another Tool in the Carpenter's Chest." In program book for Festival of
American Folklife, Smithsonian Institution, June 30–July 8, 1973.

"Broadside Art." *JEMF Quarterly,* no. 31 (Autumn 1973): 109–15. Graphics 26.

"The New Market Wreck." *JEMF Quarterly,* no. 32 (Winter 1973): 160–65.
Graphics 27.

"Report on the American Folklife Preservation Act." American Folklore
Society, December 31, 1973. (Three-page offset print sent to members.)

1974

"Billy the Kid." *JEMF Quarterly,* no. 33 (Spring 1974): 19–22. Graphics 28.

Foreword to *The Hell-Bound Train,* by Glenn Ohrlin, xi–xviii. Urbana:
University of Illinois Press, 1974.

"Gene Autry's Films." *JEMF Quarterly,* no. 34 (Summer 1974): 62–67.
Graphics 29.

"The Carter Family." *JEMF Quarterly,* no. 35 (Autumn 1974): 110–15.
Graphics 30.

"The Archive of American Folk-Song." *JEMF Quarterly,* no. 36 (Winter 1974):
157–64. Graphics 31.

"The Folklife Act in the Ninety-Third Congress." American Folklore Society,
December 31, 1974. (Eight-page mimeograph sent to members.)

1975

LP liner notes for *Hard Times,* by various blues performers, edited by Dick
Spottswood. Rounder 40007, February 1975.

"The National Folk Festival Association." *JEMF Quarterly,* no. 37 (Spring
1975): 23–32. Graphics 32.

"A Resettlement Administration Song Sheet." *JEMF Quarterly,* no. 38
(Summer 1975): 80–87. Graphics 33.

"Rail Lore." In program book for Festival of American Folklife, Smithsonian Institution, June 25–July 6, 1975.

"The NFFA, That's Who." In program book for National Folk Festival, Wolf Trap Farm Park, Vienna, Va., August 13, 1975. (Adapted from *JEMF Quarterly*, no. 37.)

"Midnight and Other Cowboys." *JEMF Quarterly*, no. 39 (Autumn 1975): 137–52. Graphics 34.

"Henry Thomas' LP Set." *JEMF Quarterly*, no. 40 (Winter 1975): 184–90. Graphics 35.

1976

"P.L. 94-201: A View from the Lobby." American Folklore Society, January 18, 1976. (12-page offset sent to members.) Reprinted in *The Conservation of Culture*, edited by Burt Feintuch, 269–81 (Lexington: University Press of Kentucky, 1988).

" 'Daddy Please Don't Go Down in That Hole Today.' " *Goldenseal* 2 (January–March 1976): 23–30. (Adapted from *Only a Miner*.)

"Dobie's Cowboy Friends." *JEMF Quarterly*, no. 41 (Spring 1976): 21–29. Graphics 36.

"Thomas Hart Benton's Folk Musicians." *JEMF Quarterly*, no. 42 (Summer 1976): 74–90. Graphics 37.

"Chulas Fronteras." *JEMF Quarterly*, no. 43 (Autumn 1976): 138–46. Graphics 38.

"Peter Tamony's Words." *JEMF Quarterly*, no. 44 (Winter 1976): 202–11. Graphics 39.

1977

Introduction to *Folklife and the Federal Government*, compiled by Linda Coe, 1–9. Washington, D.C.: American Folklife Center, Library of Congress, 1977.

"Bradley Kincaid's Folios." *JEMF Quarterly*, no. 45 (Spring 1977): 21–28. Graphics 40.

"Brunswick's Folksong Discs, 1928." *JEMF Quarterly*, no. 46 (Summer 1977): 73–78. Graphics 41.

"Visual Footnotes to *Black Culture and Black Consciousness*." *JEMF Quarterly*, no. 47 (Autumn 1977): 127–37. Graphics 42.

"Miguel Covarrubias' Jazz and Blues Musicians." *JEMF Quarterly*, no. 48 (Winter 1977): 183–95. Graphics 43.

1978

"John Held, Jr.: Jazz Age and Gilded Age." *JEMF Quarterly,* no. 49 (Spring
1978): 23–37. Graphics 44.

"*The Great South.*" *JEMF Quarterly,* no. 50 (Summer 1978): 80–85. Graphics 45.

"Industrial Lore: A Bibliographic-Semantic Query." *Western Folklore* 37 (July
1978): 213–44. Reprinted in *Working Americans: Contemporary Approaches to
Occupational Folklife,* edited by Robert Byington, 71–102, Smithsonian
Folklife Studies No. 3 (Washington, D.C.: Smithsonian Institution, 1978).

LP brochure notes, preface to *Songs of Steel and Struggle,* by Joe Glazer. United
Steelworkers of America disc (unnumbered), September 1978, and
Collector Records 1930.

"Reflexive Regionalism." *Adena* 3 (Fall 1978): 3–15. (Literary journal,
University of Louisville.)

"John Henry Depicted." *JEMF Quarterly,* no. 51 (Autumn 1978): 126–43.
Graphics 46.

"Labor Song as Symbol." *JEMF Quarterly,* no. 52 (Winter 1978): 178–97.
Graphics 47.

1979

Review of *American Realism,* by Francois Mathey. *Wilson Quarterly* 3 (Spring
1979): 149.

"Fred Becker's John Henry." *JEMF Quarterly,* no. 53 (Spring 1979): 30–37.
Graphics 48.

"Portraits of Appalachian Musicians." *JEMF Quarterly,* no. 54 (Summer 1979):
99–106. Graphics 49.

"Charles Louis Seeger (1886–1979). *Journal of American Folklore* 92 (October
1979): 391–99.

"A Suggested Museum Show." *JEMF Quarterly,* no. 55 (Fall 1979): 157–65.
Graphics 50.

LP liner notes for *The Merle Travis Story.* CMH 9018, November 1979.

"String Bands." *JEMF Quarterly,* no. 56 (Winter 1979): 215–24. Graphics 51.

"Folk Culture and the Humanistic Tradition." Transcribed talk in *Government
and the Humanities,* edited by Kenneth Tolo, 27–32. Austin, Tex.: Lyndon B.
Johnson School of Public Affairs/Lyndon Baines Johnson Library, 1979.

1980

"A Folklorist's Creed and a Folksinger's Gift." *Appalachian Journal* 7
(Autumn–Winter 1979–80): 37–45.

"Kerry Awn's Soap Creek Saloon Calendars." *JEMF Quarterly,* no. 57 (Spring 1980): 24–33. Graphics 52.

"Folk Music in Folk Art." *JEMF Quarterly,* no. 58 (Summer 1980): 81–88. Graphics 53.

"Early Country Music Journals." *JEMF Quarterly,* no. 59 (Fall 1980): 140–46. Graphics 54.

"Palmer Hayden's John Henry Series." *JEMF Quarterly,* no. 60 (Winter 1980): 199–213. Graphics 55.

1981

Introduction to *Radio's "Kentucky Mountain Boy," Bradley Kincaid,* by Loyal Jones, 1–8. Berea, Ky.: Appalachian Center/Berea College, 1981.

"Austin's Cosmic Cowboys: Words in Collision." In *"And Other Neighborly Names,"* edited by Richard Bauman and Roger Abrahams, 152–94. Austin: University of Texas Press, 1981.

"Clare Leighton." *JEMF Quarterly,* no. 61 (Spring 1981): 24–34. Graphics 56.

"Old Dan Tucker." *JEMF Quarterly,* no. 62 (Summer 1981): 85–94, 106. Graphics 57.

"Dan Tucker in *Roanoke.*" *JEMF Quarterly,* no. 63 (Fall 1981): 139–54. Graphics 58.

"Vernacular Music Albums." *JEMF Quarterly,* no. 64 (Winter 1964): 201–14. Graphics 59.

1982

"Regionalism Is a Forever Agenda." *Appalachian Journal* 9 (Winter–Spring 1982): 172–80.

"The Roots of Labor Lingo." *Carpenter* 102 (May 1982): 9.

Review of *The Smithsonian Collection of Classic Country Music* (LP collection), edited by Bill Malone. *JEMF Quarterly,* nos. 65/66 (Spring/Summer 1982), 41–58.

"Michael Adams' Honky-Tonk Paintings." *JEMF Quarterly,* nos. 67/68 (Fall/Winter 1982): 155–65. Graphics 60.

1983

"Etymologies of Americanism: A Checklist of Peter Tamony's Articles." San Francisco: privately distributed, February 1983. Reprinted in partial form in *Maledicta* 7 (1983): 14–20.

Afterword to *Songs of American Labor, Industrialization and the Urban Work*

Experience: A Discography, edited by Richard Reuss, 95–107. Ann Arbor: Labor Studies Center, University of Michigan, 1983.

"John Henry Revisited." *JEMF Quarterly,* no. 69 (Spring 1983): 12–31. Graphics 61.

"Interpreting Folklore Ideologically." In *Handbook of American Folklore,* edited by Richard Dorson, 351–58. Bloomington: Indiana University Press, 1983.

"Sound Recordings, Use and Challenge." In Dorson, *Handbook of American Folklore,* 434–40.

"The Library of Congress' Cowboy Exhibit." *JEMF Quarterly,* no. 70 (Summer 1983): 85–102. Graphics 62.

"A Folk Music Exhibition." In *The Ballad Image: Essays Presented to Bertrand Harris Bronson,* edited by James Porter, 97–127. Los Angeles: Center for the Study of Compartive Folklore and Mythology, UCLA, 1983.

"General's Folk Albums." *JEMF Quarterly,* no. 71 (Autumn 1983): 174–87. Graphics 63.

"Farewell Tony." *JEMF Quarterly,* no. 72 (Winter 1983): 231–40. Graphics 64.

"Images of Appalachia: A Critical Discussion." Transcribed remarks in *The Appalachian Experience,* edied by Barry Buxton, 3–9. Boone, N.C.: Appalachian Consortium Press, 1983.

1984

"Marcus Daly Enters Heaven." *The Speculator* (Winter 1984): 26–33. (Cultural journal, Butte, Mont.)

"Signifying Banjos." *JEMF Quarterly,* no. 90 (Spring/Summer 1984): 19–32. Graphics 65.

"Bascom Lamar Lunsford's First Album." *JEMF Quarterly,* no. 74 (Fall/Winter 1984): 94–99. Graphics 66.

"Tom Benton's Folk Depictions." In *Thomas Hart Benton: Chronicles of America's Folk Heritage,* edited by Linda Weintraub, 33–67. Annandale-on-Hudson, N.Y.: Blum Art Institute, Bard College, 1984.

"Folklore and America's Future." *Kentucky Folklore Record* 30 (July–December 1984): 65–78. (Tape-recorded lecture transcribed by Tom Hulsey.)

1985

"Reflections on 'Keywords' in Public-Sector Folklore." *Practicing Anthropology* 7, nos. 1–2 (1985): 4–5.

"The Visual Arkansas Traveler." *JEMF Quarterly,* nos. 75/76 (Spring/Summer 1985): 31–46. Graphics 67.

Review of *Minstrel of the Appalachians,* by Loyal Jones. *Appalachian Heritage* 13 (Summer 1985): 66–70.

"The Naming Tag 'Public-Sector Folklore': A Recollection." *Public Program Newsletter* (American Folklore Society) 3 (September 1985): 16–17.

"Singlejack/Doublejack: Craft and Celebration." In *By Land and by Sea,* edited by Roger Abrahams et al., 95–111. Hatboro, Pa.: Legacy Books, 1985.

"Winding Down." *JEMF Quarterly,* nos. 77/78 (Fall/Winter 1985): 99–115. Graphics 68.

1986

"The Archive's Shores." In *Folklife Annual 1985,* edited by Alan Jabbour and James Hardin, 60–73. Washington, D.C.: American Folklife Center, Library of Congress, 1986.

"Public Sector Attention to Folklore in the United States." In *Louisiana Folklife: A Guide to the State,* edited by Nicholas Spitzer, 245–50. Baton Rouge: Louisiana Folklife Program, 1986.

"Championing Crafts in the Workplace." In program book for Festival of American Folklife, Smithsonian Institution, June 25–July 6, 1986, 83–86.

LP liner notes for *Work's Many Voices,* by various performers. John Edwards Memorial Forum JEMF 110 and 111, November 1986. (Two-volume reissue set from 45-rpm discs.)

1987

"Bertrand Harris Bronson (1902–1986)." *Journal of American Folklore* 100 (July 1987): 297–99.

"At the Hall, in the Stope: Who Treasures Tales of Work?" *Western Folklore* 46 (July 1987): 153–70. (Originally delivered as Archer Taylor Lecture, California Folklore Society.)

1988

"Stitching Patchwork in Public." In *The Conservation of Culture,* edited by Burt Feintuch, 17–32. Lexington: University Press of Kentucky, 1988.

"Fink, the Labor Connection." *Comments on Etymology* 17 (May 1, 1988): 1–28.

1989

[With Charles Wolfe]. LP liner notes for *The Blue Sky Boys in Concert, 1964.* Rounder 0236, April 1989.

"Cultural Conservation." Transcribed remarks in *From the Inside Out:*

Perspectives on Mexican and Mexican American Folk Art, edited by Karana
   Hattersly-Drayton, 111–19. San Francisco: The Mexican Museum, 1989.
"Working with Laborlore." *Labor's Heritage* 1 (July 1989): 66–75.
"The Folklorist as Cultural Critic." In *Time and Temperature,* edited by Charles
   Camp, 26–27. Washington, D.C.: American Folklore Society, 1989.
Foreword to *A Bearer of Tradition: Dwight Stump, Basketmaker,* by Rosemary
   Joyce, vii–x. Athens: University of Georgia Press, 1989.

1990
"Let Us Now Praise John Handcox." *Tradition,* no. 6 (Winter 1990): 6–7, 11.
   (University of Missouri Cultural Heritage Center.)

1991
"Labor Song: An Ambiguous Legacy." *Journal of Folklore Research* 28
   (May–December 1991): 93–102.
Afterword to *Sounds of the South,* edited by Daniel Patterson, 183–88. Chapel
   Hill: Southern Folklife Collection, Wilson Library, University of North
   Carolina, 1991.

1992
"The Homestead Ballad." In *"The River Ran Red": Homestead 1892,* edited by
   David Demarest, 222–23. Pittsburgh: University of Pittsburgh Press, 1992.
"The Folk Language of Labor." Op-ed piece, *San Francisco Examiner,*
   September 7, 1992.
"Public Folklore's Name: A Partisan's Notes." In *Public Folklore,* edited by
   Robert Baron and Nicholas Spitzer, 49–63. Washington, D.C.:
   Smithsonian Institution Press, 1992.

1993
*Labor Tales: Workers' Yarns, Legends, Jokes, Whoppers, and Windies Told on the Job
   and at the Hall.* San Francisco: Labor Archives and Research Center, San
   Francisco State University, 1993. (Chapbook gift for LARC contributors.)
CD brochure notes for *Merle Travis — Folksongs of the Hills — Back Home / Songs of
   the Coal Mines.* Bear Family BCD 15636, March 1993.
"Portrait of a Pile Driver, Frank Gallegos (1900–1992)." *Organized Labor,*
   March 22, 1993. (San Francisco Building and Construction Trades Council
   newspaper.)

"Vernacular Music: A Naming Compass." *Musical Quarterly* 77 (Spring 1993): 35–46.

"Boss, Workman, Wife: Sneaking-Home Tales." *Journal of American Folklore* 106 (Spring 1993): 156–70.

Wobblies, Pile Butts, and Other Heroes: Laborlore Explorations. Urbana: University of Illinois Press, 1993.

"The Campus Folksong Club: A Glimpse at the Past." In *Transforming Tradition,* edited by Neil Rosenberg, 61–72. Urbana: University of Illinois Press, 1993.

"A Literary Contribution to the Creation of an American Folk Hero: Dan Tucker in *Roanoke.*" *North Carolina Folklore Journal* 40 (Summer–Fall 1993): 49–69. (Adapted from *JEMF Quarterly,* no. 63.)

"A Guide to Labor's Landmarks in San Francisco." Op-ed piece, *San Francisco Examiner,* September 5, 1993.

"San Francisco's Labor Landmarks." In *1893–1993: A Century of Progress.* San Francisco: San Francisco Labor Council, 1993. (Centennial ad-book.)

"Conversations with Archie Green." *Folklore in Use* 1 (1993): 5–14. (Transcribed talk with David Shuldiner.)

"Goodnight Irene, Goodbye Dick." In *Songs about Work: Essays in Occupational Culture for Richard A. Reuss,* edited by Archie Green, 15–19. Special Publications of the Folklore Institute, no. 3. Bloomington: Folklore Institute, Indiana University, 1993.

"Woody's Oil Songs." In Green, *Songs about Work,* 208–20.

1994

"How Blue-Collar Preservationists Restored the Ferry Boat Eureka." Op-ed piece, *San Francisco Examiner,* March 10, 1994.

"Raven, Mallard, and Spotted Owl—Totems for Coalition." In *Conserving Culture: A New Discourse on Heritage,* edited by Mary Hufford, 245–52. Urbana: University of Illinois Press, 1994.

"San Francisco's Blue-Collar Preservationists." *Carpenter* 114 (May/June 1994): 10–11. Reprinted in *Commemorating 100 Years of Excellence in Craftsmanship 1896–1996,* 40–41. San Francisco: San Francisco Building and Construction Trades Council, February 1996.

"Popsicle Man, Popsicle Union." *Tributaries* 1 (Summer 1994): 96–104. (Alabama Folklife Association.)

"Remembering Jack Fitch, Pile Butt and Artist, on Labor Day 1994." Op-ed piece, *San Francisco Examiner,* September 5, 1994.

1995

"Labor Landmarks: Past and Present." *Labor's Heritage* 6 (Spring 1995): 26–53.

"Appalachia: The View from San Francisco." *Journal of the Appalachian Studies Association* 7 (1995): 6–17.

1996

"Tin Man and Copper Man: Trade Sign and Union Symbol." In *Commemorating 100 Years of Excellence in Craftsmanship 1896–1996,* 96–97. San Francisco: San Francisco Building and Construction Trades Council, February 1996. (Centennial ad-book.)

Review of *The Quest of the Folk,* by Ian McKay. *Canadian Historical Review* 77 (March 1996), 122–25.

"Twin Mysteries of Andrew Furuseth." *West Coast Sailors* 59 (March 22, 1996): 3. (Sailors' Union of the Pacific newspaper.)

"Labor Landmarks." *Carpenter* 116 (March/April 1996): 25–28.

Calf's Head and Union Tale: Labor Yarns at Work and Play. Urbana: University of Illinois Press, 1996.

"Explaining Scissorbill." *Comments on Etymology* 26 (December 1996): 18–25.

1997

"Stuart Kaufman, 1941–1997." *Labor's Heritage* 8 (Winter 1997): 15. (A memorial reminiscence.)

"Carlos Cortez and Wobbly Artistry." Introduction to *Where Are the Voices?,* by Carlos Cortez, 5–8. Chicago: Kerr, 1997.

"Eugene Barnett Talks about the Centralia Conspiracy." *Columbia* 11 (Summer 1997): 10–17. (Transcribed sound recording with comments on provenance by William H. Friedland and by Archie Green on "Revisiting Gene Barnett—a Reflection.")

"Preaching by the Choir: Songs from the Commonwealth of Toil." Op-ed piece, *San Francisco Examiner,* September 1, 1997.

"The Reel Union: Video Captures the Voices and Spirit of the ILWU." Video review, *The Dispatcher* (October 1997): 15. (International Longshore and Warehouse Union newspaper.)

"Unions Preserve Skills of the Past." Op-ed piece, *San Francisco Examiner,* December 9, 1997.

"The Lowdown on 'Salmonbellies.'" *West Coast Sailors* 60 (December 19, 1997): 6.

1998

"Crimping: Scourge of the Waterfront." *West Coast Sailors* 61 (March 20, 1998): 5.

"Rene Latour—Metal Sculpture." In *Florida Folklife,* edited by Stephen Stuempfle, 66. Miami: Historical Museum of Southern Florida. (Catalog for exhibit opening September 25, 1998.)

"John Edwards." In *The Encyclopedia of Country Music,* edited by Paul Kingsbury, 162. New York: Oxford University Press, 1998.

"JEMF (John Edwards Memorial Foundation, now Forum)." In Kingsbury, *Encyclopedia of Country Music,* 262.

1999

"Industrial Workers of the World Songs." In *Encyclopedia of the American Left,* 2d ed., edited by Mary Jo Buhle, Paul Buhle, and Dan Georgakas, 362–63. New York: Oxford University Press, 1999.

"Torching the Fink Books." *West Coast Sailors* 62 (March 19, 1999): 5.

"The Odyssey of Captain Healy." Film review, *The Dispatcher* 57 (March 1999): 12.

"Tin Men on Parade: The Art of Sheet-Metal Workers." *Labor's Heritage* 10 (Spring/Summer 1999): 34–47.

Foreword to booklet with CD, *Spirit of Steel.* Birmingham, Ala.: Sloss Furnace National Historical Landmark, November 1999.

"Buckoism Lives." *West Coast Sailors* 62 (December 22, 1999): 5.

2000

"Snakeheads and Job Sharks: Shanghaiers Reborn." *West Coast Sailors* 63 (December 22, 2000): 6.

"Pier-Head Jump." *West Coast Sailors* 63 (October 20, 2000): 8.

"Birds of a Feather: Gorbeys and Petrels." In *Northeast Folklore: Essays in Honor of Edward D. Ives,* edited by Pauleena MacDougall and David Taylor, 207–39. Orono: University of Maine Press and Maine Folklife Center, 2000.

"An Unreconstructed Do-Gooder." *Folklore Forum* 31, no. 2 (2000): 5–6.

INDEX

Puckett, Riley, 17, 25, 27
Putnam, Herbert, 137

Quillen, James, 58, 59
Quilts, 115

Race records, 12, 13, 14, 15, 16, 19, 139,
    189–90, 195
Radio, 10, 14, 16–18, 23, 26, 30, 32–35,
    77, 92, 190
Rand, Anne, 185
Randall, Isabelle, 71
Randolph, Vance, 36, 109, 127
Reagan, Ronald, 153
Rector, John, 21–22, 23
Reid, Jan, 77, 81, 90
Reinert, Al, 88
Reisman, David, 11–12
Reiss (painter), 109
Remington, Frederic, 74
Reneau, Blind George, 26, 27
Renwick, Roger, 206
Reuss, Richard, 206
Reuther, Walter, 61
Rey, Charles, 15, 36
Rhythm and blues music, 87, 101
Richardson, Jerome, 189
Riggs, Lynn, 130
Riis, Jacob, 145
Rindy, Dean, 84
Rinzler, Ralph, 58, 147, 155–56, 205
Ritter, Tex, 31, 75, 118
Roberts, Lawrence, 199–200, 216
Roberts, Randy, 196, 197
Robertson, A. C. (Eck), 27–28
Robinson, Earl, 61
Robison, Carson J., 30, 34, 117
Rockabilly music, 79, 81, 101
Rock and roll music, 77, 81–82, 87, 101,
    191
Rockwell, Norman, 215
Rodgers, Jimmie, 78, 118, 132, 191
Roediger, David, 196
Rogers, Roy, 31, 75
Rogers, Will, 33, 72

Ronstadt, Linda, 65, 78
Roosevelt, Franklin D., xiv, 53, 114,
    188, 202
Roosevelt, Theodore, 71, 135, 140
Rosenberg, Neil, 211
Rosenfeld, Paul, 128
Ross, Edward, 143
Rossini, Giacchino, 31
Roth, Don, 77
Rourke, Constance, 125, 146, 158
Rowan, Peter, 74
Rowland, Bud, 189
Ruggles, Carl, 117, 127
Russell, Charles, 74

Sacco, Nicola, 210, 212
Sacred Harp singers, 17, 19
Sahm, Doug, 77, 92, 96
St. John, Powell, 80
Samuels, Joseph, 14
Sandburg, Carl, 86, 115, 125
Santayana, George, 143, 145
Sapir, Edward, 146
Schoolcraft, Henry Rowe, 125, 158
Scotland, 9
Scott, Walter, 137, 157
Seeger, Charles, 55, 109, 117, 127, 141
Seeger, Pete, 47, 61, 100
Self-determination, xv, xvi, 59
Shahn, Ben, 119
Shapiro, Henry, 56
Sharp, Cecil J., 55–57, 64, 65
Shaughnessy, Tom, 196
Sheeler, Charles, 119
Shilkret, Nat, 28
Shiva's Headband, 81, 82
Sierra Club, 59, 148, 160
Sinclair, Upton, 174
Sloan, John, 119
Slobodek, Mitch, 185
Sly and the Family Stone, 88
Smith, Bessie, 191
Smith, Bobby Earl, 80
Smith, Hazel, 76
Smith, Mamie, 12, 14

Smithsonian Institution, 141, 146–47
Socialism, xvii, 113, 202
Spain, Irene, 18, 29
Spencer, Jesse Ames, 125
Spitzer, Nick, 206
Sprague, Carl T., 31, 32, 37, 38
Staten, Henry, 82–83
Steiner, Herb, 91–92
Stevens, James, 174
Stewart, Cal, 14
Stokstad, Marilyn, 126
Stoneman, Ernest V. "Pop," 21, 23, 37, 38
Strachwitz, Chris, 206
Structuralism, 55
Stuart, "Uncle Am," 26, 28
Sutphin, James, 21
Swift, Jonathan, 68
Switzerland, 144

Taggart, Charles Ross, 14
Tamony, Kathleen, 197
Tamony, Peter, x, 3, 37, 186–98, 206–7, 209–10
Tanner, Gid, 25, 27, 28, 29
Taylor, Paul, 201
Texas, 8–9, 66–68, 74, 76, 77–90, 99, 100, 101, 135, 207
Thirteenth Floor Elevators, 81, 82
Thomas, Jean, 35–36
Thompson, Jimmie, 17
Thompson, Virgil, 129
Threadgill, Kenneth, 83
Tosches, Nick, 777
Travis, Merle, 204
Twain, Mark, 126, 137, 157

Unionism: and taking sides, vii; and Green, ix–x, xvi, 51, 171, 212; and libertarianism, xvii; and labor lore, 47, 171–75, 212–13; and coal miners, 59; and finks, 178–82; and folklore, 205; and Carwardine, 207; and conservation, 212, 213. *See also* Labor lore

United Auto Workers, 61, 124
United Mine Workers of America, 51, 60

Value relativism, 146
Vanzetti, Bartolomeo, 210, 212
Varesi, Edgar, 127
Vernacular culture, 158, 199, 200, 214
Vernacular music, 67, 138, 195, 210
Victor records, 14, 22, 24, 27–31, 138
Virginia Breakdowners, 19, 21
Virginia Reelers, 19
Vitaphone, 24
Vocalion-Brunswick Records, 24
Vocalion Records, 26, 27

Wade, Stephen, 215
Walker, Frank, 25, 38
Walker, Jerry Jeff, 77, 87, 89, 90, 99
Wallace, George, 84
Waller Creek Boys, 80
Warhol, Andy, 215
Warner's Seven Aces, 15, 16, 17, 18
Watters, Lu, 185
Wells, Kitty, 118
Wendell, Barrett, 135, 138, 141–42, 143, 144, 147, 158
West, George, 128
West, Josie, 128
West, Sabrina, 128
West, Tom, 50
Western Electric, 30
Western music, 31, 87
Western swing music, 79, 100, 101
Weston, George M., 12
Whisnant, David, 204
White, Bob, 15, 17
White, Josh, 61
Whitman, Walt, x, xx, 10, 131, 144
Whitter, Henry, 18, 19, 21, 23, 25, 26, 27, 28, 38
Wiesner, Jerome B., 47
Wiggins, Gene, 207
Wiggins, Lanny, 80
Wilcox, Gary, 88